LATIN AMERICA AND THE NEW INTERNATIONAL ECONOMIC ORDER

Latin America is undergoing a significant shift towards a development strategy of outward-orientated growth. Most countries have 'opened up' their economies to international trade and have become closely integrated into the world capital markets. Great hopes are placed on the impetus which this new strategy might give to economic growth in the region.

However, the available knowledge in Latin America regarding the present nature of the world economy is quite limited. On the other hand, it is paradoxical that, at the time when Latin America is turning towards the international economy, it appears to hold a less clearly defined position in the debate on how it ought to function.

This book is intended chiefly to analyse the implications for Latin America of the recent transformations of the world economy in three fields: financial and monetary relations; trade in primary products and trade in manufactured products; and industrialisation. Particular attention is given to the analysis of alternative external policies which the Latin American countries can apply in order to cope with the problems or take advantage of the opportunities that have appeared in each of the three fields mentioned. The possibilities of cooperation among Latin American and Third World countries with the aim of setting up a new economic order are especially emphasised.

All topics are examined from a Latin American perspective, stressing the importance of structural rigidities in the economies, the prevalence of high unemployment, the dependence on exports of raw materials, instability and other similar characteristics.

St Antony's/Macmillan Series

General editor: Archie Brown, Fellow of St Antony's College, Oxford

This new series contains academic books written or edited by members of St Antony's College, Oxford, or by authors with a special association with the College. The titles are selected by an editorial board on which both the College and the publishers are represented.

Titles already published or in the press are listed below, and there are numerous further titles in preparation.

LATIN AMERICA AND THE NEW INTERNATIONAL ECONOMIC ORDER

Edited by
Ricardo Ffrench-Davis
and Ernesto Tironi
Senior Researchers, CIEPLAN

M

in association with
St Antony's College, Oxford

First published 1982 by
THE MACMILLAN PRESS LTD
London and Basingstoke
Companies and representatives
throughout the world

ISBN 0 333 30074 2

Printed in Hong Kong

Contents

vi   *Contents*

Tables and Figures

TABLES

FIGURE

Preface

This volume presents the papers prepared for a conference organised by the Corporación de Investigaciones Económicas para Latinoamérica (CIEPLAN) in Santiago, Chile, on 'The International Economy and Developing Countries', in May 1978.

The conference was unusual in that it is not common for specialists of Third World countries to host academic meetings on international economic issues. These meetings are mainly held in the industrialised countries and show a strong bias towards the analysis of purely theoretical issues or topics more relevant for those countries. The success of the conference emphasises the need for further ventures of this kind with a more balanced exchange of views between academics from the North and the South, and between theoretical approaches and policy issues relevant for the less developed countries (LDCs).

The conference, like this book, was concerned with three main topics, each analysed from two different perspectives. The topics were international financial and monetary problems, trade in primary products, and trade in manufactures. Each topic was analysed on the one hand in terms of the LDCs' perception of the major changes that have occurred in the world economy and, on the other hand, in terms of their repercussions and policy implications for developing countries.

To conclude, we would like to acknowledge the co-operation of the many people who made this publication possible. First, the Ford Foundation for their support in undertaking the conference for which these papers were prepared. In the second place, the paper-writers, commentators and participants in this conference for their active contribution to the venture. In the third place, the researchers of CIEPLAN for their support and its staff for their patience in transcribing various versions of these papers. Finally, we are grateful to Rosemary Thorp, who first read the manuscript in Spanish and encouraged us to have it translated into English, the Fellows of St Antony's College, Oxford, who accepted the book for its series with Macmillan, and to Paul Cammack and Peter Goode, who did most of the translation.

The editors and publishers wish also to thank the following who have kindly given permission for the use of copyright material: General Agreement on Tariffs and Trade (GATT) for the table from *International Trade, 1976–77*; Professor Gerald K. Helleiner for the table from 'Intrafirm Trade and the Developing Countries: Patterns Trends and Data Problems', 1977; Inter-American Development Bank for the tables from *Latin America in the World Economy*; Johns Hopkins University Press for the extract from a table in *World Tables, 1976*; Mr Donald B. Keesing for the table from 'Recent Trends in Manufactured and Total Exports from Developing Countries' (Washington, DC, 1977); United Nations Economic Commission for Latin America for the table from *Cuaderno de la Cepal*, no. 7, 1975; World Bank for the tables from the 1973–7, 1977, 1978 and 1979 editions of *Commodity Trade and Price Trends*.

List of Abbreviations

AER	*American Economic Review*
CEPAL	Comisión Económica para América Latina
CIEPLAN	Corporación de Investigaciones Económicas para Latinoamérica
CIF	Cost, insurance and freight
DC	Developed country
ECLA	Economic Commission for Latin America
EEC	European Economic Community
EFTA	European Free Trade Association
FOB	Free on board
GATT	General Agreement on Tariffs and Trade
GDP	Gross domestic product
GNP	Gross national product
GSP	General System of Preferences
IBRD	International Bank for Reconstruction and Development
ILDIS-FLACSO	Instituto Latinoamericano de Investigaciones Sociales
IMF	International Monetary Fund
IPC	Integrated Programme for Commodities
ISI	Import Substitution Industrialisation
ISIC	International Standard Industrial Classification
JUNAC	Junta del Acuerdo de Cartagena
LDC	Less developed country
MFN	Most Favoured Nation
NIEO	New International Economic Order
OECD	Organisation for Economic Cooperation and Development
OPEC	Organisation of Petroleum Exporting Countries
PREALC	Programa Regional del Empleo para América Latina y el Caribe

SDR   Special drawing rights
SITC   Standard Industrial Trade Classification
STABEX   Stablisation Fund of Export Earnings
TNC   Transnational corporation
UNCTAD   United Nations Conference on Trade and Devel-
                    opment

Note Billions are US billions (one thousand million) throughout the book.

Notes on the Contributors

EDITORS

RICARDO FFRENCH-DAVIS, Senior Researcher, Corporación de Investigaciones Económicas para Latinoamérica (CIEPLAN); former head, Research Department, Central Bank of Chile; Visiting Fellow, St Antony's College, Oxford, and Boston University; former Professor of Economics at the University of Chile and Catholic University of Chile. He has published widely on development issues, including *Comercio Internacional y Políticas de Desarrollo*, with Keith Griffin (Mexico City: FCE, 1967), *Políticas Económicas en Chile: 1952–1970* (CIEPLAN, 1973) and *Economía Internacional: teorías y políticas para el desarrollo* (Mexico City: FCE, 1979), plus many other articles in Spanish and English journals. (PhD, University of Chicago).

ERNESTO TIRONI, Senior Researcher, CIEPLAN, Santiago, Chile; Visiting Fellow, St Antony's College, Oxford, and Institute of Latin American Studies, University of London; former Professor of Economics at the Catholic University of Chile; and Visiting Lecturer at Boston University. He has edited several books published in Latin America, including *El Cobre en el Desarrollo Nacional*, with R. Ffrench-Davis (CIEPLAN, 1974), *Pacto Andino: Caracter y Perspectivas* (Lima: IEP, 1978) and *Desarrollo Nacional e Integración Andina* (Lima: IEP, 1979), plus articles in Spanish and English journals. (PhD, MIT, USA).

CONTRIBUTORS

EDMAR L. BACHA, Professor of Economics, Catholic University of Brazil, Rio de Janeiro; former Head of the Department of Economics, University of Brasilia, and Visiting Fellow, Harvard University.

CARLOS F. DÍAZ-ALEJANDRO, Professor of Economics, Yale University; Visiting Fellow, Nuffield College, Oxford; editor of the *Journal of*

International Economics. He has published widely on development issues.

ENRIQUE V. IGLESIAS, Executive Secretary, Economic Commission for Latin America (ECLA); member of the board of the Third World Forum, the Centre for Research on the New International Economic Order, Oxford, and many other official and unofficial international organisations.

ROBERTO JUNGUITO, Director of FEDESARROLLO, Bogota, Colombia. Former Colombian representative in the International Coffee Organisation, London. He has published widely on Colombia's economic problems.

JORGE KATZ, Head of the UNDP-IDB Research Project on Technology Transfer in Latin America, Buenos Aires, Argentina. He has published extensively on multinational corporations and technology in developing countries.

GUILLERMO PERRY, Senior Economist, FEDESARROLLO, Bogota, Colombia; former Head of the Department of Economics and Centre of Economic Development Studies (CEDE), Universidad de los Andes, Colombia.

DIEGO PIZANO, Professor of Economics, Universidad de los Andes, Colombia, and researcher at FEDESARROLLO.

DISCUSSANTS

DRAGOSLAV AVRAMOVIC, Head of Research Department of the Brandt Commission Secretariat; formerly at the World Bank.

WILLIAM R. CLINE, Senior Economist, Brookings Institution, Washington.

ALBERT FISHLOW, Director of the Concilium on International and Area Studies, Yale University, and former Director of the Department of Economics of the University of California, Berkeley.

NORBERTO GONZALEZ, Head of the Foreign Trade Division, Economic

Commission for Latin America (ECLA), Santiago.

PEDRO MALAN, Professor, Department of Economics, Catholic University of Brazil.

PATRICIO MELLER, Senior Economist at CIEPLAN and Professor of Economics, University of Chile, Santiago.

DUDLEY SEERS, Professorial Fellow and former Director of the Institute of Development Studies (IDS), University of Sussex; President of the European Association of Development Institutes.

SIMON TEITEL, Senior Economic Adviser, Interamerican Development Bank, Washington; former Visiting Professor, Yale University.

1 Latin America and the NIEO: an Introduction

RICARDO FFRENCH-DAVIS AND
ERNESTO TIRONI

The developing countries have certainly not played a major role in the setting up of the prevailing international economic order, despite the significance of the external sector for their national development. Only recently have these countries begun to participate actively in the search for a new order which might offer them greater possibilities of a type of external relations which would contribute more effectively to their development.

The political will to modify existing relations is, without doubt, a necessary condition. Nevertheless, it is not sufficient. In the field of international economics there are still numerous gaps in the knowledge about the most suitable economic strategies and policies which might contribute to more autonomous, permanent and egalitarian development.

Conventional literature on international economics has a marked bias in favour of free trade. Critiques of this theory, in spite of their important contributions, also show deficiencies in their definition of the concrete means to create an alternative economic order. Given these deficiencies, in less developed countries (LDCs) there is a notorious intellectual dependence on free trade models or on excessively general and utopian approaches.

The purpose of this book is to identify the topics in international economics on which it is most urgent to carry out new research, as far as Latin America is concerned, in order to implement an alternative economic order.

Research carried out in LDCs has concentrated predominantly on internal problems. Nevertheless, many Third World economies have recently been following strong outward-oriented growth policies.

1

Indeed, nowadays great hopes are frequently placed on the impetus which this new strategy might give to economic growth in Latin America. However, the available knowledge in the region regarding the nature of the world economy is limited. Significant changes have occurred within it during the last few years – and still more are in gestation. But they have apparently not been incorporated into the diagnoses and policy recommendations now being formulated. Furthermore, insufficient attention has been devoted to the repercussions which different forms of opening the economy have at a domestic level. Hence the importance of the subject of this book.

Paradoxically, at a time when Latin America is turning more towards the international economy, it appears to hold a less clearly defined position in the debate on how it ought to function. This contrasts sharply with the situation in the 1950s, when the region exercised a definite leadership in the formulation of the demands which LDCs as a group made to the international community. For instance, Latin America played an important role in bringing about the creation of UNCTAD as the main forum in which to discuss the problems of trade confronted by Third World countries. Today, however, the region finds itself divided on many issues discussed in UNCTAD. Is it, perhaps, that the changes which have occurred in the world economy and in Latin America have placed the interests of the region nearer to those of the industrialised nations than to those of the less developed countries?

In this introduction we analyse briefly the nature of the major recent changes in the world economy, and the as yet unanswered questions concerning the implications which a new international economic order (NIEO) has for the development of the Third World.

1 CONCEPTIONS OF THE NEW INTERNATIONAL ORDER

It is not uncommon for people to believe that they are discussing the same subject when in fact they are referring to different matters. It is therefore useful to define what the concept of NIEO is taken to mean in the countries of the North and the South. In particular, some understand the term 'new order' in a normative sense whilst others understand it in a factual or positive sense. According to the first meaning, the NIEO would be the result of the changes, actual or desired, in the *norms* that regulate the international economy; whilst in the second sense the new order would be the result of changes in the *structure* of trade and factor movements – that is, in the results of international economic exchange.

The absence of a clear distinction between these concepts has led to major misunderstandings in the debate. It is the origin, for example, of the frequent contentions in the North that a new economic order already exists by virtue of the substantial transformations which have flowed from the creation of OPEC, the rise in oil prices, the predominance of flexible exchange rates and other changes of that nature in the world economy. Nevertheless, it is contended in the Third World that we have advanced little, if at all, in the constitution of a new order. The reason for this difference of opinion is that the former understand the concept of NIEO in its factual sense, whilst the latter take it in a normative sense.

As a general rule, the concept of NIEO is used here in the normative sense, but special emphasis is placed on the recommendation of new policies arising from a more up-to-date and comprehensive understanding of the transformations which have in fact occurred in the structure and functioning of the international economy. That knowledge is indispensable if we are to know *what* to change and *how* to change the international norms which govern the world economy. In spite of its importance, such knowledge is very limited in the developing countries.

Moreover, in this book the international economic order is seen as being made up as much of the norms or policies agreed upon within *international* institutions – such as the IMF, the World Bank, GATT – as of the national foreign policies of nation states, especially of the most powerful countries of the centre – i.e. the financial, commercial and foreign investment policies of the USA, the EEC, Japan, etc. In many of the available studies on this subject, and in proposals from LDCs for reaching a NIEO, emphasis is placed only on the former group of policies. This bias can involve certain costs. At times it would appear that, in the search to establish new global norms to regulate economic relations between states, and to reform existing international institutions, the governments of many LDCs have neglected to consider the difficulties, as well as the new opportunities, which have been created for them in other areas of the world economy.

In the first place, the countries of the periphery should pay far more attention to the internal economic evolution of the centres, their tendencies, conflicts and perceptions of the world which surrounds them. This would allow a better understanding about *which aspects* of the present order can be modified more readily in order to set up a system of more equitable international relations.

In the second place, in examining the alternatives of domestic policies for the external sector in LDCs, we are concerned also with the extent to which these policies might themselves contribute to forming an alternative international economic order which is both just and efficient. In the final analysis, international economic systems are partly the result of the confluence of the *national policies* of sovereign states, in matters concerning their relations with the rest of the world, just as 'international markets' are no more than the national markets of each country whose access to others is permitted under conditions established either by their governments or by the head offices of their transnational enterprises.

Lastly, in considering the *internal* repercussions of NIEO on LDCs and on Latin America we are concerned with their contribution to the success of the most urgent and relevant objectives for the region, such as attaining equitable growth, a fairer distribution of income, more jobs and adequate levels of national autonomy. Thus, in following this approach, we do not intend to lend support to the strategies for development which predominate in Latin America today, but rather to contribute towards modifying both the international and national economic orders simultaneously.

Our exclusive concentration on the most effective economic policies for these countries does not imply a disregard for their social, political and ideological conditioning factors. The economic measures adopted by governments are not decided upon merely as a result of their economic effects. There are many other factors which influence the choice of them, and in this sense economic policies are not entirely exogenous variables in any social system; they result from specific alliances between different agents and power groups. These considerations open the way to many important areas of research, but the impossibility of undertaking them all in depth makes necessary a certain selectivity. The studies in this book are restricted to economic considerations, albeit from a perspective which tries to emphasise distributive aspects, and the identification of the principal agents favoured or discriminated against by specific economic measures relating to the external sector. Thus, for example, none of the essays takes transnational corporations as an object of study, although most of them consider the role that these corporations play in the monetary and financial fields, as well as in trade.

Having made these general remarks, we shall analyse in the sections which follow the most relevant changes for Latin America which have occurred in the three major fields of the world economy dealt with in this book: the monetary and financial field; trade in primary products; and trade in manufactures and industrialisation. In the concluding chapter of this volume, we review the most urgent research needs which flow from the consideration of the recent changes in the international economy.

2 MONETARY AND FINANCIAL ISSUES

One of the most significant recent transformations in the international economy is the substitution of private for public sources of external finance which has taken place in this decade. In general, the Third World economies have seen a reduction of the long-term credits which they used to obtain officially from the governments of developed countries and from international financial agencies. Some nations have been able to replace these funds with short-term loans from transnational private banks. In Latin America this tendency is particularly pronounced, and is associated, moreover, with a change in the size and distribution of the total external debt. This had risen from around $15 billion in 1967 to $113 billion in 1976. Within these totals, private credits had grown from some $5.5 billion in 1967 to $75 billion by 1976. In other words, in little more than a decade these credits multiplied more than twelve times, whilst the total debt grew only just seven times; thus from representing less than a third of the total external debt of Latin America, private credits now constitute more than two-thirds of it.

Consequently, knowledge of how to gain access to private capital markets is becoming a point of crucial importance for LDCs. There are clear indications that such access is much easier for countries which are geographically large, and which are semi-industrialised or have relatively high levels of income. This situation poses a considerable problem for those nations which cannot fulfil these requirements. One should mention also the restrictions on the countries' choice between development strategies which may arise from the dependency on a sort of 'trust worthiness certificate' issued by private international banks; in particular, it may pose obstacles to a policy of social transformation in LDCs which are strongly indebted to transnational capitalist banks.

Returning to changes in the strictly international monetary and financial context, a second major change has been the emergence of floating exchange rates between industrialised countries. Knowledge of how these exchange markets work, and of their future evolution, seems crucial to the peripheral nations.

Another new phenomenon in the international economy concerns inflation in the central countries and its dissemination in the rest of the world. There one must emphasise the problems of control of international liquidity, as well as the effects of the macroeconomic adjustment policies which the industrialised nations are using to bring down inflation in their countries.

As to the internal repercussions on the developing countries of these changes in the international economic system, the fundamental questions which are raised are both numerous and varied. For instance, as regards the management of external debt, it seems a matter of urgency to determine the social criteria for deciding on the appropriate levels of indebtedness, and to analyse the interaction of external indebtedness with the internal allocation of resources, the functioning of domestic capital markets and, especially, the growth of internal savings. This topic also raises political and distributive problems of undeniable importance. Finally, several of the problems we have mentioned are closely related to the question of the exchange rate regime that should be followed by the Third World countries, in a context of floating parities in the central countries, high world inflation and volatile external financial flows.

3 TRADE IN PRIMARY PRODUCTS

This is an area of the international economy which has also seen spectacular changes, though there is full awareness of only some of them. The best known is the rise in the price of oil, which has meant the doubling in the importance of this product in international commerce, from around 10 per cent of total world exports in 1970, to more than 17 per cent in 1978. The clear predominance of LDCs as a group in the export of oil and, in particular, that of a few countries which are members of OPEC, has allowed a considerable increase in the share of these nations in the world economy. To be precise, it has allowed a temporary reversal of the tendency towards the diminution in the participation of LDCs in world trade, but in a very concentrated form which favours only few countries.

A second very important change in commodity trade at a global level – but one which has been little recognised – consists of the significant fall in the share of LDCs in world exports of primary products other than oil. Contrary to what is generally believed, it is many years since the developing countries were the principal world exporters of raw materials, especially those of mineral origin. These countries accounted for less than 36 per cent of exports of these products in 1978, compared with a share of almost 44 per cent in 1960. This phenomenon has been the principal cause of the decline in the LDCs' share of total world trade (excluding oil), since the expansion of their manufactured exports has not been sufficient to compensate for the slow growth of their exports of primary products. Moreover, these tendencies have been more pronounced in the case of Latin America than in the other Third World countries.

A third major phenomenon which can be observed in trade in primary products is the significant decline in the participation of transnational companies in their production and commercialisation within LDCs. Especially in Latin America, the nationalisations carried out at the end of the 1960s and early 1970s have led to the practical elimination of the control which foreign companies exercised over the production of copper, iron, zinc, bauxite, manganese, bananas, and even oil. This poses new challenges for research, and can have many other consequences which require examination.

Lastly, the considerable increase in the instability of world markets of primary products is a significant change in the world economy, as is the emphasis which LDCs have been placing – through UNCTAD – on rectifying the situation. Price fluctuations intensified in the case of almost all basic products during the five-year period 1972–7, compared with the previous decade. Two-thirds of the eighteen basic products chosen in Nairobi to make up the Common Fund have seen the intensity of their price fluctuations at least double in this decade. The need for research to construct a new international economic order, as regards trade in primary products, in thus becoming evident.

Some of the most urgent topics for investigation in this field concern more effective mechanisms to confront the growing instability of prices in international markets; the type of stabilising funds which should be developed; the possibilities of greater co-operation between LDCs and the industrialised countries to implement these funds; and, lastly, the cost of the reserve funds and the criteria with which they should be managed.

As for the internal impact of changes in the markets for primary products, and the most appropriate national policies in this context, there are various new themes which need to be analysed. Some of the most important concern the emphasis which Third World countries ought to put on the production and export of primary products, the role which transnational enterprises ought to play in these sectors in the future, the extent to which the growing tendency towards the export of manufactures should substitute for or support a higher production and export of primary products, and the extent to which further processing or elaboration of primary exports should be fostered and by what means.

4 TRADE IN MANUFACTURES AND INDUSTRIALISATION

In this field the outstanding feature is the effort which the developing countries are making to participate in the general expansion of the exports of manufactures, the most dynamic sector of world trade. The greater industrial base generated by import substitution, and the design of policies for the promotion of manufactured exports in Latin America, for example, have permitted an increase in the share of these within total exports for the region. Their share grew from 3 per cent in 1960 to over 18 per cent in 1978; if one takes the three countries with the greatest industrial development, the share of manufactured exports grew more strongly, from 5 per cent to around 30 per cent over the same period.

The feasibility and consequences of this strategy in the future have been little explored. The former depends basically on the degree to which the markets of the industrialised countries remain open. The growing channelling of trade in manufactures through exchanges between subsidiaries of transnational corporations (TNCs) is demonstrating that access to these markets for the Third World countries is not as free as has been believed. On the other hand, the governments of the industrialized countries show an increasing preoccupation with the inflow of manufactured products from Third World nations. Thus, increasing restrictions on this trade can continue.

At the international level, there is an urgent need to analyse the appropriate ways of making use of the potential capacity for negotiation which LDCs may have acquired in the field of trade in manufactures. Are there possibilities for utilising this capacity collectively or would it tend to be exercised individually by the most powerful developing countries? How, for example, should they use this greater influence within GATT? The viability of greater co-operation among LDCs has particular significance in this respect. One of the papers in this volume is addressed specifically to the analysis of this topic from a Latin American perspective.

From the point of view of the internal consequences of promoting manufactured exports, aside from analysing the particular effect of different policies used for that purpose, it is important to consider the role which TNCs play in exporting manufactures and the degree of complementarity between the processes of export promotion and import substitution in different contexts. With respect to transnationals, recent studies show that they account for around 43 per cent of the exports of manufactures in Brazil, and between 25 per cent and 30 per cent in Mexico. Similar levels have been estimated in Argentina and Colombia. A dilemma which these countries face, given the policies followed so far, is whether to accept a greater dependence on transnational corporations, or to see themselves limited to smaller, less dynamic and insecure external markets for manufactures. An examination of alternative forms of marketing and negotiating with foreign governments and companies assumes great significance if a sustained expansion of non-traditional exports, in a manner compatible with an autonomous national development, is to be achieved.

In relation to the global strategies and policies for trade and development, it has been suggested in different Latin American countries that the promotion of exports ought to replace import substitution, which has been the object of diverse criticism in recent years. Thus, it is important to enquire whether export promotion would be free from the vices and limitations attributed to import substitution and to analyse the areas of complementarity between the two strategies.

Finally, the possibilities of a marked increase in exports of manufactures from Third World countries, and from Latin America in particular, seem to be tied to rapid technological developments in these regions. Is this really the case, or are LDCs exporting manufactures of low technological content, such as, for example, textiles and footwear? If the latter is happening, the question which immediately arises is: How can they acquire the necessary technology? If it is through transnationals, the further problem arises of whether they will appropriate most of the profits of the growing trade in manufactures. If it can be attained through the generation of a native technology in LDCs, the fundamental question is that of which incentives should be proposed to stimulate the creation of technologies adapted to the needs of these countries. In this volume the experience of Latin America in this respect is also considered.

5 CONCLUDING REMARKS

The fore-mentioned are some of the most important aspects of the international economic order which need to be studied more thoroughly in the region. The collection of essays brought together here is intended to provide a closer examination of specific aspects of this order which seem most relevant to Latin America. Until now, the majority of studies on these topics have been undertaken in the industrialised nations and, logically, from their own point of view. In contrast, the rigorous investigation of the need for and consequences of a new international economic order, as they are visualised by the Third World countries, has been much less intense and of a more global nature, i.e. emphasising particularly the international political problems and the distribution of power between blocs.

Although the international economic system is a product of important political, social and military forces as well, the relevance of solely economic variables should not be underestimated. LDCs in general, and Latin America in particular, have been acquiring increasing power in the world economy, and their voices are heard more in the international sphere. The challenge now is to consider how this power can be used in an effective way. The nature of the international economic system, and the possibilities of transforming it, will depend more than in the past on the attitudes which LDCs adopt in regard to external economic issues. The difficulty of changing the present situation, and of winning approval for many of the proposals put forward by the Third World for structuring a new order, lies partly in the scant attention paid in these proposals to the analysis of concrete ways in which they relate with the practical functioning of the international economy and its institutions. For that reason such proposals are most of the time rejected on the grounds that they are 'vague' or incomplete, whilst those of the industrialised countries are the ones which win attention due to their supposed realism and specificity.

The level of knowledge on many aspects of international economic problems is still insufficient. Academics of the Third World are far more limited in their opportunities for research. Because of their lack of communication with one another in different countries, as well as with public opinion, governmental policy makers and business representatives in their own countries. For this reason we have judged it convenient to promote a joint effort with a group of researchers from Latin America and other countries, the direct results of which are presented in this publication. In the final analysis, the search for more egalitarian and democratic development in the Third World requires greater knowledge, on the part of *all* the community, of the external problems which confront the developing countries.

Similarly, it is necessary to evaluate systematically the policies which have been imposed in many LDCs by authoritarian governments in order to open their economies to world trade. Academics have a responsibility to clarify this debate and to suggest policy alternatives which are realistic and more permanent by virtue of the consensus they can command. Which measures or aspects of the strategies at present in operation should be retained in a democratic context? Are these external policies responsible for the increasing concentration of income and power which can be seen in many developing countries? How should those policies be reformulated by democratic governments which genuinely represent a majority and, consequently, regard it as a priority to satisfy the basic needs of their people? These are some of the more profound questions to which these studies aim to provide an answer.

2 International Finance: Issues of Special Interest for Developing Countries

CARLOS F. DÍAZ-ALEJANDRO

A central difficulty in writing on the international financial and monetary system during March 1978 is that one must avoid the Scylla of getting lost in the very latest crisis, but also the Charybdis of assuming away the post-1971 experience, expecting that the future of the world economy will be similar to the 1959–71 'golden age'.

The brute fact is that the future (say for the next ten years) of the international monetary system and of the world economy looks highly uncertain. Yet one needs a 'most-likely-projection' as a framework for a good part of the following discussion.

Here it will be assumed that the industrialised countries will grow at rates below those registered during the 'golden age', but that a 1930s-type depression will be avoided. During the next ten years the United States is unlikely to lower its annual inflation rate below, say, 5 per cent per annum. In spite of 'favourable' demographic trends, unemployment within the industrialised countries, particularly among the young and marginal groups, will remain higher than during the 'golden age'. Thus, protectionist pressures will remain strong and may affect LDCs with particular strength.

The world economy should witness a continuation of the trend toward policentrism, with semi-industrialised countries becoming increasingly visible in the struggle for world markets. One can foresee the emergence of 'two, three, or more Japans'.

These preliminary considerations raise the issue: What is 'research' in the area of international finance, especially viewed from an LDC perspective?

LDC researchers could join the ranks of those elaborating new models about exchange rate determination in a world of floating rates, participating in the debates on the uses and abuses of global monetarism, the elasticities approach, etc. (on which more below).

At the other end of the spectrum, LDC researchers could simply monitor their own country's experience in international financial markets (conditions of external credit, evolution of the debt), as well as the impact on their own countries of fluctuations in such key exchange rates as those between the US dollar and the German Mark, and the US dollar and the Japanese yen. While these tasks seem descriptive and unexciting, one may note that outside LDC treasuries and central banks there is very little done on these subjects. Scholarly or academic papers on these matters are quite scarce.

A more ambitious project would be to monitor the evolution of the whole system, including changes in the role played by institutions such as the International Monetary Fund. At present, it seems that within LDCs this type of monitoring is done almost solely by civil servants in Treasuries, Central Banks, and Foreign Ministries. An analytic-historic description, from a long-run and 'non-Northern' perspective, of the financial and monetary system would be of great interest not only in the South but also in the North.

In all of these lines of study the perspective could be *positive* or *normative*. But it should be noted that international finance has attracted perhaps too many plans, proposals and 'gimmicks', and too few detached, historical analyses of how the system really works. The travelling band of international experts puts a high price on catching the eye of influential officials. The ultimate triumph is being called a 'financial magician' by the specialised press, with plans and proposals associated with a name, rather than being the author of historical analyses that take a long time to carry out.

In what follows it will be assumed that all of the above lines of study are in principle useful, and indeed necessary. The proper balance among them, and between positive and normative concerns, will be further discussed more fully later.

1 THE THEORETICAL FERMENT IN INTERNATIONAL FINANCE

These are difficult times for teachers of international finance. Student motivation is not a problem; every session they come eagerly seeking an explanation for the latest gyrations of the dollar, Mark, and yen.

Shortages of theoretical models of the balance of payments and exchange rate determination are no problem either; indeed, recent years have witnessed important new theoretical work, associated especially with a global monetarism and the asset-market view of exchange rate determination.

The problem, of course, is synthesising the theoretical contributions into a coherent 'story' compatible with the recent experiences of major industrialised countries. One should note that the turmoil in academic international finance is related to the crisis in the theory and practice of macroeconomics in industrialised countries. In fact, the days when macroeconomics would be taught using closed economy models are long past; leading macroeconomists in the industrialised countries increasingly tackle simultaneously issues of internal and external disequilibrium.

While 'there is great confusion under heaven', some generalisations may be said to arise from the theoretical ferment. Global monetarism,[1] discarding the bizarre claims of some of its most folkloric advocates, has refocused attention on not-so-autonomous capital flows, which theorists of the exchange-control-riddled world of the 1940s and 1950s had tended to neglect. Global monetarists also called attention to the asymmetrical mechanisms of monetary expansion under a dollar standard, emphasising that the United States's balance of payments deficits did not reduce its money supply while those deficits led to a monetary expansion in the world. Somewhat ironically (to one who witnessed Latin American controversies of the 1950s and 1960s), global monetarists have emphasised the inflationary consequences of devaluation. Indeed, in their models it is precisely a devaluation-induced increase in the domestic price level, coupled with a given nominal stock of money, which makes devaluation 'work'. Some global monetarists are very doubtful that devaluation can change domestic relative prices for any significant length of time, a view held by some Latin American structuralists of the 1950s.

The asset-market view of exchange rate determination focuses on a *very* short run.[2] It argues that in such a short run exchange rates and interest rates adjust 'instantaneously' so that portfolio holders are pleased with their combination of assets. Models of this type are applied to a world of floating rates and free capital movements. Global monetarist models, on the other hand, apply to cases of either fixed or flexible exchange rates, but for a *very* long run. The asset-market view has the virtue of allowing for a Tobinesque continuum of liquidity;[3] there may be many financial assets of various characteristics, so that 'money' has no liquidity monopoly.

If in the very short run, which is the one which appears day to day in the financial pages of newspapers, the exchange rate is determined simultaneously with other asset prices, exchange rates cannot be expected to be any more stable than, say, the Dow Jones index of the New York Stock Exchange or short-term interest rates. Indeed, exchange rates could be much less stable than the more diversified indexes. Theorists have also explored the tendency of the exchange rate to 'overshoot' its longer-term level as a result of unexpected changes in monetary policies.[4] Overshooting results from the need for asset yields to be kept in line internationally before there is sufficient time for real variables to adjust to the new situation.

Where does all of this leave the concerns about the current account and the old-fashioned elasticities approach? Their place seems secure between the very long run of global monetarism and the very short run of the asset-market view. Most authors would still take seriously such notions as international competitiveness, the influence of exchange rates on domestic relative prices, and the interaction between the current account and national output, at least during a fuzzily defined 'medium run'.

The IMF, whose staff pioneered in the development of global monetarism and whose policies often relied heavily on the crudest versions of such doctrine, appears to be keeping its distance from the monetary approach to the balance of payments. A recent paper by Carl P. Blackwell, Assistant Director of the Fund's Research Department, argues that the monetary approach needs blending with other lines of analysis, while admitting that some of the monetary approach papers are '. . . characterized by excessive zeal and unduly categorical explanations of complex relationships'.[5] Determining which is the adequate theoretical framework to diagnose balance of payments problems in different LDCs is a question of obvious interest and importance, but with no obvious answer. Although institutional aspects (such as exchange controls) limit the mechanical application to LDCs of the models discussed in this section, many of the ideas arising from the 'theoretical ferment' should have influence in the analysis relevant for those countries.

2 THE POST-1971 INTERNATIONAL FINANCIAL SYSTEM: ANY LESSONS?

As with all economic history, evaluations of the performance of the 1971-8 international monetary and financial system will vary depending on the counter-factual situation against which it is contrasted.

Even advocates of flexible exchange rates will confess disappointment at the large magnitude and seeming pointlessness of fluctuations in key world exchange rates. But they will add that matters would have been much worse had the major industrialised countries insisted on pegging their exchange rates. Such policy, it is argued, would have led to enormous movements in foreign exchange reserves, and perhaps to an eventual imposition of stiff exchange and trade controls. Some advocates of exchange rate flexibility also blame the 'dirty' nature of the floating for some of the gyrations in exchange rates; it has been noted that the post-1973 era of floating has witnessed surprisingly large reserve movements. Official intervention in the markets, in their judgement, has been destabilising.

The above arguments, notwithstanding academic advocates of fixed exchange rates (for industrialised countries), who by 1970 had dwindled to a brave little band, have been gaining recruits during the last few years. Some of them, appalled by the explosion in international liquidity during 1970–1, when the United States belatedly confirmed European 1960s apprehensions and abused its 'exorbitant privilege', also advocate a return to a gold-based system of fixed parities. In their view there is no other way of checking excessive monetary creation than by forcing all countries to settle their balance of payments with this ancient asset, rather than with debt. These economists regard as endogenous a number of events which others consider exogenous to the international financial system, i.e. the 1973 increase in oil prices, and the 1973–4 boom in other commodity prices. In particular, the tendency of the dollar standard to create excessive liquidity and/or violent fluctuations in exchange rates is blamed for much of the worldwide inflation of the 1970s. (The exact meaning of terms like 'world inflation' and 'world money supply' is a matter which has attracted fresh research during the last few years.)

In spite of some gloomy forecasts of the early 1970s, floating exchange rates do not seem to have significantly blocked the expansion of international capital markets. World trade in goods and services has suffered more from declines in GNP growth rates and the rebirth of protectionism in industrialised countries than from uncertainties introduced by floating rates. (Some authors consider that the stagnation of GNP and investment is due to exchange rate instability, but the analytical base of that argument is weak.)

How have these post-1971 monetary and financial trends impinged on LDC development plans? Much detailed research remains to be done in this area. The following are some topics on which opinions abound, but solid evidence is lacking. It is likely that the answers will vary among semi-industrialised LDCs, oil-exporting LDCs and least-developed LDCs.

(a) The impact of 'key-exchange-rates' instability on LDCs

On the assumption that most LDCs will choose to keep either pegged nominal rates or almost-pegged Purchasing-Power-Parities, it is generally recognised that fluctuations in dollar-Mark, dollar-yen, dollar-Swiss franc rates are *in themselves* undesirable from the LDC viewpoint. Such fluctuations introduce instability in the LDC *effective* exchange rate, and/or in terms of trade, and complicate the management of LDC international portfolios, including both short-term assets (reserves) and long-term liabilities (debt).

LDC Central Bankers have been outspoken in their criticism of floating rates among key currencies. But a systematic look at how such floating has actually damaged LDCs during 1973–7 is lacking. It would be interesting, for instance, to determine the extent to which LDCs have used forward markets in order to cover themselves from the risk of fluctuations among key currencies. There is also the related issue of whether alternative exchange rate regimes for industrialised countries are viable without extensive exchange and trade controls which would also damage LDCs.

It may be noted that in a world of generalised floating the definition of an effective exchange rate is far from an easy task, even for LDCs with fairly simple trade flows with the rest of the world. There is first the issue of weighting trade versus financial flows. But even trade-weighted effective rates can present complications: Colombia may neither import from nor export to South Korea, but if Colombian goods compete with those of South Korea in the US market, the Korean dollar rate should find its way into Colombian calculations of effective exchange rates.

The choice for an LDC of whether to peg its exchange rate, and to what, is obviously a crucial issue for most countries.

(b) Access to international liquidity

A strong argument can be made that the rather 'Far West' conditions prevailing in international banking during the 1970s have provided

LDCs with better access to short- and medium-term international liquidity than the access contemplated in extant plans for international monetary reform. Such argument would emphasise that inflationary trends have substantially eroded the commercial interest rates, 'front-end charges', etc., which LDCs have had to pay for that liquidity. In short, the point is that during the 1970s several LDCs have joined the ranks of those who can settle their balance of payments deficits by issuing fresh international liabilities (although *not* denominated in their own currencies), rather than by losing owned international assets. This argument deserves a close quantitative scrutiny. (A related point is the magnitude of the gain to LDCs of more freedom in managing their international portfolios.)

(c) Other external influences on managing LDC internal equilibrium

The same forces facilitating access to international liquidity – i.e., the fast development of international capital markets and unregulated banking – have also demanded from LDC policy makers greater sophistication not just in their management of exchange rates and international portfolios, but also in the handling of domestic monetary and fiscal policies. The often wild swings witnessed during the 1970s in international commodity prices have also tested to the utmost LDC stabilisation instruments and skills (witness the impact on Colombian domestic economic stability of coffee price fluctuations). Frequently, at least the available instruments have been found wanting, raising again old issues about the desirability of exchange and other direct controls (in combination with other policies).

3 THE POST-1971 INTERNATIONAL MONETARY SYSTEM: WHERE DO WE GO FROM HERE?

Although floating exchange rates have been more erratic than expected, although they have *not* insulated national economies from most types of external shocks (something which perhaps should never have been expected), and in spite of the resurgence of 'the case for fixed parities', it is very unlikely that the industrialised world will soon return to a Bretton Woods-type of fixed but adjustable parities. Divergent rates of inflation within the OECD community plus the ever-increasing mobility of international financial capital limit the power of nostalgia for the Bretton Woods system. If such a restoration of Bretton Woods were accomplished at the expense of introducing substantial exchange and trade controls and/or OECD deflationary policies, the outcome would be quite undesirable for the LDCs, in spite of their preference for fixed parities among industrialised countries.

Control over international liquidity was one of the key targets of the efforts at world monetary reform during 1971–4. At least in this area, reform attempts were a failure. The 1970s, contrary to the preoccupations of the 1960s, have witnessed a liquidity glut and a merry extension of the habit of settling deficits by writing IOUs, in one currency or another. It is debatable whether this state of affairs is viable in the long run, particularly given the growing unhappiness of major creditor countries, such as the Federal Republic of Germany, with the way in which the United States regards the dollar standard. The danger exists that conflicts over exchange rates will spill over into trade and financial relations.

If the world is expected to remain in a system of floating parities, it may be asked why international reserves should be a serious concern. The answer, of course, is that completely free floating is unacceptable to most countries, so that intervention in the exchange market by Central Banks has been and will remain a reality.

Alternatives to the present non-system[6] of international liquidity appear difficult to negotiate. A return to asset settlement with expensive gold is a proposal which has its uses in academic seminars, but which is unlikely to advance far in the near future. For several well-known reasons, not least the prominence of South Africa as a supplier of gold, LDCs are unlikely to benefit from such a restoration of the 'barbarous relic'.

From a cosmopolitan and technocratic viewpoint, some sort of move toward the SDR as the major (or only) international reserve asset remains the most rational long-term solution. That solution is not without costs to LDCs, however, as has already emerged in the discussions on international monetary reform. *All* countries would have to give up their freedom to choose reserve composition as they saw fit, chasing the highest returns and best expectations of appreciation. Some LDC Central Banks have developed considerable expertise in this game, and would be reluctant to submit themselves to systemic discipline, preferring to remain 'free riders'. On the other hand, the consolidation of an SDR standard offers LDCs a sharing in the seignorage gains of international liquidity creation, although at the moment such gains seem distant. Those gains, of course, would exist even without the adoption of a 'link proposal'.

Discussions about the link seem remote and unrealistic in 1978. Yet, eventually, they may again become topical. The growing political muscle of the Third World in international organisations, including the IMF, could at that time assure a swift and surprisingly easy victory for one or another of the link proposals.

Not so long ago, representatives of the largest industrialised countries considered whether SDRs, not to mention discussions about the international monetary system, should be limited to a handful of nations (i.e. themselves). That world (of the early 1960s) seems for ever gone. The IMF is likely to remain the major institutional mechanism for discussing proposals regarding the evolving system. While that institution still shows birthmarks from an era dominated by the two victorious Anglo-Saxon powers, it seems a very different animal from its 1944, or even 1965, version. The growing financial weight of OPEC countries has been reflected in recent institutional changes. The future may bring a greater weight to some large semi-industrialised countries and perhaps greater participation from socialist countries.

The recession of 1974–5 witnessed the emergence of some of the largest semi-industrialised LDCs as stabilising elements in global macroeconomics. The apparent national vice of large balance of payments deficits financed by borrowing turned out to be cosmopolitan virtue which held up world purchasing power. Realisation of this fact and of its growing quantitative importance could give such LDCs a greater voice in world macroeconomic councils, historically dominated by a handful of industrialised countries. Such a trend will not be welcomed by those industrialised countries generally favouring tight fiscal and monetary policies. Semi-industrialised LDCs, as large international debtors, are likely to favour expansionist policies even at the expense of a rising 'world price level'. (Recent experience seems to indicate that interest rates do not fully adjust to increasing inflation.)

4 INTERNATIONAL CAPITAL MARKETS

Throughout its history, international capitalism has had as one of its major mechanisms an international capital market. A notable exception to this (not too surprising) generalisation was the period of the Great Depression and the Second World War. At Bretton Woods many feared (or hoped) that international capital markets had disappeared for ever;

the World Bank was to become its Fabian-New Deal replacement. The upsurge in international financial activity during the late 1950s and 1960s may be viewed as a 'getting back to trend', rather than a passing fancy. The robustness of the born-again international capital markets has been demonstrated during the 1970s, for they responded fairly well to the challenge of intermediating the financial imbalances generated by post-1973 OPEC orderly marketing agreements.

Participation by LDCs in those private markets has been viewed with different degrees of surprise, anxiety and alarm. Only recently is it becoming recognised as a subject for research outside Treasuries, Central Banks and private banks. As in the case of commodity markets, there is a lack of industrial-organisation-type of analysis focusing on major actors and the possible imperfections of financial markets. Most of the work so far concentrates on such topics as the burden of the debt (actual and projected) and probabilities of default for individual countries or groups of LDCs. The following are some issues of both positive and normative interest for which present knowledge seems deficient:

(a) Both the national financial markets of industrialised countries and the unregulated international (Eurocurrency) financial market have concentrated lending to LDCs via instruments of relatively short maturity, and with floating interest rates. Long-term lending at fixed interest rates (bonds) has been limited, although this may be changing.[7] It is unclear whether this is wholly the outcome of the 'free' market, or whether it is influenced by national regulations of industrialised countries. (The presumptions are of course different as between the Eurocurrency and the national markets.) It would be of great interest to carry out a detailed analysis of the costs and terms of loans to different countries, of the way in which they evolve during the cycles and of the long-run trends of those variables.

(b) The earlier question of international demand for different types of LDC liabilities is related to the flexibility LDCs have in managing their external debt, including possibilities for prepayment, funding or consolidating debts, so as to minimise servicing costs and avoiding the bunching of repayments. Here, too, there is some evidence of increasing flexibility. Indeed, some international banks have been perplexed by prepayments from some LDCs (at a time, incidentally, when some observers worried about defaults).[8]

(c) During 1977 nine countries accounted for 80 per cent of all syndicated bank lending to non-oil LDCs and regional development institutions. Yet altogether sixty LDCs have managed to tap the Eurocurrency market.[9] Infant borrower and infant lender learning curves remain obscure.

(d) The additional degree of freedom provided by the option to borrow from private international markets should be welcomed by LDCs (as well as by centrally planned economies). Yet one must wonder whether the relative ease of borrowing abroad may lead not only to well-known excesses, but also to delays in the development of *domestic* capital markets (and efficient tax systems).

(e) If the most dynamic LDCs turn increasingly to international capital markets for their external financial needs, what is to be the role of those public financial intermediaries devised to substitute for private markets, i.e. the World Bank and the regional development banks? Besides remaining a source of finance for LDCs unable to go on their own to private financial markets, those public intermediaries are likely to seek new forms of association with private lenders as well as with direct foreign investors. Some of this has been happening for several years, as with the International Finance Corporation. More is likely to happen with large mining projects, where one can foresee packages involving LDC public enterprises, the World Bank, private banks and mining companies from industrialised countries. The positive and normative analysis of these trends should be of great interest. Another topic to be investigated is the interaction and co-ordination between the IMF and the international private banks. Several observers are worried by the possible creation of a 'credit cartel' directed by the IMF for lending to LDCs.

(f) LDC public enterprises have been heavy borrowers during the last few years. LDC private and public financial institutions are also participating in international capital markets both as borrowers and as lenders. This trend is likely to continue, and not just for OPEC countries. Such a trend opens up, *inter alia*, possibilities for new forms of intra-LDC co-operation. Much of the lending of LDC financial institutions will be related to LDC export drives, following the well-worn path blazed by the industrialised countries.

5 A FINAL OBSERVATION

There is no point in repeating here the research suggestions listed in this paper. What about priorities? Such priorities will depend on whether one is thinking of policy needs, or whether one ranks topics according to the intellectual curiosity they arouse. If one follows the first of these criteria, priorities will differ between Chad and Saudi Arabia, or between India and Paraguay. The matter of what a scholar should be aroused by, is perhaps best left to the judgement of consenting adults.

I shall depart from this agnostic tolerance only to suggest that there is a keen need for more Third World scholars to concern themselves with topics which look at the international monetary and financial systems as a *whole*, yet involve exploring the nuts-and-bolts of those systems. Too often in international seminars the role of LDC scholars is limited to telling their 'country story' or vaguely complaining about biases in the international system. Scholars from industrialised countries typically maintain a monopoly of knowledge about the intricacies of the machinery of international finance, giving them a kind of witch-doctor aura which carries over into more general discussions of how the system as a whole does or should operate. Northern scholars benefit from the relatively easy communication which exists between Northern Treasuries and Central Banks, on the one hand, and Northern scholarly centres. During the last ten years impressive expertise must have been accumulated among Southern officials involved in international monetary discussions. Perhaps Southern Scholarly centres could exploit and encourage such expertise, while Southern Central Banks and Treasuries could financially support longer-term thinking, in detail and in depth, about the issues discussed in this paper.

NOTES

1 The literature on the monetary view of the balance of payments is staggeringly large but repetitive. For a good survey see Whitman (1975).
2 For clear presentations of this view, see Branson (1976), and Dornbusch and Krugman (1976).
3 James Tobin, through his work, has emphasised the need to include a variety of financial assets, aside from simple money, in all macroeconomic models.
4 See for example Calvo and Rodríguez (1977).
5 See *IMF Survey*, 20 February 1978.
6 I follow Williamson (1977).

7 In 1977 non-oil LDCs doubled their take from international bond markets, reaching 9 per cent of the total volume from those markets. See *The Economist*, 4–10 March 1978, p. S–10.
8 See 'Bankers Wince as LDCs Prepay Their Loans', *Business Week*, 27 February 1978, p. 86. See also 'International Borrowers Squeeze International Banks', *The Economist*, 18 March 1978, p. 113.
9 See *The Economist*, 4–10 March 1978, pp. S–6 and S–10. The big nine (in order) were: Mexico, Brazil, South Korea, Argentina, Morocco, the Philippines, Chile, Taiwan and Hong Kong.

REFERENCES

Branson, W. H. (1976) 'Asset Markets and Relative Prices in exchange Rate Determination', Seminar Paper no. 66, (University of Stockholm, Institute for International Economic Studies, December).

Calvo, G. and Rodriguez, C. (1977) 'A Model of Exchange Rate Determination under Currency Substitution and Rational Expectations', *Journal of Political Economy*, June.

Dornbusch, R. and Krugman, P. (1976) 'Flexible Exchange Rates in the Short Run', *Brookings Papers on Economic Activity*, 3.

Whitman, M. (1975) 'Global Monetarism and the Monetary Approach to the Balance of Payments', *Brookings Papers on Economic Activity*, 3.

Williamson, J. (1977) *The Failure of World Monetary Reform, 1971–74* (New York University Press).

3 International Finance: Issues of Special Interest for Developing Countries: a Comment

WILLIAM R. CLINE

Carlos Díaz-Alejandro's preamble predicts slower growth in industrial countries and at once suggests an area for research: How can the periphery achieve rapid growth in an era of slow growth at the centre? Díaz also notes the opposite direction, the buoying influence of LDC demand on developed country (DC) economies. On the basis of LINK models, UNCTAD has estimated that a 3 per cent increase in growth in the LDCs causes a 1 per cent increase in DC growth. Considering the relative magnitudes of the respective economies this estimate seems grossly exaggerated. More work is needed on both directions of growth linkage between industrial and developing countries.

The growing literature on global monetarism has also neglected an important topic: What is the optimal policy response of the developing country in the face of expansion of the money supply in industrial countries at historically higher rates? As for the burden of shifting exchange rates among key centre economies and their disturbance of LDC external accounts, I agree with Díaz-Alejandro's final conclusion, that such disturbances are minor compared to those that would occur if the key currency countries sought to maintain rigidly fixed exchange rates. In fact data for the floating period through 1975 indicate lower fluctuation of key exchange rates than during the so-called fixed exchange rate regime (for the period 1958–73; see Cline, 1976).

One of Díaz's more provocative insights is that the LDCs joined the centre currency countries as beneficiaries of the rapid expansion of international credit in the 'go-go years' of the early 1970s. Both groups of countries relied on increased foreign debt to settle their external accounts. An ironical implication of this view is that it casts doubt on the critique of some new international economic order reformers, that the reserve centre currency system discriminates against the developing countries (on which more later).

Díaz cites the increasing maturity of LDCs in international borrowing. In this area there is a need for research on the limits to the model of debt-led growth, and on optimal time paths for external debt. What happens when a country such as Brazil passes into a new phase during which increased debt can no longer supply a major source of savings because of limits to credit-worthiness? Much of the existing literature examines amortisation and interest payments relative to GNP, but it is necessary to incorporate foreign exchange constraints.

In another evolving policy area, Díaz anticipates the expansion of joint public- (multilateral) private investments. Development of new instruments in this field could make an important difference for world efficiency, allowing (for example) the exploitation of high yielding mineral deposits in LDCs prior to that of much lower yield deposits in the politically safer terrains of industrial countries. Work is needed on the 'Son of [Kissinger's] Natural Resources Bank.' Moreover, LDC economists are well positioned to do research that will be credible to both sides, because it was LDC suspicion that torpedoed the initial proposal.

Expanding on two themes raised by Díaz, I would like to offer some additional thoughts on the subjects of international monetary reform and world business fluctuations, in both cases with respect to the interests of the developing countries.

Ndeqwa and Triffin (1976) have called for a new monetary order. The current one has the following flaw, in their view: it creates reserves not by international agreement, but by the extension of credit to reserve centre currency countries (a channel which accounted for 97 per cent of increased world reserves from 1970 to 1974). This phenomenon means a perverse flow of real resources *to* these particular industrial countries. It means a failure of monetary reform to phase out reserve currencies in favour of SDRs. And it contributes to world-wide inflation (financing high demand in the centre countries and causing excess liquidity in other countries through unwanted accumulations of reserves). The remedy: consolidate reserve currencies into a substitution account of SDRs or something similar.

But is this diagnosis a correct one from the standpoint of the LDCs?

The United States had no deficit in 1975, and its deficits in 1976 and 1977 were the result of unco-ordinated OECD growth rates – which eroded competitiveness – and a faltering energy programme, not the consequence of the reserve currency system. Moreover, have past US deficits helped or hurt the developing countries? The former case is stronger. The 'perverse resource flow' has been not from the LDCs but from other industrial countries (now OPEC) to the United States. As for the LDCs, the very outflow of dollars from the United States in the early 1970s facilitated their growth by easing their access to external credit, largely through the US-deficit-fed Eurocurrency market. If LDC growth were internal-resource-constrained, there might be more bite to the critique of the reserve centre system. But more often LDC growth is foreign-exchange-constrained, and since larger US dollar outflows have meant easier global credit, they have probably boosted LDC growth instead of hindering it.

The proposed remedy of consolidating exchange reserves into SDR (or other) accounts would have one supposed benefit for LDCs: the end of the special advantage of seignorage for the reserve centre currencies (or, rather, the extension of seignorage to all IMF members in future SDR allocations). But has the seignorage benefit really been significant for the United States and the United Kingdom? These countries pay a market interest rate on the assets held by foreign countries as reserves. The reluctance of Germany and Japan to allow foreign countries to hold official Mark and yen assets as reserves seems to be adequate evidence that, in terms of revealed preference, the real net value of seignorage is perceived as negative, presumably because of the additional constraints it puts on policy options.

The practical problem with consolidation is that countries, including LDCs, prefer to have the freedom to choose and hold reserve currency assets (as Díaz aptly notes), so that it would be difficult to enlist much support for consolidation even from the supposed beneficiaries (again including the LDCs).

There is a clear need for research on the features of world monetary reform that would be in the best interests of the developing countries. Should they favour the consolidation of exchange reserves into a substitution account (either with or without an SDR-aid 'Link'), and would such a reform be viable? Should they favour instead the current regime of foreign exchange reserves *cum* ample credit for LDCs? Does the reserve currency system discriminate against LDCs? Does it cause global inflation, which can hurt LDCs? Enlightened LDC analysis of these issues is all the more important because, as Díaz notes, the developing countries have now secured a firm role in the negotiating process on monetary reform.

Finally, a word about world business fluctuations. The 'great inflation' of 1972–4 followed by worldwide recession represented a new source of instability for the developing countries. In recent research on this subject at the Brookings Institution, we have reached a number of preliminary conclusions. First, there was transmission of external inflation to internal inflation in nearly all developing countries. Statistical tests relating inflation to monetary growth, import prices and other variables show that, for a panel of thirty developing countries, import price inflation typically explained as much as half of the acceleration in domestic inflation in the period 1972–5. Imported inflation had begun even earlier through the monetary channel, as many countries accumulated reserves in 1971 and 1972 (in part as the result of US dollar outflows) with consequent increases in their domestic money supplies. In Latin America, case studies confirm that imported inflation ended decades of price stability (Central America) or helped reverse earlier trends towards reducing inflation (Brazil).

Second, the welfare effects of world inflation were mixed for the developing countries. Their terms of trade declined from 1970 to 1975 (for non-oil-exporting LDCs), but their terms-of-trade excluding oil improved. For their part, commodity prices became markedly more unstable than in the 1960s. The real capital requirements of the LDCs actually declined, as the impact of export and import inflation on the nominal trade gap was to increase it more slowly than international prices generally. At the same time, concessional aid (though inadequate to begin with) increased by more than enough to cover the increased trade gap (for poor countries) caused by world inflation. Furthermore, there was a clear windfall gain to LDCs from the inflationary erosion of their external debt (after netting out the erosion of their real foreign exchange reserves). Finally, detailed calculations indicate that the inflation in traded commodities from 1972 to 1975 had an equalising, but extremely small, impact on the world distribution of income. In sum, these impact analyses suggest that on balance the LDCs may actually have gained from world inflation, but only at the price of much higher uncertainty in their planning process.

Third, simulations concerning growth linkages found that a steady growth policy in industrial countries could enable the LDCs to reach income levels that were 25 per cent higher, after a period of five years, than would severely anti-inflationary policies of slow growth in industrial countries. Oscillating 'go-stop' policies in industrial countries would leave the LDCs at an income level midway between these two extremes.

There is a need for further research on the implications of new global instability upon LDC growth prospects. It is necessary to derive rules of how LDC policy makers can best neutralise, or even take advantage of, external inflationary and recessionary shocks. Specific issues include the common practice of pegging to the dollar. Some LDCs may find it preferable to appreciate the domestic currency in order to neutralise external inflation (ideally, however, only after first reducing import protection as an alternative means to the same end). As another specific instance, commodity price stabilisation would appear to be all the more important to LDCs now in the new period of cyclical disturbances that is aggravating commodity price fluctuations.

REFERENCES

Cline, W. (1976) *International Monetary Reform and the Developing Countries* (Washington, DC: Brookings Institution).
Ndeqwa, D. and Triffin, R. (1976) 'The International Monetary Order', in Jan Tinbergen (ed.), *Reshaping the International Order: A Report to the Club of Rome* (New York: Dutton).

4 International Monetary and Financial Issues from a National Perspective

EDMAR L. BACHA

This chapter elaborates on research themes on macroeconomic policy-making in open semi-industrialised capitalist economies suggested by the recent Brazilian growth experience,[1] and will deal successively with financial capital flows, debt management, money and credit, and exchange rate regimes.

1 ACCESS TO THE EURODOLLAR MARKET

The development of international banking, as structured in the Eurodollar market, seems to be the most relevant new theme in international finance from the point of view of semi-industrialised LDCs. Both the availability of international finance to medium income LDCs (as measured, say, by the ratio of capital inflows to exports of these countries) seems to have increased, and the financing of current account deficits seems to have become less dependent than before either on direct investments or on bilateral and multilateral loans. The expansion of the Eurodollar market probably increased the freedom of action of at least some LDCs to determine by themselves the limits of their external indebtedness without the prior approval of First World multilateral and governmental financial institutions. In the debates on the NIEO, the trends in the institutionalisation of international banking are one of the most important subjects for semi-industrialised LDCs. It seems necessary to force changes in both the internal power structure and the ideological outlook of the IMF before it can be allowed to act as an international central bank. At the same time, a new institutional framework needs to be devised to allow longer-term capital flows through decentralised means.

Governmental agencies and public enterprises in LDCs apparently can have a pivotal role in enhancing the LDCs' access to Eurodollar funds. The Brazilian experience with Eurobras, government bond issues and public enterprise borrowing deserves careful scrutiny, for it can further our understanding of the rules of the game of the private international financial market, as well as of the new opportunities that it offers to LDCs with an entrepreneurial governmental structure.

The balance of payments surpluses of the oil-producing countries are the most important determinant of the growing importance of the Eurodollar market. The four-fold increase in the dollar price of oil resulted in a massive transfer of income mostly from the industrial North to a group of countries with an extremely high marginal propensity to hoard. Notice the potentially disturbing effect of this fact on North-South economic relations. On one hand, the command over financial-capital deployment tends to escape the industrialised North. (The horror that the developing countries foreign debt causes in Northern academic and governmental circles must be imputed at least in part to this loss of control.) On the other hand, the increase in world savings creates the possibility of financing a higher level of investment in non-oil-producing LDCs, without increasing the links of dependence to the industrial North. This certainly is too rosy a picture of the results of the oil crisis; but such considerations need to be explored in order to temper at least the Northern propaganda against the oil cartel. They also point to the need for institutional research directed at establishing decentralised South-to-South mechanisms of financial intermediation to further competition with the Northern international banking system and improve the conditions of access of less privileged LDCs to the oil-induced surpluses.

2 FOREIGN DEBT MANAGEMENT

Many international meetings have been held on the LDCs' debt *problem*. One wonders if it would not be appropriate to dedicate some to the LDCs' debt *solution*. Institutional mechanisms may be inadequate, but the increased availability of foreign financial capital at least to some LDCs is to be welcomed. In a world where willing borrowers have increasing access to decentralised sources of finance, the issue of debt management assumes paramount importance. Many interesting questions arise in this context. One that seems particularly relevant is the issue of liquidity considerations (or the critical ratios approach) versus rate of return calculations. What is a sound debtor country? Is it one that has a low ratio of debt services to exports (or of net debt to GDP, or of some other similar critical ratio), or one in which the expected rate of return to capital is much higher than world interest rates? Maybe relevant theoretical insights can be developed from thinking about the debt problem as one of finding the ratio of net debt to GDP that equates the expected rate of return to the rate of interest. We may find that the rate of return of additional borrowing in domestic currency is high enough. However, the repatriation of interest requires the generation of additional foreign exchange. *Ceteris paribus*, this imposes a proportional devaluation of the domestic currency (*vis-à-vis* its value when the borrowing occurred). Let the rate of return in domestic currency be r and the proportional devaluation, d. Then, the rate of return of additional borrowing in foreign currency is $r^* = r - d$. It is r^* that is relevant for the decision to borrow. And it may be smaller than the world interest rate even as the latter is only a fraction of r, as measured, say, by the average countrywide profit rate.

Perhaps this point can be rephrased in shadow pricing terms by the observation that rates of return should be calculated using shadow exchange rates rather than observed ones. Both ways of approaching the problem suggest the need to study the microfoundations of the two-gaps approach to development planning, as a means of developing analytically solid and empirically relevant approaches to foreign debt management in LDCs.

Theoretical microeconomics will not exhaust the analysis of available policy options. For good practical reasons, generally these are considered in a structural context. It is frequently argued that there are rigid limits to export expansion or import substitution, and that these limits are outside the control of the investing country. Fruitful empirical research could be designed to investigate if this really is the case. Possibly many instances will be found where export expansion is constrained by supply considerations rather than limited by foreign demand. In the literature, this problem has been analysed from two different perspectives. One, traditionally stressed by orthodox economists, is designed to castigate with extraordinary historical naïveté the 'irrational' trade policies of LDCs. The other perspective may be summarised as the *international trickle-down*. Developing countries can export more (and hence grow faster) only in the measure that industrial countries are growing rapidly and hence importing a lot. Several empirical exercises are suggested by this view. For example, correlating LDCs' GDP growth with export expansion, correlating LDCs' export expansion with industrial countries' GDP growth, etc. Probably more interesting than the signs of the coefficients will be the pattern of the residuals of the regression equations and the shifts in the relevant elasticities through time (for example, the elasticity of LDC exports with respect to the industrial countries' GDP growth). Comparative historical case studies of successful export expansion and import substitution, too, would serve to illuminate these questions. At a more practical level, one wonders if 'every cloud has its silver lining'. To be more precise: isn't the Hirschmanian proposition true that the Latin American countries (LA) may find it easier to expand interregional trade when they face increasing difficulties to export to industrial countries? European economic integration was born and developed in a world of trade restrictions. *Mutatis mutandi*, LA integration may have been hindered by the trade bonanza of the 1960s, and may blossom in the decade following the oil crisis.

This discussion is intended to suggest that perhaps supply management is as important as demand constraints in the process of converting domestic goods into traded commodities. (And also that international trickle-down is a colonial relic, and the sooner it is discarded the better off LDCs will be.) Obviously, management of supply requires additional deployment of resources, and these costs need to be taken into account when calculating a value for r^* that is comparable to world interest rates.

Research efforts can be focused on the real issues, once old preconceptions are discarded and institutional mechanisms are devised to ensure the acceptance of large foreign debts with the same nonchalance that large national debts have come to be viewed. One real issue that seems particularly timely is the creation of international courts of justice to settle debt disputes. These courts might replace with advantage to the LDCs, the Paris Clubs of the present.

A final research theme on debt management suggested by the Brazilian experience has to do with the relationship between gross debt and international reserves. Brazil seems to be maintaining more than one dollar of reserves for every five dollars of foreign debt. The situation is similar to that of a commercial bank that keeps a cash reserve related to the level of its deposits in an unregulated banking system. On one hand, there is the need to maintain the confidence of bank customers, to ensure a continuous inflow of deposits. On the other hand, the bank needs to be prepared to face a run on its deposits without having to declare bankruptcy. Both theoretical models and analysis of empirical regularities may provide useful information for the policy makers in charge of debt management in LDCs. For the record, notice that the existence of this implicit reserve ratio implies that foreign borrowings have higher costs than indicated by LIBOR interest rates plus spread and fees. Let these be i, with j the interest rate on the reserves, and x the reserve ratio. Then, the effective interest rate of foreign loans is:

$$i + (i-j)x.$$

With $x = 0.2$, under current interest rates this may add from 1 to 1·5 per cent a year to the costs of foreign borrowing.

3 MONEY AND CREDIT

The money supply of most semi-industrial LDCs probably responds more or less passively to the needs of trade. Opening these economies to foreign finance may lead to an even higher degree of passivity in the behaviour of the money supply than before. In the case of Brazil, some empirical studies suggest that the monetary authorities might have managed to sterilise the foreign reserves component of the monetary base through an active open market policy. This result is doubtful. Legally, government bills are nearly as good as cash to compose the required reserve ratio of the commercial banking system. Moreover, they are highly liquid. On both counts, the velocity of circulation of base money increases as the national debt expands.[2] The final effect on the goods market should not be very different from an exogenous expansion of high-powered money.

Quite simply, powerful enough instruments of monetary policy do not seem to be available to sterilise effectively the foreign component of the money base, as its importance increases with the growth of foreign debt under the mechanism outlined in the previous section. More research on these issues is clearly needed.

Recent debates on the inflationary impact of foreign finance on the Brazilian economy suggest that the full picture is not captured by looking at the money supply side alone. The idea is that we are dealing with a credit constrained economy, in which the rate of investment and, hence, the level of effective demand is determined by credit availability. Foreign savings relax this constraint, allowing an expansion of effective demand even as the money supply remains invariant (money rates of interest may increase but this will not deter potential investors). The

mechanism of transmission would be as follows: (+) foreign credit →
(+) investment → (+) effective demand → (+) nominal income → (+)
imports. Money supply increases initially, but it declines once imports go
up. Imports increase in response to a higher nominal income, hence a
higher price level. The conclusion is that inflation is induced by the
foreign credit inflow in a manner that is largely independent of the short-
run behaviour of the money supply.

Foreign credit may result in a larger money supply but this is only a
side effect of the main transmission mechanism. For the monetary
authorities may not be willing to hold private domestic bills but quite
happy to increase their reserves of dollar-denominated deposits, as a
counterpart to an expansion of the money base. Total credit to the
private sector expands; hence, investment increases. The three-part
accounting framework would be as set out in Table 4.1.

TABLE 4.1   Accounting framework of an expansion of foreign credit

	Foreigners	Monetary authorities	Local firms
Debts	(+) Monetary auth- ority deposits	(+) Base money	(+) Foreign debt
Assets	(+) Local firms bills	(+) International reserves	(+) Investment

Additional aggregate demand materialises because an appropriate
financial intermediation mechanism was found to allow credit expansion
to domestic firms. Money creation is simply an accounting counterpart
to this process, with further effects on the economy that are of a
complementary nature.

The treatment of credit as an input required to ensure short-term
command over labour is another fruitful research avenue. Suppose that
the productive process requires immortal fixed capital, K, and one-
period circulating capital, wL, where w is the real wage and L the labour
input entering the process one period before output is produced. Present
period labour costs then are $wL (1 + h)$, where h is the one-period interest
rate. Short-term employment and levels of economic activity in this case
are influenced by credit market conditions in a much more direct manner
than suggested by the *IS-LM* framework. For a seminal paper in this
line, derived from observation of the Argentinian experience, see Cavallo
(1977).

This type of modelling may help to illuminate questions related to the
under-utilisation of fixed capital for lack of short-term credit, which

traditional macro-models are unable to deal with. The critical role of the banking sector is stressed, as well as the possibility of conflict between 'productive' and 'financial' capital.

4 EXCHANGE RATE REGIMES

Exchange rate policies raise several interesting research issues. A particularly relevant one is the relationship between minidevaluations (or the crawling peg) and the rate of inflation. The following example, derived from Lara-Resende (1978), is instructive in this respect. Assume a production process the current inputs of which are labour and an imported material. Mark-up pricing rules, with P the final product price, w the money wage rate, and e the exchange rate (a normalisation procedure is adopted such that the labour input coefficient, the dollar price of the imported material and its input coefficient are all equal to 1). The movements of w are contemporaneous and proportional to those of P, while the exchange rate is adjusted once a year, in proportion to the price level. Then:

$$P = u(w + e)$$
$$w = w_o P$$
$$e = e_o P_{-1}$$

Where u is 1 plus the mark-up rate, and w_o and e_o are the 'target' values for the real wage and the real exchange rate. After substitution, the annual rate of inflation is found to be:

$$P/P_{-1} - 1 = ue_o/(1 - uw_o) - 1,$$

a value which we assume to be positive.

Suppose now that the exchange rate starts being adjusted twice a year (a movement towards minidevaluations), so that:

$$e = e_o P_{-1/2}$$

Noting that:

$$P_{-1/2} = u(w_{-1/2} + e_{-1/2}),$$

with:

$$e_{-1/2} = e_o P_{-1}$$

and

$$w_{-1/2} = w_o P_{-1/2}$$

The appropriate substitutions can then be made to yield the following value for the yearly inflation rate:

$$P/P_{-1} - 1 = (ue_o/(1 - uw_o))^2 - 1$$

which is more than twice as large as before.

Questions may be raised about the relevance of this mark-up model. For example, it cannot deal with the effect of the minidevaluations on the variance of the real exchange rate (in both cases, the real exchange rate is constant at $e/P = (1 - uw_o)/u$). At least in Brazil, it definitely has been the case that the minidevaluation system reduced the variability of the real exchange rate, and this was supposed to have been a main contributory factor to export expansion and the access to international financial markets. Perhaps questions such as these can be dealt with by adding more structure to Lara-Resende's model.

In a private communication, Ricardo Ffrench-Davis suggests that minidevaluations, because they reduce the variance of the real exchange rate, may allow a lower target value to prevail. This reduction in e_o might more than compensate for the direct inflationary effect of more frequent exchange rate changes. Bruno and Sussman (1978), by contrast, feel that the minis tend to absolve the decision maker from taking unpopular actions in the areas of fiscal restraint and incomes policy. Maxidevaluations, with all their clumsiness, would have the advantage of at once forcing decision makers and social pressure groups into collective and simultaneous action on many fronts, leading to lower inflation rates.

A second exchange rate policy issue has to do with the relationship between the degree of exchange rate flexibility and the extent of required government controls over exchange rate transactions.

In an inflationary context, periodic maxidevaluations are really a non-starter, because the large fluctuations in the real exchange rate are extremely favourable to speculative activities. Private demand for foreign exchange tends to concentrate in the months immediately preceding a large devaluation, whereas the private supply accumulates in the months following the devaluation. Large fluctuations in foreign reserves are induced, which force the government to apply stiff controls on foreign exchange transactions. These controls tend to hinder legitimate foreign trade activities.

The question at issue is how far the minidevaluations can go in preventing speculative capital flows and, hence, in lessening the need for foreign exchange controls. Bruno and Sussman (1978) mention that the decision of October 1977 to float the Israeli pound was causally linked to the deregulation of foreign exchange controls. The new Israeli government felt that removing the controls while preserving the crawling peg might start a large outflow of capital. In Bacha (1978a), I suggested that transaction costs were not sufficiently large to prevent speculators from making large profits in the Brazilian monthly devaluation system. Carlos Díaz commented that the experience of Colombia indicated that an appropriate medicine was a shortening of the devaluation period; in that country, a degree of freedom in exchange rate transactions could be preserved while devaluing the currency once or twice a week. The 1976–7 experience of Chile seems to point in the same direction.

For a given domestic rate of inflation, the frequency of minis required to make speculation unprofitable is an inverse function of the sophistication of the banking system of the country (for this determines the relevant transaction costs). The implication is that the minidevaluation system will fade away, as our semi-industrial economies integrate more fully with the rest of the world and diversify their banking systems. This poses the problem of finding an alternative technique of exchange rate determination, for it is probable that inflation will remain with us. The recent international experience with floating suggests a new system of exchange rate targeting – or managed float – that could suit the needs of Third World countries as well.

Exchange rate targeting has been recommended for Portugal by Dornbusch and Taylor (1977), as a means of stabilising inflation rate expectations. However, governments are very reluctant to commit themselves to 'realistic' predictions of the inflation rate. Experience with Brazilian policy makers shows that they feel strongly that they can keep inflation in check only by underpredicting future inflation rates. In their view, these underpredictions allow them to control the claims of different social groups (including public sector departments) to higher nominal incomes. They understand that these claims have to be constantly frustrated in order to prevent an acceleration of the inflation rate. According to this view, not letting 'true' future inflation rates come into the open is an important instrument of social control in the hands of the government. In this socio-political context, exchange rate targeting would be a harmful policy choice, for the domestic currency would soon become overvalued. Research directed at showing that the policy makers' view of the inflationary process is at variance with reality is a precondition for the institution of targeting as an instrument of exchange rate determination.

A point of related interest, suggested by the Brazilian and Israeli experiences, is the difficulty of managing the minis once large once-for-all changes in the terms of trade occur (in this case, the quadrupling of oil prices). Israel chose to abandon the minidevaluations, maxidevalued and then floated; in addition, it abolished most trade restrictions. Brazil opted to maintain the minis and tightened import controls. Underlying both solutions was the fear that the confidence of the market in the minis could not be re-established in the aftermath of a maxidevaluation. These experiences suggest that a minidevaluation system designed to stabilise the real exchange rate cannot deal with discrete terms of trade changes; new policy alternatives need to be found to cope simultaneously with inflation and large terms of trade changes.

NOTES

1 Background material for these notes can be found in two recent papers: Bacha (1978a) and Bacha (1978b).
2 Velocity of circulation of base money = monetary multiplier × the velocity of circulation of the means of payment.

REFERENCES

Bacha, E. (1978a) 'Notes on the Brazilian Experience with Minidevaluations, 1968/1977', paper prepared for the Ford Foundation/Central Bank of Barbados Seminar on Developing Countries and the International Financial System (Bridgetown, Barbados: January).
—— (1978b) 'Brazil's Balance of Payments before and after the Oil Crisis', paper prepared for the UNCTAD/UNDP Project on the Balance of Payments Adjustment Process in Developing Countries (University of Brasilia: July).
Bruno, M. and Sussman, Z. (1978) 'Exchange Rate Flexibility, Inflation and Structural Change; Israel under Alternative Regimes', paper prepared for the Ford Foundation/Central Bank of Barbados Seminar on Developing Countries and the International Financial System (Bridgetown, Barbados: January).
Cavallo, D. (1977) 'Stagflationary Effects of Monetarist Stabilization

Policies', unpublished PhD dissertation (Cambridge, Massachusetts: Harvard University).

Dornbusch, R., and Taylor, L. (1977) 'Economic Prospects and Policy Options in Portugal — Summer 1977', (Cambridge, Massachusetts: MIT, September).

Lara-Resende, A. (1978) 'Mark-up Pricing with Indexed Inputs.' (Cambridge, Massachusetts: MIT, May).

5 International Monetary and Financial Issues from a National Perspective: a Comment

ALBERT FISHLOW

Edmar Bacha is correct in emphasising the dramatic improvement in the access of middle-income developing countries, and especially those of Latin America, to the capital markets of the North. This transformation, well under way even before the new surpluses of the oil exporters began to fuel the Eurodollar market in 1974, has had a series of profound effects; it has permitted accommodation of record developing country deficits on current account to finance continuing economic growth despite world recession and increased import requirements; it has changed the composition as well as the quality of capital inflow, diminishing the importance of both public concessional long-term finance and foreign direct investment in favour of private short- and medium-term debt; and it has diversified the linkages of these middle-income countries to a wider variety of financial centres in the North. All of these add up to a different style of economic integration between South and North, and one in which the lowest income countries have been prejudiced.

Several issues for national policy are posed by this new financial integration, as Bacha usefully suggests. Some require further research; others involve a reorientation of developing country perspectives in response to present opportunities and constraints.

Here I wish to stress four questions of particular interest for Latin America. First, what is the appropriate indebtedness for individual countries? Second, what are the implications of the larger capital inflow for internal resource allocation? Third, what kinds of macroeconomic adjustments, short- and long-run, are necessitated by greater financial integration? Fourth, what concerted international action is indicated as a substitute for, or complement to, national policies?

1 COUNTRY INDEBTEDNESS LEVELS

Recent experience seems to suggest that the behaviour rule for many countries has been one of maximising capital inflow. While providing a significant element of autonomy and independence in the short run, such unlimited enthusiasm for external finance is deceptive. It leaves to suppliers of credit decisions about national indebtedness capacity. That is a dangerous course because the banks take into account only the risks based on likelihood of repayment, not the productivity of the resources acquired. Fixed future obligations are not easily altered; their satisfaction may require the restriction of imports and slower economic growth. One may be exchanging greater independence in the present for more future dependence.

Bacha's formulation of the appropriate decision rule to determine optimal indebtedness – one equating the expected rate of return, net of the devaluation implicit in debt service, to the loan rate – begs the question. The fundamental problems are the uncertainties about future export proceeds, import requirements, availability of additional capital, and world inflation. Those variables are not entirely within the control of individual countries, but depend on global conditions as well. The fragility of the development process in the middle-income countries is precisely their greater susceptibility to reduced export demand from the industrial countries because of their need for foreign exchange to pay for imports and to service a large debt.

The debt problem, therefore, is a trade problem in two senses. In the short run, lacklustre export performance adversely influences new loans and aggravates management of the balance of payments. In the long run, creditor countries' deficits have to accommodate the surpluses of the developing debtor countries. In the absence of such a trade realignment the debt cannot be repaid. The alternative is toleration of continuing significant increases in indebtedness that postpone further to the future the day of reckoning. The critical danger is the possibility – in a completely decentralised global economic system – that neither adjustment will occur, but rather that the burden will present itself in the form of reduced developing country *and developed country* economic growth.

The optimal policy of debt accumulation for different types of countries (taking into account their flexibility of export supply as well as their particular conditions of external demand), the characteristics of their internal capital markets and the nature of their import requirements are all problems well worth analysing. While we readily know the requisite marginal conditions, the dynamics of debt-led development have not been adequately explored.

2 INTERNAL RESOURCE ALLOCATION AND FOREIGN CAPITAL

One important dimension of those dynamics relates to the implications of large external finance for the performance of internal capital markets. Does access to foreign capital reduce the pressure for domestic structural reforms that could ultimately generate more internal savings? If so, conventional calculations of the costs and benefits of foreign debt will exclude a significant negative component and bias the decision in favour of continued need for foreign finance.

Do foreign capital inflows influence the domestic allocation of resources in a 'systematic fashion, benefiting some sectors and discriminating against others – industry versus agriculture; large enterprise versus small enterprise; foreign firms versus domestic firms; exporters versus producers for the domestic market; state enterprise versus the private sector? Is greater monopoly power within the domestic financial market the result, by allowing those enterprises with access to foreign resources to grow most rapidly? Or is competition in international capital markets sufficient to prevent its occurrence? These effects upon the domestic economy have been ignored in much of the discussion focusing upon international capital inflows. Their analysis could tell us much about the continuing validity of the concept of dependent development in Latin America, and the changes in emphasis required.

These questions must be studied in a comparative mould. The role of the Brazilian state in influencing the domestic allocation of credit undoubtedly differs from the Mexican, or the Peruvian or the Chilean. Can a meaningful typology be identified as a function of the sophistication of public policy and the extent of domestic capital market evolution? Do self-obsolescing bargains also arise in the case of debt finance as internal financial institutions obtain experience as they arise in direct foreign investment, and under what circumstances?

3 MACROECONOMIC NATIONAL POLICY CONSTRAINTS

The third theme concerns the potential constraints imposed upon national policy by greater integration into international capital markets. In the short run, the capacity to sustain an independent monetary and interest rate policy is reduced. Bacha notes the practical problems of managing the money supply when financial inflows are large. He does not, however, raise the prior issue of whether developing countries *should* be passive in response to balance of payments surpluses and deficits. Some have argued that semi-industrialised countries require such external discipline to control inflation; international capital markets can then be relied upon to equalise interest rates. Bacha implicitly rejects such a view by his concern for the inability of national policies successfully to insulate the domestic economy from changes in international reserves. Elsewhere he has shown the importance of government measures regulating the conditions of capital inflow and the absence of interest rate equalisation in Brazil. He does not, however, compare such discretionary policies with one of more complete openness. Fuller analysis of other rules in other countries is indicated. Surprisingly, despite the virulence of imported inflation in many developing countries, their monetary policies have been regarded as fully autonomous despite their progressive integration into the world economy.

Another policy instrument quite obviously conditioned by such integration is the exchange rate. There is a clear relationship between the optimal exchange rate regime a country should choose and its domestic monetary and financial sophistication. The appeal of floating, or even minidevaluation, systems may be illusory in the absence of other domestic policy instruments and considerable flexibility in production. Variable exchange rate regimes do not dichotomise the economy by assuring external balance regardless of internal policies.

Conversely, domestic constraints may impede effective use of the exchange rate instrument. One prominent example, intimately related to the accumulation of foreign debt, is a reluctance to devalue because of the domestic distributional implications of doing so. Liabilities denominated in foreign currency are directly scaled up by devaluation; thus, wealth effect will influence those enterprises with foreign debt differentially. It has been alleged that Brazil cannot devalue because the burden will be especially great for public enterprises – requiring a compensating expansion of domestic credit in their behalf large enough to offset the original nominal devaluation. Yet Mexico, with a comparably large debt, did devalue. That experience could serve as an important opportunity for assessing the domestic balance sheet effects.

Finally, among the short-term adjustments not discussed by Bacha, there is the trauma of the stabilisation crisis that may befall excessive reliance on capital inflow. That is somewhat surprising in view of three instances of recent IMF active involvement in Latin America: Mexico, Argentina and Peru. Greater economic integration raises new questions. For example, it would be of considerable interest to examine carefully the domestic policies counselled and actually followed when private foreign debt is considerable, compared to earlier experience. That could shed light on the bargaining strength, rather than weakness, which an extant debt can represent. Banks can become hostage to their previous exposure.

For the longer term, an essential requirement for debtor nations successfully to cope with would seem to be a new development model that simultaneously reduces import requirements while encouraging exports. Current magnitudes of debt service are such that further resource transfers of similar net volume will require much larger gross capital inflows. A policy of import substitution alone would leave a dangerously narrow margin for essential import requirements and produce perilous susceptibility even to modest fluctuations in export proceeds. A policy of export growth that was biased against domestic production that was socially, even if not privately, profitable would be equally inappropriate for the long run.

This new model must differ from the disequilibrium process of the 1950s in which industrialisation was stimulated at the expense of the export sector, and whose inconsistencies eventually caused limited, and inefficient, growth. That transfer of resources from the export sector cannot now be justified. Yet there remains the need to obtain domestic savings for the new and more capital-intensive import substitution projects. Clearly, in such circumstances, and despite the disrepute of recent years, more serious attention to economic planning to project dynamic comparative advantage becomes indispensable. So, too, does serious reconsideration of the possibilities afforded by regional integration to make the future cycle of import substitution more efficient and complementary.

4 INTERNATIONAL ADJUSTMENT POLICIES

I come now to my final point: the potentialities of international policies to alleviate the burdens of adjustment of individual national units to the new conditions of financial integration. Four areas suggest themselves for practical action.

The first is a serious attempt by the South to place the debt problem in its appropriate trade context. Developing countries at one time pressed for a debt moratorium, but never tied financial difficulties to a fundamental commitment by creditor countries for adequate import surpluses. Clearly, a requirement to repay foreign debt, in the absence of such a world economic environment, places sanctity of private contract above considerations not only of equity, but also of global efficiency. Slower developing country growth, the inevitable consequence of reduced import capacity, would also imply slower growth for the developed. Developing a feasible means for indexing aggregate import absorption to terms of debt repayment merits more consideration than it has yet been given.

A related international innovation is a better mechanism for dealing with individual cases of debt default. Even if total developing country exports were adequate to the task of repayment, those of particular countries need not be. Relief of burdened debtors proceeds arbitrarily on a case by case basis. Paris Clubs follow no set rules; international politics count as much as economic considerations. Zaire is a recent good example. Bacha suggests that the International Court of Justice is the proper agency to resolve disputes. That presupposes exactly what is lacking – an international code of bankruptcy applicable to national units. Banks include a risk premium in their interest rates for just such an eventuality; on occasion they must be prepared to accept the consequences of their erroneous judgements, rather than transferring the burden fully to debtors.

The logical place for working through and implementing such a code should be the IMF, and not the Court. The Fund has the unique capacity to enforce its decisions by advancing the further credits needed to reconstruct a viable national policy. Its continued lending would be a powerful antidote against unhappy private sector lenders who might be tempted into reprisals against countries judged unable to repay their past obligations in full.

The Fund already acts in cases short of outright bankruptcy. Its operations are not without controversy because of its adherence to conservative and orthodox internal policy prescriptions. Yet such rules call for more serious analysis by outsiders, and not merely critical rhetoric. For example, the simple Polak identity relating permissible domestic credit expansion to the balance of payments deficit requires rethinking; even the Fund would agree. A factor inhibiting change is the

IMF's zeal for universalism, which quite likely exceeds even its predilection for monetarism. What are required are sets of rules appropriate to different classes of countries – depending, among other factors, on their financial structure, the composition of trade and its price responsiveness, and the flexibility of internal production and factor prices. Research that produced a series of conditionality rules varying by country type could be a more powerful influence upon actual policies than elaborate multinational negotiation.

Such analysis of Fund behaviour quickly extends into a more fundamental rethinking of its institutional role, and that of other international agencies. This is a third subject meriting consideration. The relative success of private financial markets in intermediating unprecedentedly large imbalances in global payments should not obscure a fundamental deficiency: market determination of the volume of total credit to developing countries, and its allocation among them, does not satisfy the requirements of international efficiency, let alone equity. Lack of information, bank lending conventions and surplus countries' liquidity preference do not add up to optimal private market performance. There is now no global Central Bank to oversee world economic activity. Should not that reform – so obviously consistent with the needs of the industrialised North – figure in the agenda of the South?

Despite the disappointing lack of progress in all-encompassing economic negotiations between North and South, the record of reform within existing institutions like the World Bank, the IMF and GATT is more encouraging. All influence economic performance in significant ways. More conscious attention to the structure of their rules and possibilities for their change may contribute more to enhanced development prospects for the South than more dramatic global compacts.

A fourth and last area worthy of attention is the potential for establishing more effective direct links among developing countries. Little serious analysis has been conducted to determine the real, and not the rhetorical, possibilities for increased trade and financial flows within the South. The attraction of channelling surplus resources from the OPEC countries directly to oil-importing developing countries, bypassing the private international banking centres of the North, is obvious but also deceptive. In recent years, a large and increasing proportion of international loans has emanated from credit creation within the industrialised countries rather than from the continuing deposit of petroleum surpluses. Direct financial intermediation on a significant scale may therefore involve greater costs in reduced resource flow than benefits in retained profits. Moreover, it resumes a commitment by the surplus countries that thus far has not been entirely evident.

There must be a similar cool appraisal of the potential gains from enhanced South-South trade. The past record of regional economic integration schemes suggests – in the absence of larger political objectives – that national units have been reluctant to accept policies in which the common good outweighs particular gains. That experience cautions against excessive optimism for the longevity of strategies that encourage merchandise trade exclusively among developing countries. This is not to rule out a likely upward trend: higher levels of income and technological sophistication in some countries, and a greater openness of economies within the South, offer more favourable opportunities than in the past. The issue, rather, is how far to go in creating additional and special stimuli. It should not be left exclusively to economists with biases on one or another side of the question.

International financial and monetary developments of the last decade thus open a rich agenda of policy questions requiring analysis. Greater international integration touches vitally on domestic decisions within developing countries, as we have seen. It also calls for research on reforming international rules and institutions. The vision of the new international economic order is very much in a normative spirit. It would be a shame if the best economists – in both North and South – failed to confront the challenge.

6 Primary Products in Latin America

ROBERTO JUNGUITO AND DIEGO PIZANO

The aim of this chapter is to delineate priority areas for research in connection with primary products for the Latin American case. It is intended not as a technical discussion, but as a review of contributions to the academic debate, and an expression of some doubts and worries.

The first section summarises the problems which primary products pose for the management of the developing economies that depend upon them as sources of exports. The analysis is carried out in terms of the variables commonly discussed in the economic literature in relation to LDCs and the export of primary products: dependence, slow growth of demand, instability of prices and incomes, the negative evolution of the terms of trade, etc.

The second section presents the Latin American case in some detail, and in a preliminary and exploratory manner analyses the dependence of the countries of the region upon primary products, and a number of exercises relating to fluctuations in the prices of those commodities and to export instability. We then go on to examine the problem of the terms of trade faced by the countries of Latin America and by LDCs in general. Finally, we comment upon regional attitudes to schemes for the control of primary products.

The third section takes up the themes related to primary products and the international economy which need to be investigated most urgently in Latin America, including the feasibility and opportuneness of the formation of cartels, price stabilisation, indexing, the role of primary products in the light of the restructuring of world industrial production and the 'optimal' division of labour, and the role of foreign investment in the production of raw materials.

1 PROBLEMS RELATED TO PRIMARY PRODUCTS

Although approximately half of all exports of primary products are made by industrialised nations, the evolution of the primary sector of the world economy is closely linked to the prospects for growth among LDCs. Of the income which these countries receive for their exports, 80 per cent comes from the sale of primary products.

We must first review briefly some of the major problems connected with these commodities, which have given rise to the search for new approaches which might regulate production and trade in the primary sector. The most significant problems can be summarised as follows: (a) the marked dependence of LDCs on a few products; (b) the slow expansion of international demand for these; (c) instability in the volume of exports and the prices obtained; and (d) the apparent deterioration in the terms of trade.

Each of these points is now examined in turn, and some of the solutions which have been proposed are introduced.

(a) The dependency of LDCs

Most LDCs depend upon two or three primary products to generate over two-thirds of their foreign exchange earnings. This situation reflects not only a high degree of concentration upon primary products as sources of exports, but also the fact that the primary sector continues to play a major part in the generation of GNP. In fact the curves of sectoral composition of GDP produced by Chenery and Syrquin (1975) suggests that growth in the majority of LDCs is heavily dependent upon the expansion of the primary sector. The importance of industry has increased, but according to a study of Leontief (UN, 1977), it still does not generate more than 20 per cent of GNP in LDCs (figures for 1970).

(b) The slow expansion of demand

With the exception of oil, and of some minerals and timber, exports of primary products have grown less rapidly than world trade in general. Between 1955 and 1972 world trade expanded at an average rate of 7.3 per cent per year, while trade in primary products (excluding oil) registered a rate of only 5 per cent per year in foods, and 4.2 per cent in raw materials. Nevertheless, studies carried out by the United Nations suggest the prospect of more accelerated growth of demand for mineral raw materials, projecting rates of growth from now until the end of the century of 3·6 per cent per year for industrialised free market economies, 5·1 per cent for planned economies, and 7·2 per cent for LDCs (UN, 1977).

In general terms, demand for primary commodities of mineral origin tends to be proportionate to the expansion of GNP; even so, rising *per capita* incomes in LDCs could induce an even more rapid increase in global demand, which if consolidated would reflect a demand derived from industry, a sector which would thus be gaining ground in terms of its contribution to GNP, as Leontief predicted.

Demand for primary products of agricultural origin, subject to Engels's law, as we know, does not seem likely to grow more rapidly in the period up to the year 2000 than it has in the past. In a study for the United Nations, Leontief estimates that the rate of growth will fluctuate between 3·5 and 4 per cent per year, depending upon whether one takes cereals or animal products.

The slow growth of demand for primary products (with the exception of some minerals) appears to be an unavoidable reality. Nevertheless, a recent study (IBRD, 1977a) estimates that if the industrialised countries were to eliminate tariff and non-tariff restrictions affecting trade in primary products, a substantial increase in demand for these products would occur. However, it is not realistic to suppose that this protection will be dismantled in the short term.

(c) Instability

There are various aspects of instability which require separate treatment: (i) causes; (ii) the relationship between instability and development; and (iii) tendencies towards increasing or decreasing instability in primary products, expressed in terms of fluctuations in prices or in volumes exported.

Among the causes, the following should be mentioned: low price and income elasticities of supply and demand; the subordination of demand for primary products to the cycles of developed countries; competition from synthetic products; poor planning and understanding of intervention in markets; speculation; political factors (strikes, wars) and natural catastrophes (frosts, floods).

As to the relationship between instability and economic growth, the existing literature on the subject comes to contradictory conclusions.

Some studies, such as those of Coppock (1962) and MacBean (1966) claim that there is no significant relationship between the rate of growth of GNP and export instability; others, such as those of Kenen (in Cooper, 1973) and Glezakos (1973), register a degree of association sufficient for them to state the contrary. The result of these exercises as a study by Garay and Pizano (1979) suggests, depends fundamentally upon the period selected and the manner in which the variables, and especially the index of instability, are defined. Analysis of the different studies leads to the conclusion that those who have found an inverse relationship between instability and development have been more painstaking in the adoption of a clear methodology.

Finally, it is of interest to note that although some authors have put forward the thesis that world export instability is decreasing, there are a number of factors operating in the international economy which could lead one to the opposite conclusion:

   (i) the more and more frequent sudden temporary entry of the Republic of China and the Soviet Union into world markets for primary products such as rubber, wheat and aluminium;

   (ii) the policies of nationalisation pursued in some LDCs, which have led in some cases to expropriation without adequate compensation, creating a climate of uncertainty in some geographic areas, and inducing fluctuations in the level of investment in primary sectors (and in mining in particular);

   (iii) the tension prevailing in the Middle East; and

   (iv) the ambitious research programmes of industries producing synthetic substitutes.

(d) The terms of trade issue

Low price and income elasticities of demand, combined with the tendency of many primary products to show surpluses over consumption needs, explain the deterioration that has taken place in the terms of trade, a phenomenon which was particularly marked between 1950 and 1970. It should be noted however that many of these commodities are subject to decreasing returns, which permits us to postulate that a trend in the opposite direction is possible. It is not therefore possible to formulate a law *à la* Prebisch valid for all countries and all times. What is clear is that, in the absence of specific measures, it does not seem likely that the terms of trade will improve significantly.

Various solutions have been proposed to the problems of instability and deteriorating terms of trade: support prices, producers' cartels, agreements between producers and consumers, a greater degree of manufacturing of primary goods, compensatory finance, indexing, stabilisation methods of the STABEX type, and so on. All these formulae are subject to problems of measurement and of a conceptual nature, which require more detailed treatment.

2 PRIMARY PRODUCTS AND LATIN AMERICA

In examining the theme of primary products in the Latin American context we intend, first, to establish the extent to which the countries of the region depend upon primary products; second, to study the impact which they have had upon foreign exchange income and export instability; and, finally, to examine the record regarding the terms of trade.

(a) Latin American dependency

Primary products are of great significance in the international trade of Latin America and, in general, of all LDCs. Some have gone as far as to argue that *the* problem of international trade for LDCs is that of primary products.[1] It is not enough, then, to establish their importance within international trade; we must also discover whether, in accordance with appropriate criteria, Latin America is more or less than 'normally' dependent upon trade in such products.

One way of throwing light upon the second point is to compare the coefficients of dependency of each country, defining this as the relationship between exports of primary products and of all goods and services,[2] with the pattern of dependency expected in a function of *per capita* income. These 'expected levels' can be derived from a recent study (Chenery and Syrquin, 1975) which identifies typical international patterns for the significance of total exports of goods and services within GDP, and for the share of total exports accounted for by primary products.[3] By dividing one coefficient by the other, we can find, for each level of *per capita* income, the 'expected' value of the relationship between primary and total exports. Figure 6.1 presents these values, comparing them with those obtained for each of the countries of Latin America.[4]

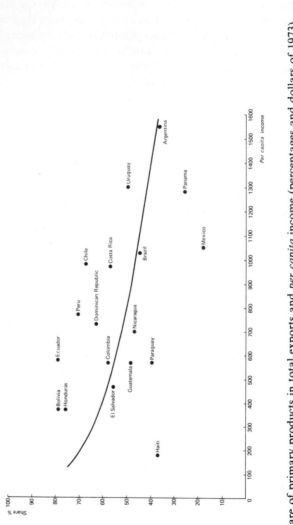

FIGURE 6.1   Share of primary products in total exports and *per capita* income (percentages and dollars of 1973)

The graph permits an answer to the question posed. The countries of Latin America show on average, a dependence upon exports of primary products which is slightly greater than that expected on the basis of their GNP *per capita*. This is due not so much to the *number* of countries lying above or below the norm as to the fact that the *deviations* of the countries above the norm are greater than those of the countries below the norm.[5]

(b) Dependency and instability

We seek now to establish the impact of Latin America's relative dependence on the export of primary products upon instability in foreign currency earnings. The issues that need clarification are: first, whether export instability in the region is greater than in the rest of the world; and, second, whether greater or lesser degrees of instability are related to or can be explained by the considerable importance of primary products or, more precisely, by the type of primary products in which the region has concentrated its production and trade.

As for the first point, the information contained in Table 6.1 reveals that Latin America has not experienced greater instability in its foreign exchange earnings than other regions of the world; its record lies close to the average. Nine countries from the region emerge in the upper half of the list of 117 nations arranged in ascending order of instability of export incomes in the period 1966–73. Nine others appear in the lower half.

As to whether the differences registered in instability of foreign exchange earnings between different Latin American countries can be explained by concentration upon primary products or by the type (or basket) of commodities exported, we should note that all the exercises carried out, admittedly of a preliminary nature, show a very low degree of statistical correlation between the variables mentioned (CEPAL, 1976a, p. 37). The first exercise undertaken was to correlate the intensity in fluctuations in foreign exchange earnings (Table 6.1, Column 1) with the degree of concentration of exports upon the three leading primary products (Table 6.1, Column 3). The second was to relate the relative importance of Latin American exports of each basic product with the degree of instability corresponding to it (Table 6.2, Columns 2, 3 and 4). This allowed us to establish that the Latin American countries have not concentrated their exports on the least stable products. Finally, we sought the correlation between the index of price instability of a basket

TABLE 6.1   Latin America: degree of concentration and instability of exports by country

Country	Degree of instability		Degree of concentration	
	Level (1)	International position (of 117) (2)	In 3 leading products, 1968–73 (3)	International position (of 117) (4)
Argentina	10.3	85	35.7	29
Venezuela	6.2	37	93.9	104
Uruguay	10.0	78	59.0	58
Panama	3.3	8	79.9	86
Mexico	8.1	60	17.8	13
Brazil	11.1	90	43.7	42
Chile	11.8	93	81.4	87
Costa Rica	6.4	41	65.3	64
Peru	7.6	58	58.1	57
Cuba	–	–	83.1	93
Nicaragua	6.9	49	54.0	49
Dominican Republic	8.9	66	69.7	68
Colombia	8.6	64	76.4	80
Paraguay	9.9	77	33.7	27
Ecuador	12.6	97	73.1	75
El Salvador	6.3	39	57.4	56
Honduras	5.5	23	70.4	69
Bolivia	7.4	57	71.4	71
Haiti	5.7	27	64.7	62
Guatemala	6.9	48	50.1	47
Average		58		62

Source: IBRD, World Tables: 1976 (Baltimore and London: Johns Hopkins Press, 1976, 1980) Table 14.

of Latin American primary exports, and the index of instability of total exports for each country, once again finding a low degree of correlation.

(c) Terms of trade

The second major disadvantage attributed to primary products is that the prices obtained for them display a secular deterioration against those of manufactured products. Thus countries exporting primary products would be prejudiced, principally because of low income elasticities of demand (in comparison with those for manufactured products) and of

TABLE 6.2   Latin American exports of primary products and international price instability 1973–5

Products	Exports Value ($ million) (1)	Percentage (2)	Price instability* Index A (3)	Index B (4)
Petroleum	14003	51.96	8.4	23.9
Coffee	2532	9.34	7.6	8.3
Sugar	2487	9.17	13.2	26.7
Copper	1485	5.48	15.5	18.2
Iron ore	975	3.60	5.6	6.8
Cotton	692	2.55	5.0	7.6
Meat	640	2.36	10.2	13.2
Maize	612	2.26	7.0	9.8
Bananas	525	1.94	3.8	4.5
Wheat	294	1.08	7.3	13.2
Cocoa	292	1.08	17.1	20.4
Silver	272	1.00		
Bauxite	250	0.92	6.1	9.8
Zinc	252	0.93	15.1	24.9
Timber	245	0.90	7.2	6.9
Tobacco	220	0.81	5.3	4.5
Wool	218	0.80	11.9	20.2
Fishmeal	213	0.78	16.2	27.0
Tin	199	0.73	7.3	10.8
Rice	129	0.47	13.9	9.8
Oil	116	0.43	14.0	18.0
Lead	124	0.46	12.9	14.8
Sisal	80	0.29	19.2	30.3
Hides and skins	60	0.22		
Manganese	56	0.21	7.0	11.6
Nuts	28	0.10	8.1	12.4
Tea	20	0.07	3.5	4.3
Rubber	7	0.02	12.8	14.2
Abacus	4	0.01		
Phosphoric rock	3	0.01	10.1	23.3

* Index A gives the average absolute percentage deviation from the five-year average. Index B gives the standard deviation from the same moving average.
Sources: Column (1): IBRD, *Commodity Trade and Price Trends: 1977* (Washington, DC: 1977); Column (3); Column (4): IBRD, *Price Prospects for Major Primary Commodities.* (Washington, DC: 1977)

the permanent tendency of the supply of primary products to react late and disproportionately to price stimuli (Singh, 1976, p. 88; Perry, 1977).

As regards the terms of trade, a number of empirical studies agree that during the second half of the 1950s and throughout the 1960s they deteriorated, to recover later, particularly in the two years 1973–4, which saw the 'commodity boom' (CEPAL, 1976a, p. 37). However, 1975 was less favourable to primary product prices, which began to recover once again from 1976 onwards.

Projections made by the World Bank suggest that prices of primary products will suffer a significant deterioration in real terms, of the order of 35 per cent, between 1978 and 1985, bringing prices by that year to a level similar to that of 1970 (IBRD, 1977a, Tables 16 and 17, pp. 34–5). Obviously, the values obtained depend upon the assumptions made with regard to the evolution of developed economies and other exogenous variables. Among the latter are agreements between producers and consumers which might be reached in coming years.

From the point of view of the present essay, the important point is to establish whether the terms of trade have been more or less favourable to Latin America than to other regions, and to identify the direct implications their evolution has had for export revenue and for the growth of the region's economies.

Table 6.3 presents the recent evolution of the terms of trade of Latin America with those of LDCs as a whole. It can be observed that in the period 1950–76 the deterioration was more acute for Latin America. No data are available to extend the comparison beyond 1976.[6] It is possible that the trend is continuing, since the increase in the prices of primary products as a group has been mainly a result of the increase in the price of oil, which contributes less to Latin American exports than to those of other LDCs.

In order to investigate why the evolution of the terms of trade should have been systematically unfavourable to Latin America we constructed Table 6.4, in which we present index numbers for the prices of primary products, unit values of exports and unit values of imports. The first thing that strikes one is that between 1950 and 1970 unit import prices increased more for Latin America than for other LDCs: this is one of the factors which explains why the terms of trade have moved more unfavourably for the region. It is possible that this result owes more to the intense process of import substitution which characterised Latin America, and which may have led to greater imports of capital goods than in other continents.

However, the most important factor in the unfavourable evolution of Latin American terms of trade is the behaviour of the price indices of primary products. These have moved far more favourably for all LDCs taken together than for those of Latin America alone.

TABLE 6.3   Evolution of the terms of trade for Latin America and for all LDCs 1950–76 (1970 = 100)

Year	LDCs (1)	Latin America (2)
1950	111	129
1951	117	128
1952	106	117
1953	105	126
1954	111	129
1955	109	119
1956	107	117
1957	103	118
1958	103	110
1959	105	102
1960	103	102
1961	100	100
1962	98	94
1963	99	95
1964	101	97
1965	99	93
1966	100	95
1967	99	93
1968	100	95
1969	101	96
1970	100	100
1971	104	99
1972	102	102
1973	112	113
1974	156	129
1975	139	113
1976	145	117

Sources: Column (1): IBRD, *Commodity Trade and Price Trends: 1977* (Washington, DC: 1977); Column (2): CEPAL, *América Latina: Relación de precios del intercambio* (Santiago 1976) and *Estudio Económico de América Latina 1977* (Santiago: 1978).

Finally, the price indices of primary products were compared with the corresponding series of unit prices of exports, with the objective of perceiving the impact of those commodities upon those values. The correlations detected indicate that in the case of Latin America the relationship is far closer than for all other LDCs taken together, and this result is consistent with the conclusion that the region displays a greater degree of dependence than the rest of the developing world upon exports of primary commodities.

To summarise, Latin America has experienced a less favourable

TABLE 6.4   Evolution of the prices of primary products for Latin America and all LDCs 1950–76 (1970 = 100)

Year	Latin America		LDCs		LA prices/ LDC prices (1):(3)	LA imports/ LDC imports
	Commodity prices (1)	Unit value of exports (2)	Commodity prices (3)	Unit value of exports (4)	(5)	(6)
1950	110	108	120	94	92	87
1951	117	140	125	117	94	88
1952	114	117	122	107	93	89
1953	115	117	126	99	91	89
1954	123	101	134	101	92	95
1955	122	104	133	102	92	93
1956	122	94	133	101	92	93
1957	116	92	132	101	88	87
1958	105	86	125	96	84	94
1959	101	86	114	94	88	94
1960	100	92	107	94	93	95
1961	94	91	106	91	89	97
1962	93	82	101	89	92	99
1963	92	93	102	91	90	98
1964	96	98	98	94	98	101
1965	97	94	98	93	99	100
1966	97	97	99	95	98	101
1967	94	95	97	94	98	101
1968	95	93	97	94	98	101
1969	97	97	99	97	98	100
1970	100	100	100	100	100	100
1971	114	113	122	108	93	97
1972	130	130	135	116	96	100
1973	184	–	196	158	94	–
1974	496	–	613	318	81	–
1975	517	–	657	311	79	–
1976	555	–	705	330	79	–

Sources: Column (1): Calculated as the weighted average of the price indices of petroleum and of other primary products from IBRD, *Price prospects for major primary commodities* (Washington, DC 1977a), adjusted in line with the weights used in Table 6.3; Column (2): CEPAL, *América Latina: Relación de Precios* . . . ; op. cit. Column (3): Based on IBRD, op. cit.

evolution of its terms of trade than the remaining developing countries. This has been due in part to the unfavourable relative movement of import prices, but the fundamental explanatory variable has been the behaviour of the prices of primary products of particular importance to Latin America. The prices of the primary products exported from the region have always lagged behind those of other LDCs, and the discrepancy was increased with the sharp rise in the price of oil.

(d) Latin America and the international dialogue over primary products

Latin America has participated actively in the consummation of agreements (either among producers, or between producers and consumers) directed at stabilising the prices of primary products and increasing foreign exchange earnings. Given that historical record, and their dependence upon a limited number of primary products, it should come as no surprise that the countries of the region gave almost unanimous support to all the schemes and proposals aimed at influencing the functioning of markets, and thus reducing price fluctuations and improving the terms of trade, stabilising and increasing foreign exchange earnings, and increasing the participation of producer countries in the total value of sales of primary products.[7]

The Latin American nations have given similar support to the initiatives which have been put forward in UNCTAD. They signed the declaration of Manila, in which LDCs put forward a programme for action relating to primary products.[8] Most of them, too, lent their support to the concept of an integrated programme and the idea of establishing a common fund for financing stocks, both of which have been taken up by the Executive Secretariat of ECLA.[9]

Latin America's preoccupation with trade in primary products is well founded, for the region continues to depend heavily upon these products. Our statistical results show that the export instability which these countries have experienced is similar to that faced by LDCs as a whole, but that trade in primary products was less significant in overall export instability, although this hypothesis should be tested by more sophisticated models and more complete statistical series. Despite the foregoing, it is possible that political initiatives in the sub-continent have been directed if anything too single-mindedly to the goal of international stabilisation. Perhaps a greater internal effort to reduce the fluctuations in exports and a better approach to negotiations for improved terms of trade and higher real prices for primary products could bring greater social benefits.

In fact the results given in the foregoing sections suggest that the Latin American countries have suffered and will possibly continue to suffer from an even more severe deterioration in the terms of trade than that faced by the other LDCs. Studies should be undertaken to establish whether, for Latin America, producers' alliances, the indexing of prices, and policies to restrict exports and production would not be more suitable initiatives than those which could be pursued within UNCTAD with the aim of establishing a common fund of buffer stocks of primary products.

3 A RESEARCH AGENDA FOR LATIN AMERICA

(a) Background

To provide a framework for a regional agenda for research, we shall first summarise some aspects of the world economy which serve to locate the international dimension of the problem of primary products. We thus provide the background information which makes possible the selection of a set of themes within which more detailed studies need to be planned and promoted. Among these aspects are: (i) the growing economic interdependence of nations; (ii) the growing importance of economic policy in the industrialised nations *vis-à-vis* problems of defence and security; and (iii) the disequilibria in the world economy in recent times.

It is now common to hear the opinion that economies are becoming increasingly internationalised, whether in LDCs, industrialised nations, or the socialist bloc. The last few years have seen a tendency for internal and external affairs to fuse together to a certain degree, within each individual nation. We are living in a time of greater mobility of commodities and of factors of production, despite the continued existence of various obstacles to the free movement of goods, persons and capital. And finally, it is no longer possible to affirm that commercial relations come down to the traditional exchange of manufactures for primary products.

In the post-war period, one of the major concerns of the industrialised nations was with national security and with the threat posed by the Soviet bloc and its expansion (Cooper and Lawrence, 1975). At the same time, with the relative success of internal policies of a Keynesian nature as an instrument for achieving stable rates of growth of GNP and of employment, concern over economic policies diminished somewhat. Nevertheless, as Professor Hicks has pointed out (see Pizano, 1977b), the industrialised countries committed the major error of supposing that there could be a permanently expanding economic universe, subject to no limits whatever. But the growing importance of various limits to economic expansion in the recent past, and the apparent incapacity of traditional Keynesian policies to resolve the problem known in the literature as stagflation, have brought economic policy back into the limelight, and in the leading role. Given the increasing interaction between nations, this enhanced importance of economic policy has also been reflected in the debate around the establishment of a new international economic order. The collapse of the monetary system designed at Bretton Woods, the world-wide generalisation of inflation, the disequilibria and disorganisation in a number of markets, the disillusion provoked by systems of external aid and by generalised systems of preference, in conjunction with increasing interdependence and the growth of consciousness that natural resources (especially those generating energy) are not inexhaustible, have all been significant antecedents of the search for an NIEO.

Furthermore, there is a tendency towards the formation of a vast bilateral monopoly at world level, with on the one side the member countries of OPEC and those LDCs who have a significant degree of control over the supply of a number of primary products, and on the other the members of the International Energy Agency, owners of the greater part of technological knowledge. Given the presence of monopolistic elements on the side of the production of primary products as well as on the side of the generation of technological knowledge, it seems unrealistic to assume that the sufficient and necessary conditions for achieving the Pareto optimum are given in the real world.

Empirical evidence suggests that there are significant disequilibria in the world economy: (i) the share of world exports attributable to LDCs, excluding OPEC, has fallen from 28 per cent in 1950 to 16 per cent in 1974; (ii) the gap between the standard of living in LDCs and in the industrialised countries continues to widen (from approximately 10:1 in the 1950s to approximately 14:1 today); (iii) demand for the majority of primary products continues to grow at a slower rate than does world trade; (iv) the LDCs' share of world industrial production continues to be very low (at around 7 per cent).

However, a number of recent events offer the opportunity to intervene against these historical trends. Among them are the withdrawal of the United States from Vietnam, the growing militancy of the poor countries, strengthened by the example of OPEC, in pursuit of correction of the disequilibria in the international economic system.

What role does the primary sector of the world economy play in the generation of these disequilibria? Examination of this theme requires specific research of the kind that we shall discuss shortly. Here we shall confine our analysis to a brief comment on the original contribution to the problem made by Professor Kaldor (1973).

Kaldor constructs a model which shows the manner in which the primary and industrial sectors of the world economy interact. Making a series of assumptions, he concludes that the expansion of the former (which depends upon land-saving technological innovations and upon technological change in the extraction of minerals) not only determines the limits of growth, but also conditions the rate of expansion of the system in the long term. A clear implication of this formulation is the following: the promotors of accelerated industrialisation and of import substitution at any cost, by ignoring the principle of opportunity cost of resources, failed to realise, for a lack of conceptual clarity, that the establishment of an exaggerated level of effective industrial protection was holding back the growth of the primary sector (through the terms of trade effect), and leading them *to sacrifice the expansion of the system as a whole.* Kaldor's thesis is, then, essentially, that for continued and stable progress of the world economy it is necessary that a given relationship be maintained between the rates of expansion of the primary and industrial sectors. Kaldor considers that the root of the current problem of inflation with recession lies in an imbalance between primary and industrial production. He concludes that the most important task for the world economy is to strengthen the mechanisms of adjustment of supply and demand of primary products. He shows, from his model, that any change in the prices of primary products, whether up or down, depresses industrial activity, and that it is therefore necessary to seek a price level *at which the terms of trade can be stabilised.*

(b) Studies on alternative economic policies

In the light of the foregoing considerations and of the exercises presented with relation to Latin America, we may now present a number of themes which demand investigation at theoretical and empirical levels. A basic criterion for the establishment of priorities should be the degree to which the research proposed takes up the problem of the imbalance between primary and industrial production, and throws light upon the process of adjustment required if the countries of Latin America are to make progress in correcting their basic disequilibria and eliminating the obstacles to more stable and balanced growth.

With regard to the establishment of a new international economic order for primary products, the most important research topics are: (i) the feasibility and advisability of the creation of cartels; (ii) price stabilisation; (iii) price indexing; (iv) the role of primary products in the light of the restructuring of world industrial production and the 'optimal' division of labour: (v) the expropriation of foreign investors and the transfer of technology, particularly in the case of mineral products; and (vi) the interrelationship between the growth of the countries of the OECD and those of the Third World. We shall comment briefly upon each of these points, before presenting a set of problems which require theoretical investigation.

(i) Cartelisation   The central questions to be asked in this area are as follows:

(1) Which primary products meet the conditions necessary for effective cartelisation?
(2) What should the basic objective of cartelisation be: to exploit monopoly power, or to use this power in negotiations to counteract monopsony and protectionism in the developed areas?
(3) Which cartels would produce common interests in Latin America, and which would produce conflict?

(ii) Stabilisation   Our analysis needs to be advanced in the following areas:

(1) Identification of the principal causes of the instability observed in primary products of interest to Latin America.
(2) A more thorough appraisal of the relationship between instability and economic growth, seeking to enquire more deeply into the following questions: Has the instability of the external sectors of the countries of the region been greater than that of those in the developed areas, although less than in other LDCs? Has it been transmitted from the external sector to the internal sector in every case? Has it prejudiced development, through its impact upon capital formation and by making the formulation of development plans more difficult?
(3) Careful analysis is required in order to select the most suitable instruments of control for each case. Price-linked flexible export quotas constitute an interesting alternative, but create incentives

to violate agreements. Buffer stocks might prove suitable in some cases, but introduce the problems of the high financial costs involved and their limited ability to flatten out the long-term cycles characteristic of many products, such as coffee.

(4) The Latin American countries should also consider the extent to which UNCTAD's integrated programme for primary products is more suitable than alternative international solutions. As far as that programme is concerned, it is particularly important to weigh up the likelihood of all leading producers (including those in the socialist bloc) participating in it, to analyse the size of buffer stocks and of the stabilisation fund that will be required and the degree to which the price of each individual primary product can be predicted into the future. It is evident that the authorities charged with the task of stabilisation will have to anticipate the principal trends in the market if their action is to be effective.

Studies should also be made of the effectiveness of past agreements, with a view to examining the feasibility of generalising systems of the Stabex type. It would also be interesting to explore in detail the working of different future markets, concentrating upon the conditions which might lead particular operations to have stabilising or destabilising effects.

Finally, if it is definitively concluded that the instability of the external sector has been prejudicial to the development of Latin America, it would be necessary to consider the possibility of proposing the increase of the IMF's compensatory funds.

(iii) Indexing   The first point with regard to indexing is to clarify the question of whether the goal is to 'freeze' the terms of trade between primary and manufactured products, or to improve those terms over the long term. Indexing can be defended theoretically, but careful attention must be paid to the circumstances in which it is desirable for Latin America, and particularly to the complementary mechanisms needed if indexing is to be effective.

(iv) Industrial production and the optimal international division of labour   On this point, the particular questions which need to be answered are:

(1) Given the limits of human and physical capital, what role might

Latin America play in an optimal international division of labour? Tinbergen (1976) has made conceptual advances in this area, and the criteria he proposes have been applied by Herman (1976).

(2) What type of tariff structures should be adopted, in developed or underdeveloped countries, to make viable a reallocation of resources such as that which emerges from Tinbergen's work? In this context, the experience accumulated in the negotiations for the adoption of the Common External Tariff in the Andean Pact should be drawn upon.

(3) A final aspect in this area which merits particular attention is that relating to the processing of primary products in their country of origin. Of equal priority is the issue of the distribution of the greater value added thus generated between the different economic actors involved (national and foreign investors, workers and government).

(v) Treatment of foreign investment and the transfer of technology In this enormous field, some points requiring urgent attention are:

(1) Would it be advisable to design an international statute for the regulation of foreign investment in the primary products sector, of a kind which does not give rise to competition between different states to attract resources?

(2) Considering that TNCs export approximately 40 per cent of primary products, how is it possible to guarantee that the macroeconomic objectives of these companies and of host governments more nearly coincide?

(3) What is the possibility that the Latin American countries will adopt a clear policy of promoting research in such fields as techniques of production of primary products?

Finally, more detailed attention should be devoted to the theme of economic interdependence between Latin America and other continents. Some simulated models of the world economy (such as Simlink, for example) consider that there is no significant feedback effect between the growth of developing countries and the OECD countries; they accept that the evolution of the former is in part determined by what happens in the latter, but do not postulate an inverse interrelationship.

(c) Theoretical research

The major themes which merit consideration in this area relate to the analysis of the theme of instability, and include the definition of an appropriate index of instability and the study of the effects of the different instruments of control (quotas, taxes, buffer stocks, etc.).

However, perhaps the most urgent requirement is to advance in the process of constructing models which enable us to understand the behaviour of world markets for primary products. The explanatory and predictive power of existing econometric models still leaves much to be desired. Their principal limitations are that they do not consider monetary factors such as the rate of international inflation (which has a very direct impact upon the price formation of many primary products), they do not take variations in exchange rates into account, they rarely consider the impact of the operation of future markets, nor do they consider the structure of the market. Explanations of price movements based upon the cobweb theorem presuppose a situation closely akin to that of perfect competition in general equilibrium models. It would be more realistic to assume that many of these commodities are enmeshed in a process of exchange which approximates more closely to a bilateral oligopoly. The dominant theory of the firm, game theory, and negotiating theory all offer interesting possibilities regarding the generation of a more appropriate conceptual framework. Finally, the available econometric models are not integrated into a more embracing simulation model of the world economy such as that developed by Hicks *et al* (1976) in the World Bank (Simlink); allowance must also be made for transport costs, as these might alter the chain of comparative advantages.

NOTES

1 Singh (1976) p. 87.
2 This is the criterion used by Chenery and Syrquin (1975) to derive their norms or international patterns. We are not asserting that it provides the best comparative index, but use it only so that consistent comparisons can be made.
3 Chenery and Syrquin (1975). The idea that countries tend to display 'expected' patterns of development in the process of economic growth results from the examination of historical trends in a wide range of different countries over different periods. The approach has been developed principally by Hollis Chenery, continuing the classic line of research of Simon Kuznets, and is used here simply as a point of reference to locate Latin America *vis-à-vis* other LDCs.

4 The figures for income *per capita* were adjusted for world-wide inflation with the objective of expressing them in 1973 dollars, and not in 1964 values, as in Chenery's data.
5 It should not be surprising that the larger countries are the ones to fall below the norm, as there is a scale effect which makes them, in general, less dependent upon exports. If the graph were corrected to eliminate this scale effect, Latin America's dependence upon primary products would stand out even more clearly. See Chenery and Syrquin (1975) pp. 67–8.
6 The definition of terms of trade utilised here is that of the quotient of unit export and import prices, or of 'barter terms of trade'. Numerous other definitions exist: see for example CEPAL (1976a) pp. 3–22.
7 It should be noted that the Latin American countries have not only undertaken favourable actions regarding producers' agreements, but have also taken upon themselves the political commitment to promote them, in the Declaration of Chaguaramas, approved by Resolution 347 (XVI) of ECLA.
8 UNCTAD, 'Declaración y Programa de Acción de Manila', TD/195, Geneva, February 1976.
9 'Exposición del Secretario Ejecutivo de la Comisión Económica para América Latina en el cuarto período de sesiones de la UNCTAD', Nairobi, March 1976.

REFERENCES

Bergsten, F. (1973) 'The Threat from the Third World', *Foreign Policy*, no. 11, summer.
—— (1975) 'The new Era in World Commodity Markets' (Washington, DC: Brookings Institution).
—— (1977) 'Access to Supplies, Export Cartels and Reform of the GATT', in Bhagwati (ed.) *The North-South Debate* (Cambridge, Massachusetts: MIT)
CEPAL (1975) 'La Coyuntura Internacional y el Sector Externo', *Cuadernos de la CEPAL*, Santiago.
—— (1976 a) 'América Latina: Relación de Precios del Intercambio', *Cuadernos Estadísticos*, no. 1, Santiago.
—— (1976 b) 'Temas del Nuevo Orden Económico Internacional', *Cuadernos de la CEPAL*, Santiago.
Chenery, H., and Syrquin, M. (1975) *Patterns of Development 1950–1970* (Oxford University Press).
Cooper, R. (1973) *A Reordered World* (New York: Potomac).
Cooper, R., and Lawrence, R. (1975), 'The 1972–75 Commodity Boom', *Brookings Papers on Economic Activity*, no. 3, (Washington, DC).
Coppock, J. D. (1962) *International Economic Instability* (New York: McGraw-Hill).

Donges, J. B. (1977) 'Problems of a New International Economic Order', *Economics*, vol. 15, Tübingen.

FAO, (1975) *Trade Yearbook*, Rome.

FEDESARROLLO (1976), 'La Industria del Azúcar en Colombia', in Garay and Rizano (1978).

—— (1978) *Economía Cafetera Colombiana* (Bogota, Colombia).

Firnger, J. M. and Yeats, A. Y. (1976) 'Effective Protection by Transportation Costs and Tariffs', *Quarterly Journal of Economics*, vol. XC, February.

Garay, L. J., and Pizano, D. (1979) *Lecturas sobre Comercio Exterior con Referencia Especial a Colombia y el Grupo Andino* (Bogotá, Colombia: Fundación para la Promoción de las Investigaciones Económicas).

Glezakos, G. (1973) 'Export Instability and Economic Growth: a Statistical Verification', *Economic Development and Cultural Change*, July.

Helleiner, G. K. (ed.) (1976) *A World Divided: The Less Developed Countries in the International Economy* (Cambridge University Press).

Herman, B. (1976) *The Optimal International Division of Labour* International Labour Office, Geneva.

Hicks, N., *et al.* (1976) 'A Model of Trade and Growth for the Developing World', (Washington, DC; Interamerican Development Bank).

IBRD, *Commodity Trade and Price Trends* (Washington, DC: annually).

—— (1976) *World Tables: 1976*, published for the World Bank (Baltimore and London: Johns Hopkins Press).

—— (1977a) 'Price Prospects for Major Primary Commodities', Report 814/77, (Washington, DC: June).

—— (1977b) *World Bank Atlas: 1977* (Washington, DC).

Johnson, D. Gale (1975) 'World Agriculture, Commodity Policy, and Price variability', *American Journal Agricultural Economics*, December.

Junguito, R. (1978) 'Latin America and the primary product trade', *Journal of Inter-American Studies and World Affairs*, July.

Kahn, H. (1976) in W. Brown and L. Martel *The Next 200 Years: a Scenario for America and the World* (New York: MacMillan Morrow).

Kaldor, N. (1939) 'Speculation and Economic Stability', *Review of Economic Studies*, October.

—— (1940) 'A Note on the Theory of the Forward Market', *Review of Economic Studies*, June.

Kaldor, N (1973) 'Teoría del Equilibrio y Teoría del Crecimiento', paper presented to a conference at the University of Barcelona.

—— (1976) 'Inflation and Recession in the World Economy', *Economic Journal*, December.

Keynes, J. M. (1971) *A Treatise on Money*, Collected Works (London: Macmillan).

Kissinger, H. (1976) 'Cooperation for Development', Organization of American States General Assembly, Santiago.

Labys, W. C. (1973) *Dynamic Commodity Models: Specification, Estimation and Simulation* (Lexington, Massachusetts: Lexington Books).

—— (1975) 'The Problems and Challenges for International Commodity Models and Model Builders', *American Journal of Agricultural Economics*, December.

Labys, W. C., and Granger, C. W. J. (1970) *Speculation, Hedging and Commodity Price Forecasts* (Lexington, Massachusetts: Lexington Books).

Lim, D. (1976) 'Export Instability and Economic Growth: A Return to Fundamentals', *Bulletin of the Oxford Institute of Statistics*, vol. 38, no. 4.

Luce, R. D., and Raiffa, H. (1957) *Games and Decisions* (London: Wiley).

MacBean, A. (1966) *Export Instability and Economic Development* (Cambridge Massachusetts: Harvard University Press).

Massell, B. (1970) 'Export Instability and Economic Structure', *American Economic Review*, vol. 60, September.

Payer, Ch. (1975) *Commodity Trade of the Third World* (London: Macmillan).

Perry, G. (1977) 'El Nuevo Orden Internacional y el Desarrollo', *Coyuntura Económica*, Bogotá, Colombia, December.

Pizano, D. (1977a) 'Un Diálogo con el Professor Tinbergen', *Coyuntura Económica*, Bogotá, Colombia, November.

—— (1977b) 'Un Diálogo con el Profesor Hicks', *Coyuntura Económica*, Bogotá, Colombia, December.

—— (1978) 'Un Diálogo con el Profesor Kaldor', *Coyuntura Económica*, Bogotá, Colombia, October.

Singh, S. (1976) 'The International Dialogue on Commodities', *Resources Policy*, 60, July.

Tinbergen, J. (1976) *Reestructuración del Orden Internacional* (Mexico City: Fondo de Cultura Económica).

UN (1977) *1999: l'Expertise de Wassily Leontief* (Paris).

UNCTAD (1975) 'An Integrated Program for Commodities', mimeo (Geneva: October).

Vovoidas, C. (1974) 'The Effect of Foreign Exchange Instability on Growth', *Review of Economics & Statistics*, LVI, 3 August.

7 Commodity Price Instability: a Note[1]

DRAGOSLAV AVRAMOVIC

At UNCTAD IV in Nairobi in May 1976, it was agreed to negotiate on the establishment of a common fund for financing commodity schemes of export interest to developing countries. It was also agreed to negotiate on the conclusion of fifteen commodity agreements, in addition to the three already existing. A year later, the countries participating in the Conference on International Economic Co-operation (CIEC) in Paris confirmed the Nairobi decision and unanimously agreed that a common fund should be established as a new entity to serve as a key instrument in attaining the objectives of the Integrated Programme for Commodities (IPC) originally proposed by the developing countries. But despite these agreements in principle, no significant advance has been made in practice.

The purpose of this note is to attempt to answer a couple of the major questions frequently raised concerning the objectives, scope and likely economic effects of the demands of the developing countries for a fairer deal in their export commodity trade.

The questions are as follows:

(1) What is the nature of the problems which developing countries face in their commodity markets, and what is the role of a common fund in solving them? and,
(2) Does the IPC, of which the common fund is the key element, aim at price stabilisation above or around the so-called market trend?

1 THE NATURE OF THE PROBLEM

(a) Insufficiency of market staying power

As matters now stand, the many financially weak producing countries, mostly low-income, have a limited staying power in the international

73

market. Financially unable to carry stocks and in urgent need of foreign exchange, the low-income countries are frequently compelled to sell competitively on a falling market the commodity surpluses which periodically arise, because most commodity production is highly variable and cannot be adjusted quickly to changing demand. These distress sales, usually accompanied by sales from speculative stocks, force even the financially stronger developing countries into competitive selling, as they become concerned about a loss in market share. This pressure of sales occurs in the face of a limited number of financially strong buyers in developed countries who postpone purchase in the expectation of still lower prices. It is these circumstances which frequently lead to extremely sharp price falls and to associated declines in producers' incomes. Even under normal circumstances, when crops are near average, the bunching of competitive sales in the face of a limited number of buyers will lead to erosion of the market price.

The losses incurred by low-income sellers in falling markets normally cannot be compensated by gains on rising markets. To achieve such gains, the sellers would need financial power to hold supplies off the market for a considerable time while it is rising. The developing countries do not have such financial power, although there are rare and temporary exceptions.

(b) Evidence

There is evidence of many cases – in cocoa, coffee and sisal – where substantial losses have been sustained by low-income producers because of inadequate financial power and improper timing of sales. In other cases, such as that of tea, the monopsony (buying monopoly) conditions in the market tend to depress its price (Avramovic, 1978, Annex A). Also the pressure of debt servicing liabilities on producers with low incomes and low assets forces them into premature and unprofitable sales. Such forced sales to pay debts and taxes are well known in domestic agriculture in many countries. The problem is the same in the international markets. But while forced agricultural sales are now avoided in a number of countries by the provision of organised domestic public credit which gives poor farmers the option of holding stocks until the off-season to fetch a better price (Lele, 1976), no organised international public credit is available to help the low-income countries to carry stocks of their export products.

During the last fifteen years the developing countries have been receiving considerably lower prices for their exports than the prevailing world market prices. Table 7.1 compares the export unit values of these countries (i.e. the average prices at which their primary products are actually sold) with market quotations. A similar comparison is made for developed countries' exports of the same products. The following emerges from the analysis of those figures: first, in 1971–5, prices actually received by developing countries averaged 85 per cent of world

TABLE 7.1   Actual export prices (unit values) received by different groups of countries as a percentage of market prices

Exports of	African countries		Developing countries		Industrialised countries	
	1961–5	1971–5	1961–5	1971–5	1961–5	1971–5
Sisal	77.6	63.9	76.0	67.0	–	–
Beef	72.1	47.0	73.1	67.3	110.4	85.2
Jute	–	–	96.1	72.4	–	–
Cocoa	96.9	78.4	95.2	78.1	–	–
Maize	80.6	74.6	79.5	79.3	90.0	94.0
Copra	86.1	81.5	85.2	81.6	–	–
Rice	129.4	114.2	83.1	81.6	104.3	103.3
Palm oil	88.8	83.6	88.4	83.8	126.7	126.2
Palm nuts and kernels	91.0	88.5	89.8	84.7	–	–
Coconut oil	–	–	89.4	85.3	98.1	104.7
Groundnut oil	113.1	81.3	108.0	85.6	107.9	101.4
Palm kernel oil	81.6	88.1	83.6	86.0	104.2	100.6
Tea	65.5	74.0	83.7	87.2	–	–
Soya cake	–	–	76.8	87.3	96.4	96.0
Rubber	101.8	94.9	92.6	91.3	–	–
Peanuts	92.8	84.3	95.4	92.0	116.9	107.5
Soya	–	–	87.4	92.8	85.9	88.8
Wheat	–	–	99.6	97.0	101.0	95.1
Soya bean oil	–	–	–	102.5	105.8	103.6*
Average						
Median	88.8	81.5	87.9	85.3	104.2	101.0
Media	90.6	81.1	87.9	84.4	103.9	100.6
Weighted**	–	78.5	–	84.3	–	94.0

* Biased towards 1971–5, as a result of the special sales of the US to the USSR in 1972–3. In other years it was sold by developed countries at or above market prices.
** Weighted by the value of exports in 1975.
Source: Unit values from FAO, 1978 *Trade Yearbooks: 1966–75*, Rome; average market prices from UNCTAD, *Monthly Commodity Price Bulletin: Special Supplement* (March 1977), Geneva, CD/CPB/92.

market prices. Second, amongst the developing countries, it was the African countries, i.e. the lowest income producers, which received the lowest prices. And, in contrast, the prices received by the developed countries were close to, or exceeded world market prices. Finally, the shortfalls experienced by developing countries have widened during the last fifteen years. For the African countries, they widened more.

The actually realised prices may fall short of market quotations for many reasons, including quality differences, transport costs and the terms of long-term contracts. But the systematic nature of the shortfalls experienced by developing countries strongly suggests that it is their low market staying-power and the corresponding weakness in their bargaining strength which is the main cause. In the London copper market the shortfall is institutionalised. The buyer is given the option of selecting, within a two-month period, the pricing days; as a result, the producers generally receive less than the average market price (Radetzki, 1976).

The problem faced by the developing countries in their export commodity markets does not stem from the physical nature of these commodities, but from their economic and financial position as countries.[2] If they had enough finance they would be able to market their export products successfully despite occasional surpluses, just as the developed countries' primary producers manage to do with their major commodity exports. If the developing countries had been more industrially advanced they could have had more alternative employment opportunities and, therefore, would have been able to avoid the overcrowding of their export markets and the associated weakness of prices, just as the developed countries succeed in doing. The problem is not in the physical characteristics of particular markets, however important they may be, but in the lack of financial strength and the overcrowding of the markets.

(c) The need for organised finance

What is needed is organised international finance to help the developing countries in marketing a wide range of their export products. In a number of cases, internationally agreed action on levels of production will also be needed. For some commodities it will be found practicable to conclude international commodity agreements. For some it may not be possible, e.g. because a major exporting developed country is not interested as it has decided to help its own producers unilaterally; in these cases withdrawing help from low-income countries' producers because there is no international commodity agreement is equal to penalising the poor because they need help most.

In the case of some international agreements, there will be internationally held stocks, like tin and cocoa; but for some products, like coffee and sugar, it may be found more practicable to operate nationally held stocks. In both groups of cases, however, there is equally a need for finance. In some cases, the finance for market support, to be effective and safely invested, needs to be combined with support of diversification measures through project and programme assistance aimed at avoiding the chronic overcrowding of export markets, or at improving the competitive position through product upgrading, research and promotion.

(d) What kind of common fund?

It is in response to the actually experienced need to improve their market staying power across a range of products that the developing countries have insisted on a common fund which would have: (i) sufficient resources at its command subscribed by governments and available for use promptly as the need for market intervention arises; (ii) the authority to intervene in a broad range of developing countries' export markets and related activities; and (iii) a structure of voting power and management control which would provide the developing countries with a share of responsibility for making decisions and implementing them commensurate with their vital interests in this field.

2 STABILISATION AROUND OR ABOVE THE TREND?

The question has been raised frequently whether the purpose of the IPC is merely to stabilise prices around the future long-term market trend, or to raise them above it (Frank, 1976; Finger and Kreinin, 1976). The question is in a sense biased, and the concept of the market trend is vague. No one seems to talk about the equilibrium price trend of automobiles, tractors or machinery, but only of rubber and coffee, as though there were some natural law determining the prices of primary products exported by developing countries, but no such law applying to the prices of manufactures exported by developed countries. In fact, the future prices of both categories of goods will be determined by the ability to manage supplies and markets, as well as by long-term production costs and possibilities of substitution.

(a) Past and future prices

The question which can be discussed meaningfully concerns the price objectives of the Integrated Programme in relation to the past price trend. The developing countries are firmly committed to an improvement in their terms of trade, i.e. in the prices of their exports in relation to those of imports. This does not mean that the prices paid by the final consumers should also rise, as there are sizeable margins accruing to intermediaries and processors, which can be squeezed.

There are four reasons why the prices of export primary products obtained by developing countries should be improved.

First, the experience of the boom years in the 1970s, with widespread shortages of primary products, has shown that the present capacity is not sufficient to meet the demand when world income expands rapidly. It follows that the prices of many primary products between the mid-1950s and the late 1960s were too low, on average, to induce the required rate of investment. Also, the resulting commodity bottlenecks were an important factor in checking the expansion in the world economy in the 1970s (Hicks, 1976). Similarly, the present disastrously low prices are expected to lead to shortages and massive increases in metal prices in the 1980s.[3]

Second, the higher prices of energy and of environmental protection will operate as significant cost-raising factors in a number of products.

Third, in order to meet the increased demand for many commodities, resources of lower quality or more remote from major markets must be exploited. Even where the potential exists for a major expansion of output, costs are likely to be higher than in the past.

Fourth, for most export primary products of developing countries, particularly of agricultural origin, the past prices have been based on incomes which are now widely considered as being intolerably low. In the mid-1970s the wages on plantations were as low as 50 cents per day. This compares with wages of production workers in manufacturing in leading industrial countries averaging 50 dollars per day. It is this enormous difference in incomes and the associated discrepancy in living standards which is at the centre of the demand of the developing countries for the establishment of the new international economic order.

The prevailing terms of trade which give rise to such enormous differences of income are fundamentally inequitable. The wage levels are likely to play a role in deciding what is an adequate price in the future (Avramovic, 1978, p. 384).

The marketing and processing margins between the export prices obtained by developing countries and the retail prices paid by the consumers in developed countries have risen sharply in the majority of products during the last two decades. In a number of instances, the traders and processors have retained the same percentage spread when the producer price has gone up, thus widening the absolute cash margin on the upswing; but they have frequently retained the same cash margin per unit, or even raised it to compensate for a declining volume of sales, on the downswing. A reversal of the trend of widening margins would make it possible for the producer (export) prices to be improved, without a proportionate increase in the prices paid by consumers. The rise in the margins is attributable to the monopolistic organisation of much of the trade and processing, and their narrowing would call for alternative forms of organisation.

(b) Feasible price support levels

In setting price support levels, a distinction must be made between commodities where the risk of substitution of other products is negligible and commodities facing the threat of synthetic substitutes. The prices of the synthetics set the limit to sustainable prices of several natural raw materials (mainly fibres and rubber). In the case of the latter, the objective of the Integrated Programme is to enable them to maintain their share of the aggregate market and possibly recapture some of past volume losses. The latter were induced by excessive fluctuations in the prices of natural products, in contrast to the stable-priced and frequently cheaper synthetics. To reverse the situation it is necessary to stabilise the prices of natural products. Price support would operate when prices fall below the level needed to maintain a competitive edge over the synthetics; prices would be kept stable during the upswing of demand by selling from stock, thus sustaining the competitive position of natural products; and the major emphasis would be placed on expanding the volume of sales by raising productivity and quality.

A considerable latitude in setting the price support level exists for commodities where the risk of substitution is not significant, i.e. for which the demand is price inelastic. Tropical beverages are well-known cases, but they are not unique. The price demand elasticity of 16 out of the 19 principal commodities is below unity; i.e. in all these commodities the revenue would increase as the price increased, probably over a considerable range of prices. Of these products, 14 play a dominant role in the exports of developing countries. The degree of a sustainable price improvement will vary from case to case, depending on the likely response of competing output in the importing countries (import elasticity of demand), the likelihood of substitution of products outside the scheme for those in it, and the ability of developing countries to control supply.

It has been argued that the possibility of expanding competing output in developed countries would severely constrain the freedom of action of developing country exporters (Laursen, 1977). On closer examination, however, this argument does not hold for most export products of developing countries. Coffee, cocoa, tea, spices, bananas, coconut oil, tin, copper, bauxite, manganese, phosphate and tropical timber are either not produced at all in developed countries or are in short long-run supply. Sugar and iron ore can be expanded in developed countries, but at a much higher cost than in the developing countries.

The Integrated Programme covers a broad product range and therefore it is possible to avoid inter-product substitution more easily than in a single product price stabilisation (e.g. copper and aluminium, coffee and tea).

It is in respect of the readiness of developing countries to jointly manage supply that the uncertainty lies. Reaching international agreements on the levels of production and exports for a large number of products will not be an easy matter. It is here that the developing countries need to make major new efforts in translating their political unity into specific co-ordinated actions. The common fund is needed to enable the producing countries to overcome the initial shocks in commodity markets and to give them breathing space in which to organise themselves and start applying policies aimed at adjusting supply, if market disturbances prove to be more than temporary. But the common fund cannot be a substitute for these policies; without them, there cannot be a sustained improvement in the terms of trade of developing countries.

NOTES

1 This note is based on the author's article 'Common Fund: Why and What Kind?' *Journal of World Trade Law*, September-October 1978.

2 This argument has been stated clearly and elaborated in detail by Emmanuel (1972).
3 Depressed prices have led to investment virtually drying up in some metal sectors, particularly copper. According to Robert Perlman, Managing Director of the Commodities Research Unit, London: 'No provision is being made to expand capacity for the future. If the past is anything to go by, this will set off massive price increases with rises of two or three-fold and even more in double quick time. The longer prices remain depressed, the surer and higher the future reaction will be' ['Metal Price Explosion by 1980s', *Financial Times*, 7 December 1977].

REFERENCES

Avramovic, D. (1978) 'Common Fund: Why and What Kind?', *Journal of World Trade Law*, vol. 12, no. 5.
Emmanuel, A. (1972) *Unequal Exchange: A Study of the Imperialism of Trade*, (New York: Monthly Review Press).
Finger, J. M., and Kreinin, M. E. (1976) 'A New International Economic Order? A Critical Survey of the Issues' *Journal of World Trade Law*, vol. 10, no. 6, December.
Frank, I. (1976) *Preliminary Statement on International Commodity Policy to the Sub-Committee on Inter-American Relationships*, (Washington, DC: US Congress, 12 August).
Hicks, J. (1976) 'Must Stimulating Demand Stimulate Inflation', *The Economic Record*.
Laursen, K. (1977) 'The Integrated Program for Commodities', draft paper, (Washington, DC: World Bank, 12 May).
Lele, U. (1976) *Considerations Relating to Optimum Pricing and Marketing Strategies in Rural Development*, mimeo (Nairobi).
Radetzki, M. (1976) *Market Structure and Bargaining Power: A Study of Three International Mineral Markets*, mimeo (University of Stockholm, Institute of International Economic Studies); also in *Resources Policy*, June 1978.

8 National Policies towards Commodity Exports

ERNESTO TIRONI

The purpose of this essay is to analyse the alternative policies which less developed countries might adopt at a national level with regard to their commodity export sectors, in matters closely connected with the attempt to establish a new international economic order (NIEO). The policies in question relate principally to the problem of the instability of primary product exports.

Just as international markets are no more than the national markets of other countries, international economic systems are no more, in the final analysis, than the result of the confluence of the national policies of sovereign states relating to their foreign transactions. One of the sectors in which trade gives rise to very important relationships between poor and rich countries is that of basic or primary products. This is the first reason for devoting specific attention to the policies which LDCs have pursued in the past and might pursue in the future with regard to the exploitation and commercialisation of those products. The character of those national policies, and the relative power they have internationally, will have a significant influence upon the new international economic order established.

Second, any multinational agreements that might be reached within the framework of the NIEO will have to be implemented in the end through the national policies of sovereign states.

Third, the greater or smaller range of alternatives in *national* policy open to LDCs, and the effectiveness of those policies, will affect the NIEO by increasing or diminishing the interest of those countries in securing international agreements more consonant with their interests. Thus, for example, countries are far more likely to show interest in reaching an *international* agreement to stabilise the prices of raw materials, and to exert pressure for such an agreement, if they have no alternative strategies *of their own* for stabilising their export revenues.

While due regard must be paid to the role of political and military power, the international order which prevailed until the early 1970s was mainly the result of the hegemony of the countries of the centre in every sphere of economic life – in production, in finance, and in commodity markets. Economic power was exercised through transnational companies and through the governments of those countries. But the past order was also a result, in part, of the 'turning inward' of a number of LDCs of importance in the world economy, such as those of Latin America. This in turn was a consequence of the firm conviction that growth based upon the export of primary products offered scant prospects for the future.

However, it appears that the prospects have changed somewhat, for while demand for raw materials of agricultural origin has been sluggish, as predicted, that for mineral products has been relatively buoyant. In addition a factor which appears to be of even greater significance is that in a large number of countries control over the production of natural resources has passed from the hands of transnational corporations into those of public enterprises. These facts at least show the need to take a new look at the implication of following a development model which has been progressively less based on primary product exports. This exercise may reveal new prospects for Latin America, but at the same time poses new problems and challenges. Foremost among them is the imperative need to take up the issue of the instability of income from such exports.

In the first section of this essay we analyse the recent evolution of the production and trade of basic products; in the second, we consider the significance of export instability for LDCs; and in the third we examine the principal national or internal policy alternatives available for individual LDCs to cope with the problems of instability. It should be made clear at the outset, therefore, that policy options which are international in character, i.e. multinational agreements, such as UNCTAD's Integrated Commodity Programme, will not be considered here.

Finally, it should be noted that reference is made primarily to Latin America. Further detailed analysis would be needed to establish the applicability of the conclusions reached here to LDCs in general.[1]

1 THE EVOLUTION OF TRADE IN PRIMARY PRODUCTS

What has been happening recently in the international trade in primary products? How important is it still for the poor nations? What has been and is now the position of Latin America in the world's trade in primary commodities and what factors have affected its evolution?

These are some of the key questions which must be answered if we are to establish the extent to which LDCs should reformulate their national policies toward their primary sectors and/or seek new international agreements with respect to them. Considerable further research is required to answer those questions with precision. Here we shall only offer some tentative answers, which may provide an up-to-date background for the discussion of alternative national policies. It is possible that policies which are being pursued today are based upon ideas which had some validity two or three decades ago, but which are no longer of any relevance.

(a) The performance of exports

Tables 8.1 and 8.2 provide some information regarding the evolution of international trade. We are principally concerned here with three of the many perspectives from which that evolution could be analysed: (i) the importance of primary products in world exports; (ii) the importance of primary products for LDCs, as compared to industrialised countries; and (iii) the importance of LDCs and industrialised countries in total exports of primary products.

The tables provided reveal, first that primary products in general (SITC 0 to 2, 4 and 68, these being foods, drinks, tobacco, agricultural raw materials, fuels and minerals) accounted for 41 per cent of world exports in 1977.[2] This compares with 48 per cent in 1960, and thus represents a relative decline, despite increases in the price of oil.[3]

But the category of basic products in general includes a number of different goods whose shares have changed considerably in the last seventeen years. In particular, oil has doubled its share in the value of world exports, passing from less than 10 per cent in 1960 to more than 20 per cent in 1976, while the share of basic products other than oil has fallen heavily, from 38 to 21 per cent, and that of manufactures has shown a modest increase, from 51 to 58 per cent. The rise in fuel prices has also had a marked effect upon the structure of trade of individual countries.

Turning to the second point, for the LDCs considered as a group oil accounted for 57·5 per cent of total exports in 1977, as against under 29 per cent in 1960. Thus, as a result of the predominance of oil, primary products in general continue to represent the overwhelming majority of

TABLE 8.1 Composition of exports: LDCs, developed countries and the world 1960, 1970, 1977 ($billion and percentages of total exports by country groups)

Country groups	1960 Value	1960 %	1970 Value	1970 %	1977 Value	1977 %	1960–70	1970–7
Less Developed	26.8	100.0 (23.9)	54.3	100.0 (19.5)	285.8	100.0 (28.2)	7.3	26.8
Primary products	24.2	90.3	43.2	79.5	233.21	81.6	6.0	27.2
Petroleum	(7.7)	(28.7)	(17.9)	(33.0)	(164.4)	(57.5)	(8.8)	(37.3)
Other	(16.5)	(61.6)	(25.3)	(46.6)	(68.8)	(24.1)	(4.4)	(15.4)
Manufactures	2.5	9.3	10.0	18.4	51.7	18.1	14.9	26.5
Other	0.1	0.4	1.1	2.0	0.8	0.3	27.1	0.0
Developed	85.4	100.0 (76.1)	224.2	100.0 (80.5)	726.5	100.0 (71.8)	10.1	18.3
Primary products	29.3	34.3	59.4	26.5	178.1	24.5	7.3	17.0
Petroleum	(3.3)	(3.9)	(7.6)	(3.4)	(36.2)	(5.0)	(8.7)	(25.0)
Other	(26.0)	(30.4)	(51.8)	(23.1)	(141.9)	(19.5)	(7.1)	(15.5)
Manufactures	54.9	64.3	160.9	71.8	537.5	74.0	11.4	18.8
Other	1.2	1.4	3.9	1.7	10.9	1.5	12.5	15.8
World Total	112.2	100.0	278.5	100.0	1012.3	100.0	9.5	20.2
Primary products	53.5	47.7	102.6	36.8	411.3	40.6	6.7	21.9
Petroleum	(11.0)	(9.8)	(25.5)	(9.2)	(200.6)	(19.8)	(8.8)	(34.3)
Other	(42.5)	(37.9)	(77.1)	(27.6)	(210.7)	(26.7)	(6.1)	(15.4)
Manufactures	57.4	51.2	170.9	61.4	589.2	58.2	11.5	19.3
Other	1.3	1.1	5.0	1.8	11.7	1.2	14.4	12.9

Composition of exports spans the 1960, 1970, 1977 columns; *Annual rates of growth* spans the 1960–70 and 1970–7 columns.

* Percentage of world exports
Source: IBRD, *Commodity Trade and Price Trends: 1978* (Washington, DC: 1978) p. 2.

LDCs' exports (82 per cent). Nevertheless, the performance of oil has failed to compensate for the sharp decline in the relative weight of the remaining basic products, as their share sank from 62 per cent to 24 per cent between 1960 and 1977. In the industrialised countries, on the other hand, the share of primary products in total exports fell only from 30 per cent to 20 per cent over the same period. As a result, primary products other than oil now account for a similar share of the exports of each group of countries, whereas that share was significantly higher for LDCs in the early 1960s.

However, the situation described above is not representative of what is occurring in the majority of LDCs when individually considered, for only a few of them export oil, and its value is so high that it makes the contribution of other exports appear small by comparison. If oil is excluded altogether, it can be appreciated that primary products are still much more important for LDCs than for industrialised countries, although much less so than a decade and a half ago. In 1977 they generated 57 per cent of the export revenue of LDCs, as against 86 per cent in 1960 and 19 per cent of the export revenue of industrialised countries in 1977.

The third aspect of the present composition of world trade which should be emphasised is that, contrary to widespread belief, the nations of the Third World do *not* have a greater share of total exports of primary products excluding oil than the industrialised nations. In fact, LDCs exported less than one-third of the value of all primary products traded in 1977, excluding fuels, a share that has fallen from almost 40 per cent in 1960. Industrialised countries exported 60 per cent of such products in 1960, and 67 per cent in 1977.

To complete this synthesis of the evolution of world trade, it should be noted that the LDCs have been able to increase their share of total international trade almost exclusively as a result of increases in the price of oil in the 1970s: otherwise, that share would have remained almost constant in the 1970s after the sharp fall during the 1960s. If oil were excluded from world trade, the LDCs' share in the world's exports would have been 15 per cent in 1977 (14·4 per cent in 1970), as compared to almost 19 per cent a decade and a half ago.

The position of Latin America in world trade in primary products is somewhat different from that of LDCs in general. First, in 1977, total exports of primary products represented 84 per cent of the region's exports, slightly above the figure for the Third World as a whole, although it had declined more rapidly, from a level of 97 per cent in 1960. Oil exports, accounting for 36 per cent of total exports in 1977, are less important in Latin America than in the LDCs as a whole, and have not increased as rapidly (they already accounted for 34 per cent of that region's exports in 1960). Therefore, the rest of primary exports have been relatively much more important for Latin America: they represented 63 per cent of the total in 1960, and 48 per cent in 1977.

Particularly worthy of note is the significant fall – from 8 per cent to 5 per cent – in Latin America's share of the world's aggregate exports in the period from 1960 to 1975–7. The increase in oil prices was not the only cause, nor perhaps even the principal one; the cause lay as much in the slow growth of other primary exports, and in the failure to expand manufactured exports faster so as to compensate for the lower growth of primary goods.[4]

What were the factors, then, which lay behind the performance of Latin American exports? Was it the result of problems of *demand* and terms of trade, such as were predicted in the region after the end of the Second World War? Or was it, rather, a consequence of national policies which tended to work against the continued expansion in the *supply* of basic products?

The first hypothesis would be verified if it could be shown that prices of primary products have tended to fall systematically. The available evidence suggests that, even when oil is excluded, this was not the case, either for Latin America or for the Third World in general. But this method to test that hypothesis has a number of limitations, and there is a more direct method which might be used to verify it. If the cause of the unsatisfactory performance of primary exports from Latin America were sluggishness on the demand side, the share of the region's exports in world supply, or at least in that generated by all LDCs taken together, should have remained relatively constant.[5] If, on the other hand, the failure to expand the supply were the cause, we should observe a decline in Latin America's share of world trade in basic products.

The evidence available for the period 1960–77 seems to confirm the greater relative significance of an inadequate supply response (see Table 8.2). In that period, Latin America's share of world exports declined in all but five of the eighteen primary products (oil excluded) chosen by UNCTAD IV to make up its Integrated Programme[6] (in the case of jute it remained practically constant). At the same time, its share in world oil exports fell sharply, from 38 per cent in 1960 to 7 per cent in 1975–7.

What is particularly interesting is that the decline in Latin America's share of world trade in primary products is fundamentally due to the more rapid rate of expansion of exports of those same goods by the developed countries, a phenomenon which has also affected other

TABLE 8.2 Latin American, LDC and developed country shares in the world's exports of main primary products 1960–77 (%)

Commodities and their share in LA's exports (1975–7)		Less developed countries						Developed countries	
		Latin America		Others		Total			
		1960	1975–7	1960	1975–7	1960	1975–7	1960	1975–7
1 Coffee	(9.5%)	75.9	57.2	21.5	34.9	97.4	92.1	2.6	7.9
2 Cocoa	(0.8)	24.7	22.1	75.3	74.4	100.0	96.5	–	3.5
3 Tea	(0.1)	0.5	2.2	87.0	76.5	87.5	78.7	12.5	21.3
4 Sugar	(4.0)	54.2	23.6	20.4	23.8	74.6	47.4	25.4	52.6
5 Cotton	(1.5)	11.8	14.8	32.3	31.0	44.1	45.8	55.9	54.2
6 Rubber	(0)	0.5	0.3	79.8	95.8	80.3	96.1	19.7	3.9
7 Jute	(0)	–	0.1	97.6	95.7	97.6	95.8	2.4	4.2
8 Sisal	(0.1)	25.8	39.4	12.4	58.3	38.2	97.7	61.8	2.3
9 Copper	(2.8)	26.4	23.0	27.5	33.9	53.9	56.9	46.1	43.1
10 Tin	(0.5)	14.3	16.2	77.8	66.4	92.1	82.6	7.9	17.4
Sub-total 1–10	(19.4)	29.1	27.4	43.3	40.8	72.4	68.2	27.6	31.8

11 Bananas	(1.3)	79.4	75.3	14.2	21.9	93.6	97.2	6.4	7.3
12 Beef	(1.0)	28.2	12.3	1.4	1.1	29.6	13.4	70.4	86.6
13 Linseed	(0.2)	74.5	53.6	3.9	10.2	78.4	63.8	21.6	36.2
14 Timber	(0.4)	2.7	2.0	78.1	23.0	80.8	25.0	19.2	75.0
15 Bauxite	(0.6)	73.4	49.6	10.9	28.8	84.2	78.4	15.7	21.6
16 Manganese	(0.1)	23.0	16.0	47.1	33.7	70.1	49.7	29.9	50.3
17 Iron ore	(2.7)	22.6	24.8	17.4	14.8	40.0	39.6	60.0	60.4
18 Phosphoric rock	(0)	0.8	0.1	71.3	63.1	72.1	63.2	27.9	36.8
Sub-total 11–18	(25.7)	29.1	21.5	39.4	32.4	68.5	53.9	31.5	46.1
Petroleum	(19.8)	37.6	7.3	44.3	82.8	81.9	90.1	18.1	9.9
Other 15 pp	(5.3)	10.9	8.2	19.6	12.8	30.5	21.0	69.5	79.0
Main 33 pp	(50.8)	26.5	11.2	35.4	59.5	61.9	70.7	38.5	29.3
Other exports	(49.2)	1.8	3.2	4.5	6.1	6.3	9.3	93.7	90.7
Total exports	(100.0)	7.8	5.1	12.1	18.4	19.9	23.5	80.1	79.5

Source: IBRD, op. cit., 1973–7, Table 2(a).

LDCs, though not to the same extent. These facts reveal especially the limited ability of Latin American producers to compete with rival nations, whether industrialised or developing, or to capture a share of the markets opened up in the industrialised world.[7] Inability to compete with other Third World producers is in evidence principally in the cases of coffee, rubber, copper, and bauxite. Relative loss of markets to producers in industrialised nations is more marked in the cases of sugar, beef, oilseeds, and phosphate rock.[8] Of the four basic products in which the supply share of the industrial countries has fallen, Latin America has been the major beneficiary in the cases of cotton and sisal (Brazil has taken an increasing share of the hard fibres market through its sizal exports); in the cases of rubber and phosphates non-Latin American LDCs have benefited more than proportionately, hence cutting down the Latin American share of these markets.

Given its origins, the evolution we have been considering has been principally a consequence of the national foreign trade policies pursued by individual nations. In this respect, one surprising fact is that the great majority of Latin American countries saw their share of world exports in their principal product decline between 1960 and 1977, despite the heterogeneity of those countries as far as their principal export products are concerned (see Table 8.3).[9] In this area the different countries have tended to conform to a similar pattern; the only countries to increase significantly their share in the world's exports of their main commodity were Brazil and Costa Rica (coffee) and Nicaragua (cotton). Nevertheless, basic products continue to account for a high proportion of total exports for the majority of countries in the region.

It cannot be simplistically inferred from the foregoing discussion that the Latin American nations have suffered a comparative welfare loss, or that their National Income could have been higher if they had followed a different development strategy. This is an open question, and one which we shall not seek to answer here. We shall instead proceed with the delineation of the facts and of their global causes, outlining the changes which have taken place in the production of primary commodities in the countries of the region.

(b) The organisation of production

The organisation of the production of natural resources in Latin America has undergone a number of changes in the last two decades. The most important is the increased involvement of the state in the regulation of the sectors in question, and in particular the nationalisation of activities formerly under foreign control.

At the beginning of the 1960s transnational companies controlled the production of copper, iron ore, zinc, lead, bauxite, manganese, bananas and oil. Their position was dominant in practically all the minerals on the list of eighteen primary products in the Integrated Programme of UNCTAD, but much less important in the production of agricultural commodities.[10] This external control over the production of basic products had practically ended by the second half of the 1970s.[11]

The nationalisations began in the second half of the 1960s with the 'Chileanisation' of copper in that country, and culminated in Venezuela's nationalisation of its oil in 1976.[12] But the process has not been sustained or uniform, either throughout the region as a whole, or within individual countries; furthermore, the methods adopted have not been homogeneous. For example, Peru nationalised some old copper mines and left some un-nationalised, while the exploitation of some new deposits was undertaken by foreign capital; the same has occurred with petroleum. Chile, for its part, nationalised all the major copper companies, but has recently given foreign capital again the right to exploit certain important deposits.[13] In practically all Latin American mineral-exporting countries, nationalisation has been accompanied by arrangements for compensation, as a result of which the countries in question have committed themselves to making fixed payments in foreign exchange in the future, and the exploitation of major deposits has generally been entrusted to public enterprises.

As for the gradual increase in state involvement in regulating the exploitation of natural resources, it should be noted that the various acts of nationalisation were preceded by the generalisation of exchange controls (and sometimes of multiple exchange rates), increases in taxes, growing intervention in marketing (with the stipulation that the product should be sold on particular markets, such as the London Metal Exchange in the case of Chilean copper, or in a particular form, e.g. refined rather than unwrought). Finally there has been insistence upon the increased use of local inputs and the provision of social services for workers.

In the particular case of agricultural products, a further feature is the extension of price controls, especially on products which are consumed internally on a large scale, such as meat in Argentina and Uruguay. In addition agrarian reforms have affected foreign-owned export sectors, such as sugar in Peru and coffee in some Central American countries.

TABLE 8.3   Importance of primary products for the Latin American countries 1975–7

Country	Share of total exports in GDP* (1977) (1)	Main exported commodity (2)	Share of main exported commodity in			Share of all primary products in each country's total exports (1975–7) (6)
			world exports of the commodity		each country's total exports (1975–7) (5)	
			(1960) (3)	(1975–7) (4)		
Argentina	11.0	Maize	20.2	6.8	11.3	39.2
Bolivia	19.7	Tin	14.3	14.9	40.9	87.9
Brazil	6.1	Coffee	3.5	7.3	6.9	44.0
Colombia	10.9	Coffee	17.5	12.7	57.2	69.9
Costa Rica	27.8	Coffee	7.9	14.7	29.4	63.7
Chile	23.4	Copper	19.2	18.6	55.6	67.5
Ecuador	15.6	Petroleum	–	0.4	46.3	77.1
El Salvador	21.7	Coffee	4.0	4.6	52.4	69.6

Guatemala	20.7	Coffee	3.9	3.6	35.4	62.8
Guyana	64.4	Sugar	2.1	1.3	37.7	78.9
Haiti	8.7	Coffee	0.9	0.5	36.0	57.6
Honduras	24.4	Bananas	9.1	11.2	25.1	73.5
Jamaica	39.2**	Bauxite	23.8	20.4	17.0	33.4
Mexico	8.4	Petroleum	0.2	0.5	18.2	40.9
Nicaragua	24.6	Cotton	0.6	2.4	24.3	65.7
Panama	37.4	Bananas	–	7.1	25.2	45.0
Paraguay	13.8	Cotton	1.1	0.1	21.3	44.2
Peru	14.4	Copper	5.4	4.1	18.5	80.5
Dominican Republic	16.8	Sugar	5.5	4.0	43.1	70.3
Uruguay	18.6	Beef	3.7	2.2	17.8	41.4
Venezuela	11.7	Petroleum	25.8	4.3	64.1	67.3

* Refers to exports of goods and services.

** For 1973, World Bank, *World Tables: 1976* (Washington, DC: 1976).

Sources: IBRD, *op. cit.*, 1979 edition, except column 1, which is obtained from CEPAL, *Estudio Económico de América Latina* (Santiago, Chile).

To summarise, in one way or another the countries of the region were able to increase their share of the profits generated by the primary products they exported. This had the effect of reducing the profitability of foreign investment in these sectors, which probably explains part of the relative decline in Latin America's share in world markets. But that decline does not necessarily indicate a reduction in the economic benefits derived by these countries from the export of basic products. It is probable, though, that in this process avoidable costs were incurred, whether as a result of errors in the formulation of certain policies, some inconsistencies in their application or the absence of planning for the longer term. Certainly, planning of this nature is far from easy in an area of the international economy in which markets are very imperfect and control over decision-making and access to information are unequally distributed. As a result, some of the costs of these failings have also been borne by the industrial countries, who are the main commodity importers, as they have seen normal supplies of a number of basic products threatened and disrupted. Hence the need in the North as much as in the South for changes in this aspect of the prevailing international economic order.

2 CHANGES IN THE INTERNATIONAL MARKETS AND INSTABILITY

Since the end of the Second World War, international markets for basic products have been characterised by their disorganisation and by the lack of the political will of governments to improve them. The latter stands in sharp contrast to what has occurred in the markets for manufactures (through GATT), with the regulation of exchange rates and of international finance (through the IMF) and the financing of development over the long term (through the World Bank). History has proved that Keynes was correct to emphasise, as he did in 1942, the importance of organising post-war international economic relations institutionally around bodies playing the roles mentioned above, *in conjunction with* another whose mission would be to contribute to the regulation of the prices of basic products.[14] The cost of neglecting this task has been very high, not only for most LDCs, but also for the industrialised countries. The action of OPEC in the early 1970s and the world-wide 'stagflation' which followed testifies to this effect (Cooper and Lawrence, 1975; Okun, 1975; Bergsten, 1977).

(a) The organisation of markets

From the end of the Second World War until today, no real use has been made of opportunities to improve markets for raw materials, probably because they had *apparently* been functioning 'well', or at least better than they had before the war (Rowe, 1965, Chapters 13, 15). But they were functioning well only for the industrialised countries, who controlled them either through their transnational corporations or their governments. The latter intervened sporadically and unilaterally in markets by a variety of means: the imposition of quotas (in oil, for example) and tariffs (on copper, sugar, etc.) and the accumulation or release of 'strategic stocks'. Decisions on all these matters were taken with an eye only to the individual interests of the countries of the centre, to the almost complete exclusion of those of exporting LDCs.[15]

Given this context, it is understandable that LDCs, and in particular those in Latin America, sought to defend themselves with the only means at their disposal; that is, with the intervention of governments in the marketing activities of foreign companies exporting their primary products, the nationalisation of some of these companies, and the formation of cartels or organisations for producers only (such as OPEC and the Council of Copper Producing Countries (CIPEC)).

The principal repercussions arising out of these changes, and in particular out of the success of OPEC, were, on the one hand, the stimulus to other LDCs to enter into producers' agreements to defend the prices of their basic products, and, on the other hand, the change in the DCs' negative attitude towards the search for new ways of regulating international commodity markets (CEPAL, 1976, pp. 34–5).

At the same time, the growing intervention of the LDCs' governments in the marketing of their primary products has had as its major consequence that these commodities are being sold with increasing frequency, at the prices obtaining in 'free' international markets. These markets are relatively marginal in relation to world production and exchange. That is true of the London Metal Exchange, for example, which is a relatively small and segmented market, i.e. separated from the internal markets of a number of the more important countries of the centre. This separation is maintained principally by means of various real or latent restrictions imposed by the governments of those countries upon imports of primary products, normally at the request of local producers.

The prices in these international markets proper have frequently been higher than those prevailing in the industrialised nations, and to this extent the movement of the LDCs into them has been to their advantage. But because of their marginal nature, these markets are highly unstable. The prices at which LDCs sell their primary products have therefore tended to fluctuate more as a result of the shifts mentioned here.[16]

(b) Price instability and its effects

The lack of concern for the need to provide an institutional framework which would allow markets to operate adequately, or, to put it another way, the widespread acceptance of the fallacy that a 'free market' is synonymous with an efficient market, has permitted the survival of a situation in which international prices do not adequately reflect the relative attractiveness over the long term of investment in particular areas. Those problems were aggravated in the 1970s by the devaluations of the dollar, the international monetary and exchange rate instability, the increase in the price of oil and in international liquidity, and the speculative operations with some primary products.

It is more difficult and misleading than ever today to generalise about price trends for primary products as a group. In aggregate terms, if oil is excluded, the long-run changes which can be observed are not substantial, although there is a distinction to be made between agricultural commodities, whose prices have tended to fall, and minerals, whose prices have shown an upward trend (CEPAL, 1975, p. 35). Nevertheless, considerable fluctuations can be observed in the prices of individual products. Furthermore, these fluctuations became more marked in the 1970s, moving in general in the same direction, with minor discrepancies as to the turning points but with far larger variations as to their intensity.

The average degree of fluctuation in prices increased in the early 1970s for all basic products (see Table 8.4). Of the ten major commodities selected by UNCTAD for its Integrated Programme, four have seen a doubling of the intensity of their price fluctuations in this decade as compared to the last. These are coffee, cotton, sisal and tin. In an intermediate position, with an increase of over 50 per cent in the intensity of these fluctuations, are tea, rubber and copper. Only jute prices have remained relatively stable. As for cocoa and sugar, increases in price instability were hardly to be expected, given the high levels of fluctuation recorded in the past.

The literature on export instability in LDCs is relatively abundant, if somewhat out of date.[17] It has concentrated mainly upon such aspects as (a) its causes and origins; whether and to what extent it is a result of price instability, volume instability, or a combination of the two (income instability); and whether it is related to shifts in demand or in supply (UN, 1952; FMI-BIRF, 1969); (b) the comparative effect of such instability as between poor and industrialised or large and small countries (Massell, 1970); and (c) the welfare effects, i.e. costs and benefits of instability for exporting LDCs (Coppock, 1962; MacBean, 1966; Yotopoulos and Nugent, 1976, Chapter 18).

The causes and origins of instability differ considerably from one product to another as well as from one country to another, depending upon the range of commodities exported. The distinction between these two aspects is crucial, and the relationship between them should he analysed with extreme care. Simple generalisations in this field are dangerous: a country may enjoy a relatively high level of stability in its total income from exports of basic products despite high levels of instability in sales of individual products, and vice versa.

As for the comparative intensity of fluctuations in price, volume, and income, practically all the empirical studies carried out for both individual countries and individual products show that instability of export *income* is greater than that of prices or of quantities exported (Helleiner, 1972, p. 80).

Furthermore, there is general agreement at present that the prices and volumes exported by the poorer and smaller countries, and the incomes derived from them, fluctuate more than those of the richer and larger countries (Erb and Schiavo-Campo, 1969; Massell, 1970).

The evidence regarding the *costs* of price or income instability is less clear, owing to the complex manner in which such effects are generated. It is necessary to consider who bears the costs and enjoys the benefits or, in other words, the distributive impact of instability. At an aggregate level, the impact of instability upon economic welfare may be analysed from a microeconomic or a macroeconomic perspective. The majority of theoretical studies on this theme adopt the first approach, and have been able to establish that, contrary to what was intuitively believed previously, producers did not benefit from greater price instability when this originated predominantly from aleatory fluctuations in demand, and vice versa. But this microeconomic focus is a partial one since it considers only some of the effects of instability upon a country's development. Furthermore, it has been shown recently that propositions based upon microeconomic analysis rest upon a number of assumptions of doubtful validity, such as the existence of linear supply-

TABLE 8.4   Fluctuations of prices of main primary products 1949–76 (percentages and dollars of 1975)

	1949–64		1965–70		1971–6	
	Fluctuation index[a]	Average price[b]	Fluctuation index	Average price	Fluctuation index	Average price
1 Coffee	14.1	114.1	9.7	87.6	23.7	95.5
2 Cocoa	23.2	76.3	26.3	63.1	33.0	80.7
3 Tea	9.2	285.0	7.8	238.6	10.9	159.0
4 Sugar	22.0	11.8	2.8	13.2	43.6	17.6
5 Cotton	5.8	64.8	5.6	61.1	22.7	68.9
6 Rubber	20.5[c]	171.7	16.5	103.4	26.8	82.6
7 Jute	24.1	463.5	8.6	577.4	10.7	410.1
8 Sisal	23.8	702.8	11.2	399.2	50.1	645.8
9 Copper	14.5	1,591.7	15.6	2,771.3	24.4	1,849.3
10 Tin	8.5	5,376.3	6.1	728.8	17.3	7,114.8

	1.1	36.0	3.2	32.0	3.4	24.2
12 Beef	12.5	137.9	19.7	210.8	7.3[d]	409.5
13 Linseed	n.a.		n.a.		n.a.	n.a.
14 Timber	3.4[e]	83.3	7.1	77.9	29.7	93.6
15 Bauxite	n.a.	n.a.	n.a.	n.a.	n.a.	n.a.
16 Manganese	n.a.	n.a.	n.a.	n.a.	n.a.	n.a.
17 Iron ore	5.6[c]	27.8	5.7	18.9	16.5	16.7
18 Phosphoric rock	4.5	29.6	7.5	25.1	43.7	37.0

[a] Defined as the average of the absolute price differences between two successive years, expressed as a percentage of the average price over the period considered.

[b] Prices refer to dollar cents per pound in the case of agricultural products (except tea, rubber, bananas and beef which are cents per kilogram), dollars per metric ton in the case of minerals and dollars per cubic foot in the case of timber.

[c] Period 1954–64.

[d] Period 1971–74.

[e] Period 1955–64.

Source: IBRD, op. cit., 1977 edition.

and-demand functions, and the dependence of quantity upon actual rather than expected product prices (Turnovsky, 1978).

The majority of empirical studies of the global effect of instability upon the exporting countries' national income are founded upon a more macroeconomic basis. The results, in general, are not conclusive; evidence is presented to support each of the three possible positions, and the arguments marshalled in each case are very different. Some writers argue that instability has positive effects upon economic growth, fundamentally as a result of the greater tendency to save and invest which is supposedly generated as a result of temporarily high incomes obtained in periods of high prices.[18] A second group considers that, in net terms, instability has no significant effect upon economic growth. Finally, a third group of authors argue that it definitely reduces economic growth. This is because of (a) the cost of maintaining greater foreign currency reserves to avoid interruptions in the supply of imports; (b) the cost of *uncertainty*, translated into lower production of the commodities affected; (c) the inefficiency implicit in leaving investment projects unfinished, having excess installed capacity and seeing un-employment generated in periods of scarcity of funds for investment; and (d) the macroeconomic costs and inflationary spirals provoked by the downward rigidity of prices and the difficulties in compensating for the monetary impact of variations in fiscal receipts and of excessive balance of payments surpluses or deficits.

Beyond these conventional economic problems, there are others of a less tangible nature but of equal significance. They include, for example the 'rentier' rather than 'industrious' mentality which tends to be generated among the population of a country in which the growth of incomes depends more upon exogenous conditions, such as the unstable prices of export products, than upon individual efforts at production.[19] To this we should add the problems of internal income distribution mentioned previously, and the social costs resulting from the *political* instability which so often has its origins in a crisis in the external sector.

These considerations indicate how difficult it is to make a quantitative estimate of the costs and benefits of export instability. Nevertheless, a number of partial empirical studies on the subject have been carried out. Some authors have found a statistically significant favourable effect of such instability upon the rate of growth of GDP (Coppock, 1962; MacBean, 1966; Yotopoulos and Nugent, 1976). But these same authors, with the exception of Yotopoulos and Nugent, are sceptical as to the validity of their own assumptions and results.[20] Furthermore, other partial studies show opposite results (Glezakos, 1970). Hence, considering *all* the costs of export instability (not always reflected in immediate changes in GDP) there is little doubt that it poses a serious problem for LDCs.

What is even more worrying, however, is that in this decade there have been at least three events which have increased the *costs* of instability for Third World countries.

First, the processes of nationalisation have, on the one hand, added a fixed foreign exchange outflow which has to be discounted from foreign currency income in order to pay for the nationalised capital. On the other hand, nationalisations have increased the share of fluctuating revenues (profits) within total foreign exchange receipts.[21] Thus, the surplus available for the acquisition of imports has become more unstable. In addition, when nationalised firms have been transfered to co-operatives or small private producers (as in the case of sugar in Peru, and bananas in Central America), the distributive problems of instability have become more acute. And when companies have been incorporated into the public sector, the inflationary effects of instability have become sharper and more direct, as a consequence of fluctuations in public revenues.[22]

Second, it is well known that official loans from governments and international agencies have given way to shorter-term loans from private transnational banks as a source for external credit for the developing countries. In this context, it is likely that LDCs will find access to international financing more difficult on account of very fluctuating export income.[23] This is particularly serious when such resources are required for the specific purpose of expanding the supply of primary products in the long term, as in the case of minerals whose production is highly capital intensive. The difficulty in obtaining these capital resources has unfavourable repercussions upon the very supply of raw materials which the industrialised countries want to secure in order to avoid seeing limits placed on their own prospects for growth in the long term.

In this context it should be noted that the transnational companies had reacted to the instability of mineral raw material prices not only by seeking an oligopolistic control of their markets, but also with vertical integration and diversification into other products. Furthermore, they had in the last analysis transferred their risks to investors in the industrialised countries, who had in turn defended themselves by diversifying their share-holding across companies involved in a variety sectors. The whole of this chain has been partially dislocated by the nationalisations, and this creates a necessity for further real and financial mechanisms which can secure sufficient investment in the production of primary products in the future.

Finally, the third change that has taken place in recent years which makes instability more costly is the level reached by the process of import substitution in the majority of LDCs. Within the range of products which they now import, the proportion corresponding to final consumer goods or goods which might easily be dispensed with is much smaller than in the past. In Latin America, in particular, the majority of imports are now intermediate goods, fuel and capital goods, so there is a smaller margin by which imports can be reduced in periods of foreign exchange shortages. Forced reductions in those imports will have a far more serious impact upon the level of domestic industrial activity, employment, and national income.

3 ALTERNATIVE DOMESTIC POLICIES REGARDING PRIMARY PRODUCTS

Which policies appear to be most efficient for LDCs seeking to derive greater advantage from the exploitation of their natural resources given the foreseeable international context? This is certainly a question which does not have a single answer valid for all cases. Besides, the level of our theoretical and empirical understanding of a number of key aspects of the problem is still insufficient. For those reasons, the policies suggested here should not be seen as a fixed package to be applied in all cases, but as a range of options upon which individual countries can draw in accordance with their own needs and circumstances.[24]

(a) Primary products and development

First, it is important to re-evaluate the relationship between development and commodity exports in Latin America in the light of the present international context and the level of development reached by the region. It seems necessary to revise the idea, still very widely accepted in the region, that it is neither possible nor desirable to obtain a faster growth based upon the export of primary products. Some of the empirical facts on which that position was based have not prevailed unqualified in the recent past. The idea that there is a 'progressive deterioration in the terms of trade of primary products' has been generalised somewhat indiscriminately by followers of this line of thought. First, there has been insufficient attention paid to the experience of some particular commodities. Second, exports of the same primary product can present very different problems, depending on the country which exports it; as a consequence, it is not advisable to offer the same recommendations to countries in very different conditions.

More specifically, the role of commodity exports as promoters or obstacles to development should be re-evaluated. In a certain sense, we must undertake once again the type of work done so brilliantly by Prebisch at the end of the 1940s, but this time in the light of the new internal conditions of the producing countries. It seems essential also to update our knowledge of the *specific* production and marketing characteristics of the different primary products.

Among these characteristics are: (a) the long run price which basic products are likely to command in the future, as a consequence of international economic and technological developments, and the possibilities for producing them in industrialised countries or other LDCs; (b) the extent to which they are capital or labour intensive, and the national value added which they generate; (c) the backward or forward linkages which they may have; (d) the implications of national or foreign control over elements which are essential for their exploitation (from technology to marketing); and (e) the relative magnitude of the surpluses generated by the production of primary products and the capacity of countries to use them productively.[25]

Although it is one of the logical extensions of the pioneering thought of Raúl Prebisch, very little attention has been paid to the study of the organisation and policies best calculated to maximise the contribution of natural resources to development. In global terms, this involves, first, the determination of the optimum *size* of the sector and the forms by which it can be achieved; the degree of diversification of exports and of the economy in general, and the levels of protection (negative or positive) to be granted to the primary sector in relation to other activities (industry and agriculture, in particular). Second, it involves decisions, political as well as economic, regarding the structure of ownership (foreign or national, private or public) of firms in the sector. Finally, it involves the design of specific *sectoral policies* capable of regulating more efficiently the functioning of companies under different systems of ownership and of new *forms of internal organisation* of public enterprises participating in the production of basic products in LDCs.

Another area of crucial importance which has received scant attention relates to alternative policies to counter the instability of revenue from the export of primary products. The optimum weight of these products in the overall structure of production and foreign trade of a country will depend also upon the specific instability of their prices or quantities, and the policies available to combat them.

The excessive fluctuations in the *value* of commodity exports can be faced by directly *stabilising* the prices or quantities of the primary products sold, or by *neutralising* (or compensating) their changes in value through the application of special financial mechanisms. What has to be borne in mind though is that the autonomous *national* capacity of a country to take either line of action, and the costs involved, will vary from one country to another. One of the key variables which determine this autonomous capacity for stabilisation is the specific source of the fluctuation in export income.[26] If it is *price* instability, there is very little that an individual country can do alone unless it controls a very high proportion of total supply. And even when this is the case, the co-operation of the consuming nations in jointly financing the stabilising stocks required would considerably reduce the costs involved.

In theory, it can be shown that the optimal form of reducing or eliminating excessive fluctuations in the value of primary exports consists of a multi-national regulation of prices and quantities sold, by means of the creation of stabilising stocks.[27] Nevertheless, if this mechanism is adopted in isolation for a few commodities only it can run into significant international political difficulties, arising out of the distributive effects of stabilisation, which render it only partially effective. Therefore, while we recognise the importance of the initiatives being undertaken in this area – essentially in connection with UNCTAD's attempt to set up the Common Fund and the Integrated Commodity Programmes – we feel that it is wise to explore alternative national policies to stabilise export incomes.

(b) National policies for stabilisation

It seems crucially important to make a rigorous classification of the national stabilising policies possible for LDCs, and their principal effects. There are several areas in this field which call for more detailed investigation. First, there is a need to examine the criteria for the selection of the most suitable stabilising policies. Foremost among those criteria are: (a) their *economic efficiency* (especially their capacity to balance out the discrepancies between the private and social costs of instability; (b) their *political viability* at a national level and their internal distributive effects; and (c) the *contribution* which they make (or the obstacles which they present) to the implementation of international stabilising policies theoretically superior to those merely national in scope. Second, attention must be paid to the domestic institutional organisation which should be set if the viability of particular policies is to be assured.

We shall proceed therefore to review the principal policies applied or suggested as a response at national level to problems of instability, classifying them in three basic groups: (i) policies relating principally to balance of payments problems; (ii) policies designed to correct fiscal and macroeconomic disequilibria; and (iii) policies affecting the producers of basic products.

In practice, LDCs have tended to direct their attention primarily to the first category of policies. But the impact of instability in the other two areas can be equally or more significant, despite its remaining hidden or diffused. For that reason we propose the broader classification adopted here, recognising of course that a number of policies act at all three levels, and could appear in more than one category.

(i) Policies relating to the balance of payments   Historically the main policy adopted by Latin American countries (partly, though by no means primarily) aimed at combating the instability affecting their primary products was that of deliberately stimulating import substitution. This is one way of freeing consumption and internal investment from the excessively fluctuating income derived from commodity exports.

The second policy, also relatively global in nature, has been to diversify exports, especially by providing incentives for the export of manufactures through subsidies of various kinds.

Without denying the logic of applying these policies to some degree with the objective of achieving a faster overall development, it should be pointed out that they have possibly proved too costly as methods of reducing export instability by inducing a failure to exploit valuable resources to the extent that might have been possible otherwise. In any case, other types of export diversification, linked more closely to the exploitation of the comparative advantages enjoyed by particular countries, merit more consideration than they have received heretofore.[28]

The third policy of internal adjustment which has been frequently employed in Latin American countries is the imposition of temporary quantitative restrictions or delays on imports, by means of the introduction of varied obstacles to importing during periods when the prices of primary exports are low. Among the drawbacks of mechanisms of this nature are their regressive impact upon income distribution and the indirect costs arising out of their often untimely application.

The fourth stabilising mechanism employed in Latin America has been the manipulation of foreign currency reserves or borrowing on a short-term basis. In general, however, this has proved extremely insufficient. With the recent emergence of policy makers committed to free trade in positions of influence in the region, the idea that instability could and should be combated only at national level, and largely through these financial mechanisms, has gained ground. But the system implies that the bulk of the costs of adjustment will be borne by the exporting nation in isolation: The level of reserves needed if the mechanism is to prove effective is very high, and it is to be doubted whether countries experiencing periods of reduced income of uncertain duration could afford to obtain the necessary resources.[29]

The response of the free trade theorists to these doubts is to propose that the exchange rate should be also determined freely in the market as a means of maintaining the balance of payments automatically in equilibrium, in spite of sudden fluctuations in the proceeds from raw materials exports. We have criticised this proposal more extensively elsewhere (Tironi, 1977), arguing that it would probably prove counter-productive, as the rate of exchange would fluctuate as much as export prices. But the latter is a macroeconomic variable which has wider macroeconomic effects, so it would magnify the transmission of the initial instability to the economy as a whole, make investment decisions more difficult and render the allocation of resources less efficient.

With the exception of the accumulation and manipulation of foreign currency reserves, it seems that the other national policies for stabilising export income reviewed in this section should play a less central role than in the past, and be replaced by others capable of achieving the same objective more efficiently. Aside from the limitations which we have indicated, they have not provided solutions to two other key problems connected with external instability: fluctuations in fiscal revenues and in producers' revenue (which act as a disincentive to production). In other words, even if it were possible to maintain the balance of payments in perpetual equilibrium through the use of the instruments considered thus far, significant problems would still remain.

(ii) Fiscal and monetary equilibrium   Some of the most serious effects of export instability are those transmitted to the economy through the fiscal and monetary disequilibria which they generate. Nevertheless, this

is one of the areas into which little research has been carried out, and in which there is an urgent need to study alternative compensatory mechanisms.

Some countries have recently introduced a number of interesting instruments, such as public bonds given to exporters in exchange for their foreign currency earnings, which temporarily sterilise the monetary effects of excessive balance of payments surpluses in periods of very high prices.[30]

Some authors have suggested the possibility of introducing forms of taxation of foreign companies in the primary sector which transfer to them a greater proportion of the risk of export income instability. Given that they are in a better position to absorb the fluctuations in the prices of the raw materials they produce, the governments of host countries could design tax mechanisms which would assure a more stable flow of fiscal revenue, without provoking a very negative effect upon the volume of foreign investment (Tironi, 1977).

Among the forms of taxation which might be considered are: (a) the application of taxes upon the income or profits 'expected' in the long term by foreign companies, calculated as a function of a reference price or a 'normal' price (for example, a moving average over three to five years);[31] (b) the charging of a 'royalty' per unit of the product exported, without this necessarily substituting all the tax on income; and (c) the payment of a fixed annual rent for the use of deposits or of land, to be determined by an initial auction of these among the different companies interested in exploiting them.

Finally, an option that should be explored to complement these measures is the idea of manipulating a number of import tariffs over varied periods of time, with the objective of compensating in part for the excessive ups and downs of income derived from primary exports. Some of the characteristics and fundamental advantages of such a scheme have been discussed in greater detail elsewhere (Tironi, 1977, Section 4). In summary, it would be a question of selecting a very small group of goods not produced domestically (preferably durables whose consumption could be foregone temporarily), upon which high tariffs would be raised when the prices of primary products exported were low, and vice versa; i.e. tariffs would be lowered as commodity prices rose and the capacity to import increased. In this way the rest of the economy (and in particular the level of employment and overall economic activity) would be isolated from the instability of the prices of a limited number of products, whereas this is not the case with a free exchange rate policy. In addition, this scheme permits some compensation for the loss of fiscal revenue provoked by temporary declines in the prices of primary products exported.[32]

(iii) Stabilisation of producers' incomes   Even if optimal stabilisation policies relating to the balance of payments and to fiscal and monetary equilibrium could be devised and implemented, it would still be necessary to ensure that more stability was adequately transmitted to the producers of primary products themselves. What is required is that they should receive correct profitability signals in the long term, so that their levels of investment and production are adequate. Nevertheless, the stabilisation of producers' incomes may at times have an additional distributive intent.

The question of which policies will be most efficient at this level depends once again upon the specific characteristics of the products exported, and in particular upon the source of income instability. In a case of excessive fluctuations of price only, the most effective course will be to regulate prices. If instability of supply is more important, it may be necessary to apply direct public policies such as the provision of credit or storage facilities.

Hence, it is unwise to make simple generalisations as regards the manner in which the incomes of national producers of basic products might be stabilised. Research is needed throughout this area in order to determine which internal policies for stabilisation are best suited to each type of product, establishing above all whether small, medium or large producers are involved. The reactions of each to the same government measure may be very different, and thus give rise to different allocation and distribution effects.

In global terms, it seems clear enough that the best strategy for avoiding the negative effects of excessive income instability deriving from the export of primary products consists of the application of a *set* of various complementary policies. Any policy applied in isolation tends to involve growing costs for the economy if it is taken beyond a certain point. One of the areas which this study reveals as being most ripe for analysis is, therefore, the theoretical and empirical determination of the optimal point to which different policies should be applied in order to achieve a more stable flow of benefits from the exploitation of the natural resources which are so abundant in LDCs.

Finally, something must be said with regard to the institutional and political requisites for the implementation of these internal stabilising policies. One of the most relevant issues is to define the characteristics of the co-ordinating body or governmental agency responsible for applying stabilising measures, and to set *a priori* the time at which they should be applied. This would include the determination of the decision-making authority of this agency within the public administration as a whole, and the criteria according to which it should operate. Among the latter is the complex practical problem of defining the 'normal' price of the key primary product exported by each country, and of designing the indicators which reveal when a given market situation is 'transitory' or 'permanent'.

The clearly political nature of the problem of stabilising widely fluctuating export incomes should not be overlooked. The basic question is how to prevent the government affected from succumbing to the temptation to use immediately the extraordinary resources obtained at times when exports of primary products command high prices in world markets. The problem is not only to maintain the necessary international reserves or stocks, but to ensure that the relevant authorities organise public spending as a function of 'normal' fiscal revenues over the long term. The objective appears complex, but not unattainable. After all, it is closely analogous to that which gave origin to the formation of Central Banks to regulate the supply of money within individual countries. What is important now is to increase consciousness of the relevance of these problems, and to promote their systematic investigation.

NOTES

1 Nor should the reader expect that conclusions will be reached here with regard to policies for particular countries. It bears repeating that it is dangerous to generalise about the situations and needs of LDCs, which are very *heterogeneous* as regards the characteristics of the primary products they export.
2 All these are World Bank data taken from IBRD (1978) p. 2.
3 It should be borne in mind that by making comparisons across time we are risking failing to take into account changes over time in the characteristics of the products exported. By 1976, for example, the minerals being sold may have been more highly refined than previously. But the problem applies to other exports as well. However, since the figures are given here in terms of value, that phenomenon is partly taken into consideration to the extent that it is reflected in commodity prices.
4 Excluding oil, Latin America's share of world trade fell from 5·7 per cent in 1960 to 4.7 per cent in 1975–77.
5 Unless the discovery of new mineral reserves or the expansion of agricultural frontiers had been systematically concentrated outside Latin America. The second point seems to have some bearing on the African case.

6 In world exports of four products – sugar, beef, bauxite and manganese – Latin America's share fell by more than one-third.
7 To appreciate the competitive position of particular countries, or the advantage which they take of their competitiveness in world markets, the ideal procedure would be to compare their shares of world *supply* of each product, i.e. considering not only exports but also production for internal markets. Unfortunately, these figures are far harder to obtain.
8 In the cases of bauxite and coffee, part of the market shares lost by Latin America was gained by producers in industrialised countries also.
9 The 21 countries which appear in this table do not, as might be assumed, have common interest in the same few basic products: *ten* different products are involved. The most common are coffee, oil and cotton. The former was the major export product of six countries in 1975–7.
10 Nevertheless, towards 1958 North American companies were generating approximately 37 per cent of Cuban sugar exports, and substantially higher proportions of those of Haiti and the Dominican Republic. See Grunwald and Musgrove (1970, p. 349).
11 See ONUDI (1978), Baklanoff (1975), Mikesell (1970), Ffrench-Davis and Tironi (1974), and Girvan (1974). A general survey of expropriations in LDCs appears in Weekly (1977).
12 See *Comercio Exterior*, vol. 26, no. 1, January 1976, pp. 100–3.
13 An excellent synthesis of the new forms of contract between LDCs and foreign companies from the end of the 1960s appears in Smith and Wells (1975).
14 See 'The International Control of Raw Materials', reproduced in *Journal of International Economics*, August 1974.
15 See Girvan (1974) and, in particular, the excellent article by Bergsten (1977).
16 We should add here that the problem of instability in 'marginal' markets also strongly affects other LDCs who import primary products.
17 For a more extended discussion and an analysis of the relevant literature, see Helleiner (1973, Chapter 5) and Adams and Klein (1978). A survey of empirical studies will be found in Yotopoulos and Nugent (1976, Chapter 18).
18 The theory holds that the marginal propensity to save out of the transitory component of income is greater than the propensity to save out of the 'normal' or 'permanent' component of income.
19 Wallich (1960) stresses the point that instability engenders a 'speculative' mentality in businessmen.
20 The estimates made by Yotopoulos and Nugent are based on Friedman's 'permanent income theory', which assumes among other things that the propensity to consume out of the transitory component of income is zero. This clearly affects their results.
21 Furthermore, the total profits of nationalised companies will be more unstable than those previously obtained by foreign companies, as they will have to place a larger proportion of their production on marginal international markets, where prices are characterised by their higher propensity to fluctuate.
22 It should be added here that some authors suggest that the exploitation of natural resources by state enterprises has increased *per se* the instability of

prices, as those enterprises do not seek to maximise profits and face greater rigidities (or have more scruples) regarding the dismissal of workers in periods when prices are low. This is possible in theory, but the consequence is not necessarily to reduce the producing country's 'social welfare' because there will be less temporary unemployment generated by fluctuations in price. In this sense, one effect of nationalisation is to change the country which has to bear the costs of instability. Is it not logical to assume that when faced with lower prices transnational companies would tend to reduce production – and to sack fewer workers – in their countries of origin than in the LDCs in which they have investments?

23 Furthermore, world-wide inflation has reduced the real value of the compensatory funds of international public bodies, which would otherwise have been more effective in countering the temporary falls in price of the export products of LDCs.

24 A very interesting review of topics for further research, but which pays insufficient attention to the perspective of the LDCs, is that of Bergsten (1973).

25 This is a key issue, particularly in the case of highly capital intensive sectors, which employ little labour, and whose investments are indivisible and discontinuous (Tironi, 1978).

26 For this reason the *general* recommendations for the use of financial mechanisms (Wallich, 1960, Brooks *et al.*, 1977) or market regulation agreements appear to miss the point.

27 Bhagwati (Bergsten, 1977, Chapter 6) provides an indirect demonstration of this proposition. It would be useful, however, to have more complete theoretical studies, with a rigorous ordering of the efficiency of alternative policies.

28 Consider for example the promotion of exports which use as raw materials certain natural resources of the country, but which generate more highly elaborated products whose prices are more stable than those of the raw materials themselves. This implies going beyond simple refining. See Radetzki (1977).

29 See Ffrench-Davis (1978, Chapter XII, Section 1) for a description of the official credit facilities currently available.

30 Colombia used this device during the recent boom in coffee prices.

31 A very interesting proposition relating to this idea, and one that could be extended to take in the problem of instability more directly, has been advanced by Garnaut and Ross (1975).

32 Exercises which apply this formula to the Chilean case, using imported cars as an example of a good to which compensating tariffs might be applied, demonstrate that such a scheme would offset a significant proportion of the instability of copper revenues.

REFERENCES

Adams, G., and Klein, S. (1978) *Stabilizing World Commodity Markets: Analysis, Practice and Policy* (Lexington, Massachusetts: Lexington Books).

Avramovic, D. (1978) 'Common fund: Why and What Kind', *Journal of World Trade Law*, 12, no. 5, September–October (Summary in this volume).

Baklanoff, E. (1975) *Expropriation of U.S. investments in Cuba, Mexico and Chile* (New York: Praeger).

Bergsten, F. (1973) *The Future of International Economic Order: An Agenda for Research* (Lexington, Massachusetts: Lexington Books).

—— (1977) 'Access to Supplies and the New International Economic Order', Bhagwati (ed.) *The North-South debate* (Cambridge, Massachusetts: MIT).

Brooks, E., Grilli, E., and Wealbrook, J. (1977) 'Commodity Price Stabilization and Developing Countries: The Problem of Choice', *World Bank Staff Working Paper*, no. 262 (Washington, DC: July).

CEPAL (1975) 'La Coyuntura Internacional y el Sector Externo', *Cuadernos de la CEPAL*, no. 7, Santiago.

—— (1976) 'Temas del Nuevo Orden Económico Internacional', *Cuadernos de la CEPAL*, no. 12, Santiago.

Cohen, B. I. (1968) 'The LDCs' Exports of Primary Products', *Economic Journal*, vol. 78; no. 310.

Cohen, B. I., and Sisler, D. (1971) 'Exports of Developing Countries in the 60's', *Review of Economics Statistics*, no. 53, November.

Cooper, R. N. and Lawrence, R. (1975) 'The 1972–75 Commodity Boom', *Brookings Paper on Economic Activity*, no. 3.

Coppock, J. D. (1962) *International Economic Instability* (New York: McGraw-Hill).

Díaz-Alejandro, C. (1974) 'North-South Relations: The Economic Component', Discussion Paper no. 200 (New Haven: Yale University Economic Growth Center, April).

—— (1976) 'International Markets for Exhaustible Resources, LDCs and Transnational Corporations', Discussion Paper, no. 256 (New Haven: Yale University Economic Growth Center).

Erb, G. F., and Schiavo-Campo, S. (1969) 'Export instability, Level of Development and Economic size of LDCs', *Bulletin of the Oxford University Institute of Economics Statistics*, vol. 31, no. 4.

Ffrench-Davis, R. (1978) *Economía Internacional: Teorías y políticas para el desarrollo* (Mexico City: Fondo de Cultura Económica).

Ffrench-Davis, R. and Tironi, E. (1974) *El Cobre en el Desarrollo Nacional* (Santiago: Nueva Universidad–CEPLAN).

FMI-BIRF (1969) *El problema de la Estabilización de los Precios de los Productos Primarios* (Washington, DC).

Garnaut, R., and Ross, A. (1975) 'Uncertainty, Risk Aversion and the Taxing of Natural Resources', *Economic Journal*, vol. 85, June.

Girvan, N. (1974) 'Corporaciones multinacionales y subdesarrollo dependiente en economías exportadoras de minerales', in Sweezy *et al.* (eds) *Teoría y Práctica de la Empresa Multinacional* (Buenos Aires: Periferia).

Glezakos, C. (1970) 'Export Instability and Economic Development: A Statistical Verification', unpublished PhD thesis (University of Southern California).

Grunwald, J., and Musgrove, P. (1970) *Natural Resources in Latin American Development* (Baltimore: Johns Hopkins Press).

Helleiner, G. K. (1972) *International Trade and Economic Development* (Harmondsworth: Penguin).

IBRD, *Commodity Trade and Price Trends* (Washington, DC: annually).

Iglesias, E. (1975) 'América Latina: el Nuevo Escenario Regiònal y Mundial', *Cuadernos de la CEPAL*, no. 1, Santiago.

MacBean, A. I. (1966) *Export Instability and Economic Development* (Cambridge, Massachusetts: Harvard University Press).

Massell, B. F. (1964) 'Export Concentration and Fluctuations in Export Earnings: A Cross Section Analysis', *AER*, vol. 54, no 2.

—— (1970) 'Export Instability and Economic Structure', *AER*, vol. 60, no. 4.

Mikesell, R. (1970) *Foreign Investment in the Petroleum and Mineral Industries* (Baltimore: Johns Hopkins Press).

Okun, A. (1975) 'Inflation: Its Mechanisms and Welfare Costs', *Brookings Papers on Economic Activity*, no. 2.

Onudi (1978) 'Las empresas transnacionales y la elaboración de materias primas: repercusión sobre los países en desarrollo' (Vienna: Organización de las Naciones Unidas para el Desarrollo Industrial) Document ID/B/209.

Radetzki, M. (1977) 'Where Should Developing Countries' Minerals be Processed?', *World Development*, vol. 5, no. 4, April.

Rowe, J. W. (1965) *Primary Commodities in International Trade* (Cambridge University Press).

Smith, D. N., and Wells, L. T. (1975) 'Mineral Agreements in Developing Countries: Structures and Substance', *The American Journal of International Law*, vol. 69, no. 3, July.

Tironi, E. (1977) 'Issues in the Development of Resource-rich LDCs: Copper in Chile', in L. Krause and H. Patrick (eds), *Natural Resources in the Pacific Area* (San Francisco: Federal Reserve Bank of San Francisco).

——(1978) 'Recursos naturales y desarrollo: generación de empleo y excedentes en el cobre', *Estudios Cieplan* 28, Santiago, October.

Turnovsky, S. J. (1978) 'The Distribution of Welfare Gains from Price Stabilization: A Survey of Some Theoretical Issues', in Adams and Klein (1978).

Wallich, H. (1960) 'Estabilización de los ingresos provenientes de la exportación de materias primas', in H. S. Ellis (ed.) *El desarrollo económico y América Latina* (México City: Fondo de Cultura Económica).

Waugh, F. V. (1944) 'Does the Consumer Benefit from Price Instability?', *Quarterly Journal of Economics*, 58.

Weekly, J. (1977) 'Expropiación de inversiones multinacionales', *Perspectivas Económicas*, no. 20.

Yotopoulos, P. A., and Nugent, J. (1976) *Economics of Development: Empirical Investigations* (New York: Harper & Row).

9 National Policies towards Commodity Exports: A Comment[1]

SIMON TEITEL

To begin with, it should be noted that as a result of the nature of primary products LDCs face problems of two kinds: one of a long-term nature, arising out of the existence of adverse terms of trade, and another affecting them in the short term, and consisting of the instability of incomes derived from their exports of these products. Tironi's work deals with these problems, and with others that go beyond international trade and bear upon aspects of the organisation of the production of primary resources (and minerals in particular) and upon problems of distribution (securing control of the profits).

Accepting the existence of these problems, two types of solution are available. The first is to change the structure of national production, whether by diversifying exports to reduce the weight of a particular product or group of products, or by processing traditional exports, so that they cease to be 'primary' products. The second is to mitigate the adverse consequences mentioned previously by means of stabilisation funds and/or the securing of more resources for development by indexing the prices of exports of basic products. Some thought might also be given to the possibility of using primary products to advantage in negotiations with industrialised countries and in particular with those who depend upon continued access to some of those products (Bergsten, 1977).

As Tironi well observes, then, it is not possible to generalise about all LDCs, or about all primary products; more specifically, it is necessary to focus upon particular countries and particular products. Indeed, Latin America itself might prove too large a region for generalisations in this area.

TABLE 9.1   Relative importance of principal primary products exported by Latin America and leading exporting countries 1970–2

Principal products*	Percentage of total LA exports	Leading exporting countries and share of LA exports (%)			
Petroleum	13.0	Venezuela	(92.8)		
Coffee	11.7	Brazil	(47.4);	Colombia	(22.6)
		Central America	(17.8)		
Copper	6.3	Chile	(76.3);	Peru	(20.8)
Sugar	4.2	Brazil	(25.0);	Dominican Republic	(21.4)
		Mexico	(14.1)		
Beef	3.9	Argentina	(49.9);	Brazil	(14.2)
		Uruguay	(11.6)		
Iron ore	3.2	Brazil	(44.3);	Venezuela	(31)
Cotton	2.7	Brazil	(35.3);	Mexico	(17.3)
Bananas	2.4	Ecuador	(27.3);	Honduras	(23.3)
		Costa Rica	(18.0);	Panama	(17.1)
Maize	2.1	Argentina	(78.1)		
Fishmeal	1.7	Peru	(95.9)		
Wheat	1.4	Argentina	(94.2)		
Seafood	1.0	Mexico	(47.2)		
Cocoa	1.0	Brazil	(60.5)		
Soya beans	1.0	Brazil	(97.9)		
Wool	0.8	Argentina	(51.0);	Uruguay	(35.1)
Total	56.4				

* Products accounting for 1 per cent or more of the exports of the region in at least one of the years 1970–2.
Source: BID, *América Latina en la Economía Mundial: Evolución Reciente y Tendencias* (Washington, DC: 1975).

1 LATIN AMERICA AND PRIMARY PRODUCTS

We must first enquire which primary products are significant for Latin America. The answer is given in Table 9.1, the first column of which shows Latin American exports of 15 primary products which accounted for at least 1 per cent of total exports in at least one of the three years 1970–2. The list contains 3 mineral products and 12 agricultural products, and during the period they generated an average of 56·4 per cent of the total exports of the region. The 4 leading products – crude oil, coffee, copper and sugar – represented more than one-third of this total. The 3 minerals accounted for 22·5 per cent of the total, while the agricultural products accounted for 33·9 per cent. Other minerals which are important for individual countries in the region but have less weight in the overall total are tin and bauxite.

It should be remembered that exports of practically all these products are dominated by a few countries; this is shown clearly in the final column of Table 9.1, which indicates for each of the 15 primary products of most importance to the region the proportion of the total exported which is accounted for by the one or two leading exporters. For 6 products (coffee, sugar, iron ore, cotton, cocoa and soya) the first place is taken by Brazil, and for 4 more (meat, maize, wheat and wool) it is taken by Argentina, and these are the most industrialised countries in the region.

We might still ask, however, just how dependent the countries of Latin America are upon the export of their primary products. The answer to this question is found in Table 9·2, which reveals that for 17 of

TABLE 9.2   Relative importance of primary products in the exports of individual Latin American countries 1970–2

Percentage of total exports	Countries
Under 20	Bolivia, Jamaica, Trinidad and Tobago
20 to 40	Mexico, Paraguay
41 to 60	Argentina, Barbados, Brazil, El Salvador, Gautemala, Uruguay
61 to 80	Colombia, Costa Rica, Ecuador, Haiti, Honduras, Nicaragua, Panama, Peru, Dominican Republic, Venezuela
Over 80	Chile

Source: BID, op. cit.

the 22 countries of the region these products account for more than 40 per cent of total exports; furthermore, for 11 of them they represent more than 60 per cent. This conclusion is confirmed if we consider that the 3 countries which exhibit a low level of dependence upon *these* products are in fact dependent upon other primary products not included in the 15 taken into account here. Trinidad-Tobago, Jamaica and Bolivia depend upon refined petroleum, tin, and bauxite and aluminium for 77 per cent, 55 per cent and 62 per cent of their exports respectively.

If primary products still represent, as we have seen, a significant proportion of the exports of the countries of a semi-industrialised region such as Latin America, does this mean that primary products are mainly exported by LDCs? The answer can be drawn from the material presented in Table 9.3, which shows, for each of the fifteen major products, the major world exporters and the proportion of total world exports for which they were responsible, on average, in the period 1971– 3. The situation has been summarised in Table 9.4, which shows the groups of countries occupying first place, the first three places, and the first five places in world exports of the fifteen primary products. As can be seen from Table 9.4, Latin America takes only 4 first places, compared to 8 for the industrialised countries and 7 for all LDCs, and 8 second or third places.

Using an arbitrary system of weighting for the different placings – 5 points for first place, 3 for second or third, and 1 for fourth or fifth – it is possible to construct what might be called an index of the importance of the various groups of countries in the export markets of the fifteen products selected, and it provides the following results: industrialised countries 95 points, Latin America 54 points, and other LDCs 46 points.

That is to say, *exports of the primary products which are important for Latin America are not in general dominated by countries from the region, but by industrialised nations.* Thus, it is not the case that comparative advantages clearly separate the North and the South, except for a few tropical crops such as coffee and bananas.

Tironi argues that Latin America's share in international trade has declined; since at the same time its share of manufactured exports has increased, this indicates that it has been able to compensate, in part at least, for the decline in its exports of primary products. This is in line with its growing comparative advantages, and I do not see much reason to regret it. The changes which have taken place have been fundamentally shifts towards LDCs in the Middle East and Africa, in the case of products for which advantages of location and climate are decisive, such

TABLE 9.3 Principal world exporters of the primary products most important for Latin America and their shares of total exports 1971–3 (in cumulative percentages)

Product	First place Country	%	2nd and 3rd place Countries	%	4th and 5th place Countries	%
Petroleum	Saudi Arabia	(19.8)	Iran, Kuwait	(46.0)	Libya, Venezuela	(62.3)
Coffee	Brazil	(33.2)	Colombia, Ivory Coast	(50.2)	Uganda, Algeria	(60.6)
Copper	Zambia	(16.9)	Canada, Chile	(43.5)	Zaire, Belgium	(61.4)
Sugar	Cuba	(24.8)	Brazil, Australia	(47.4)	Philippines, Dominican Republic	(60.4)
Beef	Australia	(22.2)	Argentina, New Zealand	(48.2)	Ireland, France	(60.5)
Iron ore	Australia	(17.7)	USSR, Canada	(38.9)	Brazil, Sweden	(56.4)
Cotton	USA	(22.2)	USSR, Egypt	(45.1)	Turkey, Brazil	(58.7)
Bananas	Ecuador	(20.5)	Costa Rica, Honduras	(47.8)	Panama, Guatemala	(59.7)
Maize	USA	(52.2)	Argentina, France	(71.3)	South Africa, Thailand	(83.3)
Fishmeal	Peru	(37.5)	Norway, South Africa	(52.0)	Chile, Angola	(57.8)
Wheat	USA	(41.1)	Canada, Australia	(73.9)	France, USSR	(91.2)
Seafood	Japan	(18.6)	USA, Spain	(39.3)	South Korea, Denmark	(55.3)
Cocoa	Ghana	(28.9)	Nigeria, Ivory Coast	(58.0)	Brazil, Cameroon	(73.6)
Soya beans	USA	(79.0)	Brazil, China	(92.3)	Holland, Canada	(93.9)
Wool	Australia	(49.6)	New Zealand, South Africa	(77.2)	Argentina, Uruguay	(85.1)

Source: BID, op. cit.

TABLE 9.4   Places occupied by different groups of countries in exports of Latin America's leading fifteen primary products 1971–3 (frequencies in absolute value)

Groups of countries	1st place	2nd and 3rd place	4th and 5th place	Points*
Industrialised	8	15	10	95
Latin American	4	8	10	54
Other less developed	3	7	10	46

* Five points for 1st place, three for 2nd or 3rd and one for 4th or 5th.
Source: BID, op. cit.

as coffee, oil and cocoa, and towards the industrialised nations in the case of meat, sugar and oil seeds.

2 STABILISATION AND PRICE INCREASES

Once it has been confirmed that trade in primary products is significant for Latin America, and once the problems faced in the relevant markets have been noted, two principal goals arise in the international field for the countries exporting those products: (i) reducing variations in prices from one period to the next; and (ii) raising the level of the prices they receive. From the point of view of the generation of resources for development, the second objective is the more important.

As we know, it has been proposed that price instability should be reduced by means of the operation of buffer stocks. The principle is simple: the stock-piling authority buys when prices are low and sells when they are high, thus reducing variations in price levels. Given that excessive price instability has a series of undesirable consequences – such as the cost of the incorrect allocation of resources deriving from (i) uncertainty, (ii) the possible downward rigidity of prices, and (iii) the cost of the greater foreign currency reserves needed – it could be argued that manipulation of such stocks should be of benefit to producers and to buyers.

Two possible cases can be distinguished in this respect: one in which supply varies more than demand, and another in which demand varies more than supply. The results of the analysis of these two cases are asymmetrical (Johnson, 1977; MacAvoy, 1977).[2] In the first case, price stabilisation benefits *the producers*, as their income increases more on account of higher prices in periods of surplus than it falls as a result of lower prices in periods of shortage. In the second case, *the opposite occurs*: when demand varies more, the buyers gain and the producers lose with stabilisation, as the gains to the former from prices being held steady in times of high demand exceed the losses which they suffer during periods of slack demand when prices are kept up through purchases for the buffer stock.

The existence of this dichotomy, if it should prove valid, is of importance for Latin America if we take into account the nature of the variations observed in the prices of the leading primary products of the region. In general terms, it can be said that the first case (in which supply varies more) corresponds to agricultural products, while the second (in which demand varies more) corresponds to mineral products. *Prima facie*, then, as most of the primary products which interest Latin America are agricultural, for which supply varies more than demand, *the region should benefit by stabilisation through buffer stocks*. However, as MacAvoy observes, for some products, such as wool and cotton, variation on the demand side predominates. This is probably due to the influence of substitution by synthetic fibres, a phenomenon, on the whole, of a long-term nature. It must also be borne in mind that although the benefits accrue to the producers, some of them are industrialised nations, as in the case of wheat. Clearly more research into these matters is needed.

As producers gain more from stabilisation when the variation is greater on the supply side, and buyers gain more when it is greater on the demand side, co-operation from which both sides would gain might be sought. The costs of operating buffer stocks are estimated to be substantial, and the benefits would not outweigh them in all cases, but it might still be asked why such stocks are not organised. It could be because there are high costs attached to organisation itself, while the benefits constitute a public good, for once the stocks are formed it is not possible to exclude from the ensuing gains those who have not contributed to those costs. This, too, is an area in which further research is needed.

As for restrictive agreements to increase the prices of primary products, MacAvoy is of the opinion that the best possibilities would be for wool, wheat, rice and sugar. Apparently the signing of agreements regarding such products could generate additional income in the order of tens of thousands of millions of dollars, depending upon the exact level of the rate of increase in prices established as a goal. Even so, it should be pointed out that the industrialised nations are responsible for a significant proportion of exports of these products, and it is probable that LDCs as a group would lose out with wheat and rice, while gaining with sugar. It should also be noted that the poorest of the LDCs would lose in most cases from restrictive agreements, and could only gain if there were to be an agreement to redistribute part of the additional income in their favour. In this area, too, there is a need for a detailed study of specific countries and products.

3 SOME MINOR CRITICAL OBSERVATIONS

I should like to make some minor observations on Tironi's chapter which might help to clarify some points. Although he excludes alternative international policies from consideration here, the problem of primary products cannot in fact be approached in a fragmentary manner, as national policies are a function of international agreements not only of the nature of the Integrated Programme for Commodities of UNCTAD, but also between producers (and consumers) of specific products. Take for example the impact upon Bolivia of the possible sale of surplus tin from the US strategic stockpile, or the effect of the fixing of production quotas for coffee or import quotas for sugar upon producers of these commodities.

Furthermore, the capacity of the LDCs to apply pressure in pursuit of price stabilisation agreements for raw materials does not depend upon whether or not they have alternatives *of their own* for stabilising their income, as Tironi suggests. If they had such alternatives they would not need to sign agreements with third parties. What is more, the bargaining power of a country or a particular group of countries, to which Tironi refers, is not necessarily – and I would say not generally – associated with the sector, problem or product in question, nor possessed by the actors directly involved. For example, the OPEC countries have had some success in the North when defending the South on various aspects of economic and financial policy, as a result of their power based upon oil.

Ernesto Tironi points correctly to the need to distinguish between the different primary products, agricultural and mineral, and to study in a detailed manner their markets and production functions, but goes on instead to concern himself with the manner in which the results of their exploitation should be disposed of (including the distribution of profits, the role of the state, etc.), these being policies of a more general nature rather than relating to international trade proper. The same can be said of the arguments concerning nationalisation with exploitation by the state, or other forms of ownership such as co-operatives, etc. (Section 1.b). In contrast, insufficient attention is given to the major national policies relating to primary products, which are, as Tironi notes at the outset, the diversification of exports and a greater degree of processing applied to them.

Although they are not really germane to the central theme under discussion, I should like to make some comments upon some of the points Tironi makes with regard to the expropriation (nationalisation) of companies producing primary products. I believe that if it is correct to argue that the greater participation of the countries owning natural resources in the profits which they generate made investments in other places or sectors relatively more attractive, it is incorrect to argue that the *cost* of investment has increased. Tironi makes two other observations on this theme (Section 2.b): (i) that the instability of (net) income in foreign currency from nationalised companies is greater, since they have to pay a fixed element of the same as compensation for the capital acquired; and (ii) that the sales of such companies will be made in marginal markets, which are inherently less stable. The first argument is purely one of accounting, rather than of economics, as the cost of capital or of investment will always be present as a fixed cost. If there were imperfections in the capital market, there might be differences between the cost of this capital, depending upon whether it were obtained in that market or through the retention of profits. Furthermore, it could be argued, if the payment is not indexed, that, as with every loan upon fixed conditions, the debtor will gain from the prevailing rate of inflation. As for the second point, it is valid only in so far as the highest prices in the marginal market do not compensate for the greater instability of the same. Detailed research is required on this point.

4 CONCLUSION

To conclude, I should like to point out that while in recent years, as Tironi observes, there may have been an apparently favourable conjuncture for a development strategy based upon international trade in primary products – as a result of (i) positive changes in the terms of trade, and (ii) a greater degree of national control over the profits – as far as development is concerned it makes little difference if a country remains a leading exporter of primary products, as the United States with cereals and Australia with meat have been. This does not constitute a strategy in contradiction with industrialisation, as it can be combined with an advanced degree of industrialisation and of control over decision-making. Indeed, as Kaldor (1976) argues, on the basis of historical experience industrialisation needs to be complemented by a certain degree of development of the domestic market based upon agriculture.

I would like to finish by saying that I share W. A. Lewis's (1978) view that the importance of international trade in the development of LDCs has been often exaggerated. Technological progress, rather than trade, should be the motor of growth; the latter may help sometimes by acting as a 'lubricant but is not a fuel'. Therefore, to avoid frustrations, one should not expect trade to be a substitute for technological change.

In the particular case of Latin America, a region at an intermediate stage of the process of industrialisation, attention should be turned, as a priority, to the productive activities which are conducive to the creation or introduction of technology in those countries.

NOTES

1 I am grateful to Carlos Diaz-Alejandro for his comments.
2 Clearly, the analyses in question are based upon a number of simplifying hypotheses: linear demand curves, low elasticities of supply and demand (considerably less than unity), a negligible effect of income on welfare, and no consideration of secondary effects.

REFERENCES

Bergsten, C. F. (1977) 'Access to Supplies and the New International Economic Order', in J. N. Bhagwati (ed.) *The New International Economic Order: The North-South Debate* (Cambridge, Massachusetts: MIT) Chapter 7.
BID (1975) *América Latina en la Economía Mundial: Evolución Reciente y Tendencias* (Washington, DC) Chapter 111.
Johnson, H. G. (1977) 'Commodities: Less Developed Countries' Demands and Developed Countries' Response', in Bhagwati, op. cit., Chapter 9.
Kaldor, N. (1976) 'Capitalismo y Desarrollo Industrial: Algunas Lecciones de la Experiencia Británica', in C. Díaz-Alejandro, Teitel and Tokman (eds) *Política económica en centro y periferia* (Mexico City: Fondo de Cultura Económica) Lecture 16.

Lewis, W. A. (1978) *The Evolution of the International Economic Order* (Princeton University Press).

MacAvoy, P. W. (1977) *Economic Perspective on the Politics of International Commodity Agreements* (University of Arizona Press).

10 World Markets for Manufactures and Industrialisation in Developing Countries

GUILLERMO PERRY

Many developing countries took significant steps forward in the process of import substitution during a period of some twenty years after the Second World War. However, at the beginning of the last decade there was a growing awareness that such advances were becoming more and more difficult and costly, and that the early stages of the process had not provided a satisfactory solution to bottle-necks in the external sector of these countries. In fact, the way in which substitution policies were applied was prejudicial to non-traditional exports and there was a preference for activities which were relatively intensive in imported intermediate and capital goods. On the other hand, exports of primary products continued to face traditional problems of slow growth, low prices, deterioration in the terms of trade and instabilities of quantities sold and price. In contrast, world exports of manufactured goods were proving to be very dynamic and to show greater stability and improving relative prices, so some developing countries began to focus on the promotion of manufactured exports in the hope of finding a permanent solution to the external constraints on their development.

Given the growing disillusion with the supposed panacea of foreign aid and the apparent success of those developing countries which embarked on export promotion, these hopes have gained considerable ground and many experts today actively promote the new faith in 'export-led development'. But after the favourable prospects created by the boom in commodity prices in 1973 and 1974 and by the success achieved by OPEC, there has reappeared a justifiable scepticism about the prospects for agricultural and livestock exports, and about the viability in the short term of setting up successful agreements between producers and consumers (based on the indexing of reference prices or on the integrated Programme for Basic Commodities put forward by UNCTAD: (see Singh, 1976; CEPAL, 1975; and Perry, 1977b).

Consequently it is worth reconsidering the experience gained regarding the export of manufactured goods from less developed countries, in order to see what lessons can be learned for their commercial policies and to identify those aspects and problems to which priority should be given in future research.

1 EXPORTS OF MANUFACTURES: ACHIEVEMENTS AND SHORTCOMINGS

(a) Growth

Over the past few years, exports of manufactured goods from the LDCs have increased faster than their exports of primary goods, and even faster than exports of manufactures from the developed countries. This expansion, however, has been too concentrated in only a few countries (Table 10.1); three of these (Taiwan, Hong Kong and Singapore), who monopolise 37 per cent of the total export of manufactured goods from the LDCs, are insular countries containing only a minute proportion of the world population and having quite unique economic characteristics as regards population density, location and degree of urbanisation.

On the other hand, the exports of manufactured goods from LDCs have gone mainly to other nations with similar characteristics, and almost exclusively to those in the same geographic area. Keesing (1977) has shown that in 1975 exports within their region represented 69, 62, 67 and 90 per cent of all manufactured exports of the Middle Eastern, Asian, African and Latin American countries respectively. Exports by developed countries to LDCs are, in contrast, substantially diversified by regions. To a great extent world trade follows North–North and North–South directions, as does the flow of direct investment and the development of trade infrastructure (transport facilities, financial services and the like). Consequently, LDCs have not been able to take advantage of the rapid growth of LDC markets in other regions of the world, nor have they exploited fully the potential of markets in the socialist countries (Perry, 1977a).

The growth of manufactured exports from the LDCs to the indus-

TABLE 10.1   Exports of manufactures by country

Country	Share in total LDCs' exports		Nominal rate of growth per year			Ranking according to total country exports in 1976	Manufactured exports as percentage of country total	Nominal rate of growth of total exports
	1974	1975	1971–4	1971–5	1975–6		1974	1971–6
Hong Kong	16.8	16.8	27	20	40.7	2	91.4	19.6
Taiwan	14.3	13.0	41	27	55.9	3	83.9	21.5
Korea	11.6	12.5	63	48	63.2	4	84.7	31.5
Yugoslavia	7.8	8.4	30	25	17.5	8	66.3	13.2
Singapore	7.1	6.7	58	40	30.9	5	39.9	6.5
Brazil	5.9	6.6	63	49	5.5	1	24.2	12.9
Mexico	6.6	5.9	48	32	10.6	10	36.9	5.4
India	6.3	6.3	23	18		7	51.7	12.2
Argentina	2.9	2.3	54	30	33.9	9	24.4	–0.5
Pakistan	1.8	1.8	16	12	19.0	14	52.6	2.4
Malaysia	1.7	2.0	64	53	11.6	6	29.3	11.8
Kuwait	1.7		68					
Egypt	1.2		22			13	26.3	–3.7
Thailand	1.2	1.2	80	56	58.5			
Colombia	1.2	1.0	64	38	13.1	12	25.0	8.8
Turkey	1.0	1.0	60	42	45.3	11	22.0	13.1
Others	10.9							

Source: D. Keesing, 'Recent Trends in Manufactured and Total Exports from Developing Countries', mimeo (Washington, DC: 1977).

trialised nations could have been substantially greater if it had not come up against a growing and discriminatory protectionism on the part of the latter (see Section 2). In fact, some of the goods on which LDC exports have concentrated (textiles, clothing, leather, footwear, etc.) follow Engels's law in the same way that the majority of basic consumer goods do; therefore, accelerated growth in this sector must occur at the expense of local production in the industrialised countries. This fact partly explains the protectionist reaction. None the less, the same phenomenon has occurred with other types of goods (electronic equipments, metal and wood products, etc.).

In the same way, several of the sectors in which a substantial flow of exports of manufactures could be generated (those related to the processing of local primary products, for example) have run up against the escalating tariff barriers of the industrialised countries and the control which the transnational corporations exert over technology and marketing (see Section 3).

It should be noted that exports from the LDCs to the industrialised countries come up against the barriers mentioned in spite of the introduction of the Generalised System of Preferences (GSP). In fact, given that the tariff barriers set up by the DCs went against the LDCs' interests, the latter began to seek non-reciprocal concessions (UNCTAD 1, 1964). The DCs accepted this demand in principle in 1966 within GATT itself. However, the extent to which anything has been done through the GSP is very limited. Instead of complete, permanent and generalised tariff reductions, the GSP allows for partial, temporary and discretionary reductions confined to non-sensitive products, which in practice excludes the main exports from the LDCs. The GSP also allows for import quotas, which have often proved very restrictive.

To cite an example, the GSP covers about 10 per cent of the total imports of the USA, Japan and the EEC from the LDCs,[1] and includes 22 per cent of the imports subject to customs duties. The percentage of manufactured exports is larger. For example, the EEC's Generalised System of Preferences covers between 3 and 4 per cent of the total imports from Latin America, and 30 per cent of its manufactured goods imported from that region. But it is normal for the GSP to exclude groups of products, such as textiles and clothing and the majority of the processed products from the agriculture and livestock sector.

On the other hand, the majority of products with a dynamic growth which are not excluded are subject to restrictive quotas. CEPAL (1975, Table 11) compares the characteristics of the different systems. There are many export products from Latin America which have been confronted with a suspension of the system of preferential treatment owing to the imposition of quotas in the EEC and Japan;[2] in fact, individual quotas have proved to be particularly restrictive given the high concentration of manufactured goods among the exports of LDCs. Mainly for this reason, the use of global quotas within the EEC system of preferences is only about 62 per cent (ITC, 1978). It has been estimated that, without them, exports to Japan from the LDCs which benefit from the system would have been three times as high as they are in practice (UNCTAD, 1977).

Even so, the effect of the GSPs is not insignificant. The most recent estimates suggest that, if these systems were not in operation, there would be a reduction of between $2 billion and $4 billion in total exports from the LDCs (approximately 10 per cent of the value of their exports of manufactured goods).[3]

The GSP of the United States (brought into effect in 1976) may be less restrictive than that of the EEC and of Japan (in operation since 1971 and 1972 respectively) and is of considerable interest to countries of Latin America (CEPAL, 1975 and 1976). Its effectiveness seems to have been hindered, however, by administrative procedure and guarantees of origin.[4]

Apart from the restrictions indicated, the GSPs of Japan, and particularly of the EEC countries, have a limited effect on Latin American exports as a result of the special advantages which these countries grant to the rest of the world (Table 10.2). The markets for manufactured goods of the EEC are open, without tariff or quota restrictions, to exports from the fifty-two developing countries of Africa, the Caribbean and the Pacific Islands who were signatories at the Lomé Convention, from the six Associated States in the Mediterranean basin (Cyprus, Greece, Malta, Morocco, Tunisia and Turkey) and from four other countries in the same area with whom there are special agreements (Egypt, Spain, Israel and Lebanon). The EEC markets are also, of course, open to exports from other member countries of the EEC and of EFTA, with whom an extensive free-trade zone has been set up. In other words, the developing countries of Latin America (with the exception of the Caribbean) compete in the European markets with limited advantages compared to the USA, Canada and Japan, but with disadvantage in relation to almost all the other suppliers of these markets. In the case of Japan, its GSP grants a certificate of origin to inputs which originate within its own territory, which effectively means a system of regional preference in favour of the Far Eastern countries, with whom Japan has extensive trade and investment links.

TABLE 10.2   Indicators related with the GSPs of the EEC, the USA and Japan (in $ million)

Origin of imports	EEC-9	UK	US	Japan
Total	116.524	21.728	45.476	18.881
From LDCs	19.821	4.886	12.401	6.754
From countries with special relations:				
Countries associated with EEC	2.239			
'Associable' countries	1.867			
LDCs belonging to the Commonwealth		2.317		
Goods imported from LDCs subject to tariffs:				
Agricultural	4.517	960	1.890	509
Non-agricultural	1.515	638	6.537	3.437
Total	6.032	1.598	3.427	3.946
Goods imported from LDCs covered by GSPs:				
Agricultural	86	58	95	22
Non-agricultural	992	423	1.110	749
Total	1.078	481	1.205	771
From this total				
From countries with special relations:				
Associated with EEC	46			
'Associable' countries	36			
LDCs in the Commonwealth		367		
From Latin America				
Total	4.395	768	5.310	1.400
Covered by GSP	176	43	753	53

Source: CEPAL, *La Coyuntura Internacional y el Sector Externo* (Santiago: 1975) Table 12.

Finally, it should be noted that exports of manufactured goods from LDCs tend to be channelled towards those industrialised nations within whose sphere of influence they find themselves (Table 10.2 and GATT, 1978). This happens partly as a consequence of advantages in transportation. However, it is also to some extent a question of the 'regional preferences' already mentioned and of the predominant presence of transnational corporations from the respective centre, as well as of other reasons with neo-colonial undertones.

(b) Instability and terms of trade

The exports of manufactured goods from LDCs has shown a concentration in products where there is strong competition in terms of supply and, except in some cases (such as textiles and clothing), where international marketing is dominated by TNCs.

Problems similar to those affecting primary products have been observed with regard to low profit margins, price instability and a tendency to a fall in relative prices (see Keesing, 1976b). So, between 1970 and 1975, the main source of deterioration in the terms of trade for LDCs, with the exception of oil exports (Table 10.3), was not a generalised decrease in the relative price of agricultural exports, which increased slightly compared to exports of manufactures (Table 10.4), but possibly to the fall in the price of manufactured goods exported by LDCs as compared to those of the industrialised nations.

Moreover, during the 1975 recession, the absolute prices of manufactured exports from LDCs decreased, while the average prices for exported manufactures world-wide continued to increase (Keesing, 1976b).

On the other hand, a large part of the manufactured goods exported, particularly by Asia and Mexico, have consisted of imported products assembled in those LDCs. The contribution of these exports to national value added and the balance of payments is small. Frequently, foreign investment appropriates part of this value added, so the net effect is even smaller; it is limited to the payment to labour and some taxes. Even if offshore assembly operations may represent an adequate temporary use of the labour force in countries which have a large labour surplus, it can hardly be seen as a response to the comparative advantages of the majority of the Latin America countries.

2 LDC PROBLEMS AND INDUSTRIALISED COUNTRY POLICIES

(a) The processing of primary products

It should be noted that the type of manufactured goods which the developing countries produce, as well as their specialisation in primary products, is in no way the result of mere comparative advantage. The effects of tariff policies and of the policies regarding the transfer of technology on the part of the industrialised nations is also a determining factor. These countries grant an increasing protection to their domestic

TABLE 10.3   Evolution of exports and terms of trade of LDCs and developed countries (DCs) (indexes, 1970 = 100)

Year	Volume			Unit value			Total value			Terms of trade		
	LDCs		*DCs*	*LDCs*		*DCs*	*LDCs*		*DCs*	*LDCs*		*DCs*
	Total	Excluding oil		Total	Excluding oil		Total	Excluding oil		Total	Excluding oil	
1950	56		23	94		74	53		17	111		89
1955	43	50	32	102	95	84	44	48	27	109		89
1960	52	62	44	94	88	86	49	55	38	103	98	96
1970	100	100	100	100	100	100	100	100	100	100	100	100
1975	121	124	134	311	180	192	376	233	257	139	84	90
1976	137		149	330		192	452	286		145		89

Source: IBRD, 'Tendencias del Comercio y de las Precios de los Productos Básicos' (Washington, DC: 1977).

TABLE 10.4   World trade trends (average annual rates of growth %)

	1960–1970	1970–1976
Volume		
World exports	7.8	6.6
World production	5.5	4.3
Agricultural products		
World exports	4.1	3.1
World production	2.4	2.5
Minerals		
World exports	7.1	1.8
World production	5.3	2.9
Manufactures		
World exports	9.8	8.0
World production	6.7	5.1
Unit value of world exports		
Agricultural products	0.8	13.8
Minerals	1.9	27.0
Manufactured goods	1.6	10.9
Value of world exports		
Agricultural products	4.8	17.3
Minerals	9.3	29.4
Manufactured goods	11.5	19.8

Source: GATT, *International Trade*: 1977/1976 (General: 1978)

production as the degree of processing of the raw materials involved becomes greater (Tables 10.5 and 10.6). So, on aggregate, manufactured goods receive a nominal protection (and especially an effective protection rate) far in excess of that afforded to primary products.[5] Taking agricultural products as an example, it can be seen that the nominal protection for raw materials ranges between 0 and 5 per cent for processed raw materials between 3 and 8 per cent, and for finished products between 6 and 13 per cent. The same applies to textiles and clothing, where the nominal protection for the latter averages about 25 per cent and climbs to as much as 160 per cent for some products.

Similarly, the protection which the present freight system grants to production reflects the degree of processing involved and not always the effective cost of transportation (Finger, 1976). This situation suggests the need for case studies on the possibility and advantage for LDCs of taking unilateral compensatory action (duties or restrictions imposed on the export of unwrought raw material or subsidies for local processing), in accordance with the characteristics of each particular market as

TABLE 10.5   Barriers on the eleven major industrialised country markets

	Average tariff rates (%)	Non-tariff barriers fraction of imports affected by quantitative restrictions (%)	Incidence
Industrial raw materials (mining and agriculture)	Very low	Not frequent (except for fuels)	
Fuels	0 to 4	20 to 30	Not very serious
Other minerals	0 to 3	8 to 10	Not very serious
Agricultural	0 to 2	15 to 20	Frequently serious
Processed food			
Low processing	3 to 8	Very common	Serious
High processing	6 to 13	Very common	Serious
Textiles and clothing	15 to 25	70	Very serious and increasing
Other manufactured exports	11 to 17	1 to 2	Not serious but increasing
Most industrial products	7 to 10	1 to 2	Not serious

Source: **IBRD**, 'Trade Liberalization and Export Promotion' (Washington, DC: 1977).

TABLE 10.6   Tariff barriers according to degree of processing of selected products in eleven major DCs (%)

Products	Average tariff rates
Iron	
Iron ore	0
Unwrought iron	2.4
Iron and steel plates	9.3
Knives, forks, etc.	18.8
Aluminium	
Bauxite	0
Oxide	3.9
Plates	5.4
Foil	12.8
Rubber	
Rubber	0.1
Tyres	9.3
Rubber footwear	16.5
Leather	
Hides and skins	9.6
Suitcases	13.1
Footwear	16.4
Wood	
Timber	0
Sawn wood	2.2
Chairs, etc.	11.5
Plywood	16.7
Textiles	
Cotton not carded or combed	1.1
Carded and combed cotton	5.2
Cotton textiles	8.2
Knit cotton	12.4
Men's and children's clothing	23.1
Knit clothing	26.9

Source: Ibid.

regards the control which transnational corporations hold over marketing and/or technology. Equally, it would seem appropriate to study the further effects of systems for the negotiation and fixing of freight charges in the international shipping conventions.

(b) The intra-firm trade of TNCs

The difficulties which the developing countries experience in undertaking the more advanced stages of processing arise partly from restrictions in the transfer of technology. This occurs predominantly as a result of the 'package-deal' which the developing host countries face from the TNCs. Thus, the LDCs face the dilemma of either not being able to develop certain processes or of being forced to allow foreign firms to internalise a large share of the potential benefits of trade.[6]

The phenomenon of the internationalisation of world trade by transnationals may be characterised as follows:

(i) Over 25 per cent of the total exports of the USA and about 20 per cent of those of the UK were accounted for by transactions between branches of transnationals at the end of the 1960s (Shonfield *et al*, 1976).

(ii) In 1971 the value of the total production of TNCs outside their country of origin exceeded the corresponding figure for world exports ($330 billion against $310 billion), while their affiliates abroad were responsible for about one-third of world trade.

(iii) The production of TNCs is more concentrated than world trade in terms of countries of origin; over 50 per cent of that production comes from North American TNCs.

(iv) The greatest increase in intra-firm trade during the 1960s took place amongst those in the industrialised countries. On the one hand, in 1960 almost half the foreign investment of the United States was placed in the developing countries; in 1971 it was less than a quarter. On the other hand, according to studies by Helleiner (1976, 1977a, 1977c) the importance of exports from the Third World to the USA which were made by firms with more than 51 per cent of US-owned capital dropped from 19 to 8 per cent between 1967 and 1975 (excluding oil). The figures suggest that the developing countries are being excluded by the transnationals from the process of internalisation of trade; in part, however, they also reflect the new policies of 'association' being applied by the developing countries, where the majority of the firms' capital must be national. In fact, 50 per cent of the exports from the Third World (25 per cent excluding oil) are intra-firm. As regards manufactured goods, an increasing percentage of the exports from the developing countries corresponds to this type of transaction, as is suggested by the increasing incidence of assembled goods. This percentage varies considerably from one country to another; in the case of the Latin American countries, it is normally in excess of 30 per cent (Table 10.7).

TABLE 10.7   Share of TNCs in the exports of manufactures of LDCs

Country	Percentage Share	Year	Exports of manufactures in 1972 ($ million)
Hong Kong	10	1972	2 635
Taiwan	20	1971	2 489
South Korea	15	1971	1 351
India	5	1970	1 320
Singapore	70	1970	893
Brazil	43	1969	740
Mexico	25–30	1970	647
Argentina	30	1969	394
Pakistan	5–10	1972	380
Colombia	30	1970	172

Source: G. Helleiner, 'Intrafirm Trade and the Developing Countries; Patterns, Trends and Data Problems', Seminar in Intrafirm Transactions, UNCTAD and IDS, Sussex, November 1977.

(v) In the developing countries, transnational corporations concentrate their activities within their areas of influence and they control a larger proportion of exports than of the value added of the respective national manufacturing industry. For example, between 1966 and 1968 North American firms controlled 10 per cent of the value added and 40 per cent of the exports of manufactures in Latin America (Vernon, 1973).[7]

The growth of TNCs over the past decades has kept pace with the growth of trade in manufactured goods among the industrialised countries. Initially, the TNCs operating in this sector sought to exploit foreign markets. Once they had consolidated their monopolistic and oligopolistic position in some particular product or process, it became more profitable to penetrate other markets on the basis of that specialisation particular to the firm. In this way a considerable trade developed which has little to do with the traditional conception of the comparative advantages of different countries, but was based, rather, on comparative advantages specific to the transnational corporations. Most of this latter type of advantage is based on the exploitation of technological knowledge which is closely protected by national legislation and international agreements. In fact, conventional theories of comparative advantages hardly explain the increase in the trade of manufactured goods between countries with a similar endowment of factors of production. Other theories, following Linder, fail to explain why the South-South trade in manufactured goods has shown such slow growth (Stewart, 1976). On the other hand, the theory of the 'product cycle', which would also make a contribution towards explaining the sharp rise in the North–North trade in manufactured goods, is found wanting in so far as North–South trade is concerned, because the latter is being carried out more and more on the basis of specialisation in processes rather than on the basis of 'mature' products. If anything, the theories of comparative advantages play only a limited role within the planning departments of the transnational corporations (Helleiner, 1977a, 1973).

Apart from intra-firm transactions, the TNCs have developed a wide network of commercial outlets. Both of these factors put the developing countries in a dilemma: either they do business with the transnationals and give away part of the profits derived from the export of manufactures, or they sell on their own in an increasingly restricted and uncertain market.

It should be noted that the TNCs have a considerable capacity for appropriating that part of the value added generated by exports which does not correspond to salaries. Underestimation (over-invoicing) of the value of exports (imports), as well as payments for technology, administration, for merchandising and financial services, represent a form of tax evasion and avoidance of exchange controls which allows the transnationals' participation in profits to be greater than their participation in their subsidiaries' capital.

Even in cases where the TNCs confine their activities to marketing administration or the provision of technological services, they are able to extract quasi-rents by virtue of their monopolistic or monopsonistic positions.

In addition to these crucial problems, which are common to import-substituting industrialisation, the internalisation of South-North trade by the transnationals frequently reduces the effectiveness of the developing countries' trade policies. Profit maximisation by the trans-nationals does not coincide with profit maximisation in their branches or subsidiaries and, therefore, the effect of the developing countries' policies on their behaviour is uncertain, to say the least.

The presence of the TNCs in trade is reinforced by the selective operation of the present schemes of protection and tariff concessions. For example, the industrialised countries rarely apply compensatory tariffs or restrictive quotas to goods which their own transnationals export to any great extent from the developing countries (see Section 3a). In the same way, these products are often included in the

Generalised System of Preferences which is granted to the developing countries. Moreover, the industrialised countries have set tariff reductions on the assembly of their own products abroad (Section 2c). The TNCs constitute a powerful domestic lobby for the selective application of trade policies in their favour.

This whole topic offers up a wide variety of research possibilities, among which it is worth mentioning the following: In which type of manufactured product is there extensive and growing participation by the transnational corporations, either in their direct production or in terms of their marketing? To what extent do the policies of the developing countries encourage or permit TNCs to capture an unnecessarily high share of the potential benefits from trade and from the industrialisation processes in general? Why does the participation of the TNCs in the export of manufactured goods from the Latin American countries seem particularly high?

(c) The assembly of products in the developing countries

It has already been noted that the internationalisation of trade by the transnational corporations is moving more and more towards the relocation of parts of the production processes, particularly those of assembly. The information available suggests that exports from the developing countries to the USA, Holland and Germany of products resulting from these processes have increased at a much higher rate than the respective export of all manufactured goods (Finger, 1975, Table 1). Assembled products are found amongst the most dynamic categories of goods in world trade: machinery and mechanical and electrical equipment. On the other hand, these exports are even more concentrated on a few sources of supply than the total of manufactured goods from the developing countries. For example, in the case of the USA, 43 per cent of the assembled goods come from Mexico, and 49 per cent from Taiwan, Hong Kong, South Korea and Singapore (Finger, 1975, p. 367, and Helleiner, 1977a).

This situation has been facilitated by the trading policies of both the industrialised and the developing countries. Several of the former – primarily Germany, Holland and Japan – have followed the example of the USA and instituted tariff concessions for the imports of offshore assembled goods. The USA has two special schemes in operation: the first allows the entry, duty-free, of components made in the USA which have been incorporated in articles assembled abroad without losing their identity (Item 807.00 of the USA trade classification); in other words, the tariff is applied on the value of the imported product less that of the components. The second scheme is confined to assembly operations, or the processing of metal products which subsequently return to the USA for further processing; in this case, the duty is applied to the value added in that operation. Schemes introduced by Germany and Holland are similar to this, but they are not confined to metal products, nor to those which require further local processing; they apply also to the fabrication of finished products, such as textiles, which come mainly from Eastern Europe (Finger, 1975, Table 1).

On the part of LDCs, their export promotion policies have favoured the assembly processes which have low national value added. They have been favoured through the use of free-trade zones (Mexico, Taiwan, Hong Kong, Singapore and Korea); the refund of duties on imported inputs; the subsidisation in proportion to the gross value of production or to the need for working capital, etc. This suggests another important area of research, namely, a study of the effects and the suitability of alternative instruments of export promotion.

3 INDUSTRIALISED COUNTRY POLICIES AND THE PRESENT ECONOMIC ORDER

(a) Discriminatory protectionism

Table 10.5 indicated that tariff and non-tariff barriers raised by the industrialised countries are concentrated mainly on those manufactured goods which constitute the principal exports of the Third World, particularly textiles and clothing.[8] In 1962, under pressure from the USA, a special transitory agreement on cotton textiles was signed within GATT with the supposed intention of liberalising that market in an 'orderly' fashion. In the course of time, both the agreement and its bilateral developments became more and more restrictive, especially after 1973 with the introduction of more permanent quotas with wider application, incorporating synthetic textiles and clothing. In 1977 the fifth renewal of this multilateral agreement was negotiated under pressures of increasing protectionism from the DC. It is estimated that the dismantling of the present restrictions on textiles and clothing would have a greater effect on the exports of the LDCs than the liberalisation of trade in all other manufactured goods and even of trade in agricultural products. (Cline *et al.*, 1977; IBRD, 1977a and 1977c).

The high degree of protection afforded by DCs to their national and (in the case of the EEC) regional production of most primary products has been justified on the basis of 'national security' considerations and of redistribution of income in favour of agricultural producers. The growing protectionism for industries like textiles and clothing has been justified on the grounds that their products are of basic consumption and create many jobs. However, it does not seem to be the case that protectionism on the part of the industrialised countries towards those of the Third World can be explained simply because the LDCs have specialised in goods which are highly 'sensitive' for DCs. As regards the argument of employment, a recent study shows that, between 1962 and 1975, the jobs lost in Germany as a result of the increase in imports from the LDCs were 9 times fewer than those lost due to the growth of imports from other DCs, and 50 times fewer than those lost as a result of technological change (Wolter 1976). A similar study has calculated that, between 1964 and 1971, the increase in imports from LDCs accounted for scarcely 0·4 per cent of the annual turnover of the manufacturing industry of the USA. Similarly, the Brookings Institution, in a study carried out for the Department of Labor of the USA, concludes that the liberalisation proposed during the Tokyo Round would, in all the DCs together, put only 1 million people out of work over a ten-year period (100,000 per year), at a time when the work force in the manufacturing industry is over 65 million and over 300 million in their economies as a whole. Moreover, the Kennedy Round liberalisation would generate over the same period at least 600,000 new jobs in additional export production, to which one would have to add an increase of the same order of magnitude to account for the global increase in national income which could be expected as a result of a more open international trade, so that the total net effect on employment would be positive (Cline *et al.*, 1977). In the light of this evidence, it is argued that exports from the LDCs displace the least qualified workers and affect local industry in the more depressed areas. It is curious that this social concern had not been exposed decades ago in view of the formidable impact which technological change and trade between the industrialised countries has had on this type of worker and industry.

In fact, the DCs' non-tariff barriers have not had the same effect on Third World exports as on other DCs' exports, even as regards the same products. In the case of the textile agreements, the restrictions are discriminatory against LDCs, since they do not affect other industrialised countries except Japan. Similarly, just when certain LDCs have begun to be successful in exporting wood products, leather goods and electrical components, they have found themselves up against restrictions which previously did not exist for trade between industrialised countries. Many European countries have made unfair use of safeguard clauses and those covering 'damage' to the domestic market, as laid down by GATT, in the face of exports from the Third World, but the use of similar clauses within the EEC has been minimal (see Tinbergen *et al.*, 1976).

It must be concluded, therefore, that in the increase of protectionism by the DCs there are other important factors involved: the inability of the LDCs to take reprisals and the smaller degree of internationalisation of their industrial structure. In fact, as we have seen, North American foreign investment over the past fifteen years has been concentrated in the manufacturing industry of other DCs. So the capacity of organising internal lobbies in support of trade liberalisation and in opposition to groups which advocate protection is very great. The same is not the case with regard to exports from LDCs, except those produced or handled by the TNCs.[9]

The case of compensatory duties applied by the USA sets a very serious precedent. Although this instrument for retaliation already existed, the United States President had seldom used it. Nevertheless, since the passing of the 1974 Trade Law, which requires decisions to be made within a fixed period, there has been an increase both in the number of claims made and in the rulings in favour of retaliation. Up to September 1977, sixty-three cases had been taken up, of which twenty-two applied to goods from LDCs.[10] In view of the manifold distortions in their economies and of their higher tariff levels, these countries have been obliged to provide more and greater subsidies for exports, and as a result have suffered a higher proportion of unfavourable rulings and higher rates of compensatory duties.

It seems absolutely necessary, therefore, to carry out studies which will anticipate the appearance of this form of protectionism in other manufactured goods and which may provide the basis for government authorities to set up internal compensation lobbies in the country in question or to prepare themselves for adopting specific measures of retaliation. This type of study, however, would be more appropriate for organisations such as ECLA or the foreign trade offices of the Latin American countries than for private research centres. Likewise, it will be crucial for the DCs to apply reconversion aid to reduce the internal pressure towards more protectionism.

Negotiations in GATT have been set up basically between countries which make reciprocal concessions, which virtually excludes the LDCs.

Under these circumstances, it is not surprising that the lowest tariff cuts have been for products in which LDCs are highly competitive, nor that the DCs have maintained a tariff structure which discourages the processing of raw materials in the LDCs.

Second, GATT does not define precisely under what conditions the safeguards and other exceptional measures may be applied, nor does it contemplate a mechanism of sanctions for those who violate its norms over and above the capacity for retaliation of those affected (Palacios, 1977). In countries like the USA, Congress has not ratified the agreement, as a result of which there are laws sanctioned – the 1974 Trade Law, for example – which clearly violate its terms. Within GATT itself there was the signing of the textiles agreement, which contradicts many of its principles: it is discriminatory; it contains permanent quantitative restrictions; it allows new barriers to be set up without having to prove the reality or even the threat of 'grave danger' to domestic production; and it does not even authorise the adoption of reprisals.

To sum up, both in the negotiating stage and in the way agreements are put into effect, the rule has been 'might is right'. Consequently, it is not to be wondered at that the present commercial order has discriminated against the LDCs in spite of the assertions made in the agreements that have been reached.

(b) The transfer of technology

The present economic order has been characterised in many areas by the absence of a free market for technology, and even by the existence of restrictions preserved under the Paris Convention on Patents (in the pharmaceutical sector, for example). Otherwise, governments in the DCs have promoted foreign investment while, at the same time, restricting in practice the access of capital into their domestic markets, and have not seen fit to create a really *long*-term international capital market open to LDCs. It was precisely because of disequilibria in the monetary order that an incipient short-term free capital market was created: that of the Euro-dollar. In the past, therefore, developing countries have had to fall back either on the so-called 'foreign aid', with all its conditions, or on the 'package' of capital and technology offered by direct foreign investment. This problem would bear no relation to the present international economic order if it were not for the fact that markets are political entities. As Diáz-Alejandro (1975) has pointed out, markets do not spring spontaneously or inevitably from economic necessities. Which markets are allowed to operate, and which are not, and under what circumstances, constitute political decisions or agreements, either tacitly or openly. The failure to liberalise capital and technology markets, and support for the joint flow of these through foreign direct investment, are key elements which make up the present order, as is the liberalisation of trade in manufactured goods between the industrialised countries.

4 PERSPECTIVES

(a) Growth and protectionism

The export of manufactured goods from LDCs to the DCs faces a less favourable external situation than in past decades for three main reasons:

(i) It would be difficult for those exports of manufactures from the LDCs which have shown the greatest dynamism in the recent past to keep growing at the same rate, in as much as they have achieved substantial volume and participation in some markets today.

(ii) The average annual growth of the DCs will probably diminish in comparison to that of previous decades.

(iii) It is possible that there will be less liberalisation of DCs' markets than in recent decades.

With regard to this last factor, it should be pointed out that while the high degree of protectionism in the DC against exports of manufactured goods from the Third World is still present, there have been several moves towards liberalisation over the last couple of decades which have had significant effects on the export of manufactured goods from the LDCs. In summary, these movements were: (i) the sixth round of negotiations in GATT, known as the Kennedy Round, after which there were substantial tariff cuts between 1967 and 1972 which, though specially favourable to mutual trade within the DCs, were not without importance for exports from LDCs; (ii) the surprising and vigorous process which opened up the Japanese economy, particularly to exports from LDCs, after it had been the country which had applied the strongest protectionist measures; this development led Japan to become within only a few years the second most important market for the LDCs; (iii) the liberalisation in the USA, Germany, Holland and other DCs with regard to the assembly of its own products abroad; (iv) in spite of all its limitations, the establishment of GSPs in the EEC, Japan and other DCs between 1971 and 1973; and (v) the preferences of the EEC, established at the Yaounde and Arusha Conventions, in favour of the member countries' former colonies.

The effect of these last two factors on the increase of manufactured exports from the LDCs to the industrialised countries over the past couple of decades may be partially superseded, on the one hand, by the likely effects of the GSPs of Canada (1975) and the USA (1976) and, on the other, by the extension of the regional preferences of the EEC as an outcome of the Lomé Convention of 1975. None the less, the effects of any liberalisation through the Tokyo Round will almost certainly be considerably smaller than those ensuing from the Kennedy Round.[11] The tariff reductions on textiles and clothing will make no greater impact on trade because of rigid quantitative restrictions.[12] This is a factor of great importance, as we have already noted.

Broadly speaking, little can be expected from the Tokyo Round as regards curtailing the tendency towards extending the use of non-tariff barriers in the DCs. It is understandable that, after the recession of 1975 and the slow beginnings of a new cycle of growth, the tendency towards liberalisation should be less marked than in the period from 1965 to 1967. This attitude could be seen in the Tokyo Round in the insistence by many DCs on giving a 'sectoral focus' to liberalisation, following the example of the textiles sector. Moreover, as long as GATT agreements are not complemented with effective supra-national legal institutions, or until the agreements are turned into national laws in all DCs, however closely the GATT's safeguard clauses are defined they will continue to be applied in a discriminatory fashion against the LDCs, who do not possess sufficient retaliatory power.

Finally, even though the LDCs have been speaking out more forcefully in international forums, their position in the Tokyo Round was eroded by two factors. On the one hand, many of them, together with UNCTAD, persistently defend the maintenance of the GSP margins of preference. Since these have, in practice, been responsible more for creating than diverting trade, and have been applied to a limited extent, it would appear that it is better for the LDCs as a whole to have a generalised, permanent and non-discretionary reduction of trade barriers (Cline *et al.*, 1977; IBRD, 1977a and 1977b). This consideration is further supported by the fact that discretionality enables the

DCs to include in their GSP those categories of goods for which they have significant foreign investments in the Third World, and to exclude those of greatest interest to the LDCs – apart from the fact that discretionality can be used for political ends.[13] However, it will be difficult to arrive at a common position on this question, in so far as each LDC will be interested in preserving margins for *certain products* and the estimates at present available show that it is better for some countries – the poorest, generally speaking – to *retain* the present margins. If, at the request of the LDCs themselves, exceptions to the norms for tariff reduction begin to be introduced, this will accentuate the tendency already observed to exclude reductions in products of considerable interest to the LDCs.

On the other hand, the countries which are signatories to the Lomé Convention are bringing pressure to bear on the EEC to maintain, as it has undertaken to do, the regional margins of preference established within the terms of the Convention. In many ways, this Convention represents a step forward in North-South relations (certainly as regards its character of absolute non-reciprocity and the establishment of new transfer mechanisms, like Stabex).[14] However, it contains a dangerous precedent for the eventual formation of commercial blocs of a distinctively neo-colonial flavour and creates divisions between the LDCs.[15]

In spite of all that has been said, it should be noted that the field is still wide open for LDCs to exploit the opportunity to export different manufactures to the DCs. It is feasible, therefore, as the apostles of the new faith in export-led growth proclaim, that the adoption of sound foreign trade policies may enable their exports of manufactured goods to expand at an even greater pace than in previous decades.

Moreover, if the LDCs manage to overcome the difficulties caused by the restrictive flow of technology, principally in the form of foreign investment, and to penetrate the fields of transportation and international marketing at present dominated by the TNCs, they would have the possibility of a faster growth of manufactured exports through the expansion of their regional exports. This would be easier after the approval by GATT of proposals allowing LDCs to set preferences among themselves only; i.e. without extending them to the DCs through the MFN clauses. On the other hand, it seems important to carry out studies about the possibilities and problems of developing trade among LDCs in different regions, as well as with socialist countries (Perry, 1977a).

A greater liberalisation of technology markets, however, is very unlikely; the industrialised countries insist on promoting foreign direct investment as the preferential channel for technology transfers. Under these conditions it is vital for LDCs to participate in the process of generating new technologies and to look at the opportunities offered by the socialist countries. This may increase their bargaining power *vis-à-vis* foreign investment.

(b) Terms of trade and instability

The problems noted in this regard will tend to become more acute for the manufactured goods exported by the LDCs. Again, only a greater diversification in terms of products and markets will make it possible for these problems to be overcome. But it is difficult to follow this alternative, given the restrictive ways in which technology is transferred and the increasing internalisation of world trade inside the TNCs. If some LDCs make progress in exporting manufactures incorporating a more sophisticated technology, is it not likely that there will be great competition on the supply side which will become a source of instability, low profit margins and decreasing terms of trade? In any case, would not the TNCs appropriate a large share of the benefits from that trade? These considerations reinforce our previous recommendations. They suggest also the need for international organisations to carry out projections about the growth of the markets for manufactures of interest to LDCs in order to avoid an excess supply of them in the future.

NOTES

1 In the case of the EEC 5·4 per cent, in that of Japan 11·5 per cent and 17·9 per cent in the USA (CEPAL, 1976).
2 See a list in CEPAL (1976).
3 IBRD (1977c) on the basis of calculations made by Baldwin and Murray (1977) and Iqbal (1975).
4 For instance 8 per cent of all Colombian exports to the USA which in principle had the right to benefit from the GSP did not in fact enjoy preferences (according to official data from the Department of Commerce).
5 The effective protection of manufactures in DCs is approximately twice their nominal protection.
6 In other cases the contracts for technology transfer impose commercial restrictions and other significant costs (see Vaitsos, 1973).
7 As suggested by Vernon's (1966) 'on product cycle theory'.
8 This characteristic of the DCs' tariff structure has been recently studied by several authors. Some of them show, in particular, that the exception to the

tariff concessions agreed in the Kennedy Round are concentrated on products which are relatively intensive in the use of skilled labour (see Helleiner, 1977a).
9 For a good discussion of the political economy of protectionism, see Schonfield *et al.* (1976) and Helleiner (1977b).
10 Figures taken from the Trade Actions Monitoring System, Executive Office of the President, September 1977.
11 This essay was written in 1978, long before the final agreements on the Tokyo Round. However, most of the decisions conformed with the expectations.
12 They could have important effects only for those countries that are far from using all their export quota allowances.
13 Naturally, since the reductions as a result of the Most Favoured Nations (MFN) clause will be partial, it is convenient for LDCs to insist *later* on an extension of the GSPs, or on a compensation for the erosion of their margins of preference. What does *not* seem convenient, in global terms, is conditioning the MFN tariff cuts to the preservation of the present preference margins.
14 The Fund for the Stabilisation of revenues from Primary Product exports.
15 The countries of the Association of East Asian Nations (ASEAN) have been pressing Japan to establish regional preferences.

REFERENCES

Baldwin, R., and Murray, J. (1977) 'MFN Tariff Reductions and Developing Countries Trade Benefits under the GSP', *Economic Journal*, March.
Brookings Institution (1973a) 'World Trade and Domestic Adjustment' (Washington, DC).
—— (1975) 'The World Economy in Transition' (Washington, DC).
—— (1977) 'Economic Prospect and Policies in Industrial Countries' (Washington, DC).
CEPAL (1975) *La Coyuntura Internacional y el Sector Externo* (Santiago).
—— (1976) *Temas del Nuevo Orden Económico Internacional* (Santiago).
Cline, W., *et al.* (1977) 'Multilateral Effects of Tariff Negotiations in the Tokyo Round', mimeo (Washington, DC: Brookings Institution).
Díaz-Alejandro, C. (1975) 'North-South Relations: The Economic Component', in Bergsten and Krause (eds) *World Politics and International Economics* (Washington, DC: Brookings Institution).
—— (1976a) 'Un-shackled or Unhinged? On Delinking North and South', mimeo (New Haven: Yale University Department of Economics).
—— (1976b) *Foreign Trade Regimes and Economic Development:*

Colombia (NBER). (New York: Columbia University Press).

Finger, J. (1975) 'Tariff Provisions for Offshore Assembly and the Exports of Developing Countries', *Economic Journal*, June.

—— (1976) 'Effective Protection by Transportation Costs and Tariffs', *Quarterly Journal of Economics*, February.

—— (1977) 'Effects of the Kennedy Round Concessions on the Exports of Developing Countries', mimeo.

GATT (1978) *International Trade:* 1977/1976 (Geneva).

Helleiner, G. (1973) 'Manufactured Exports from Less Developed Countries and Multinational Firms', *Economic Journal*, March.

—— (1976) *A World Divided* (Cambridge University Press).

—— (1977a) 'Structural Aspects of Third World Trade', Institute of Social Studies 25th Anniversary Conference, The Hague, Holland.

—— (1977b) 'International Enterprises and the New Political Economy of US Trade Policy', *Oxford Economic Papers*, March.

—— (1977c) 'Intrafirm Trade and the Developing Countries: Patterns, Trends and Data Problems', seminar on intrafirm transactions, UNCTAD and Institute of Development Studies, Sussex, November.

IBRD (1977a) 'Prospects for Developing Countries' (Washington, DC).

—— (1977b) 'Tendencias del Comercio y de los Precios de los Productos Básicos' (Washington, DC).

—— (1977c) 'Trade Liberalisation and Export Promotion' (Washington, DC).

International Trade Center (ITC) UNCTAD-GATT (1976), *Statistical Analysis of Dynamic Non-food Import Products Exported from Developing Countries to 18 Industrialized Countries, 1970–1974*, Geneva.

—— (1978) *Structural and Cyclical Changes in International Trade and their Impact on the Export Performance and Prospects of Developing Countries*, Geneva.

Iqbal, Z. (1975) 'Trade Effects of the Generalized System of Preferences' (Washington, DC: IMF).

Keesing, D. (1976a) 'Industrial Countries' Manufactured Imports from Developing Countries', mimeo (Washington, DC: World Bank, May).

—— 1976b) 'Manufactured Exports from Developing Countries: recent Trends and Prospects', SID Conference, Amsterdam.

—— (1977) 'Recent Trends in Manufactured and Total Exports from Developing Countries', mimeo (Washington, DC: World Bank, June).

Lewis, A. (1977) 'La Evolución del Orden Económico Internacional',

Janeway Conferences, Princeton University, March.

Linder, S. (1961) *An Essay on Trade and Transformation* (Stockholm: Almgvist and Wicksell).

Palacios, H. (1977) 'El Nuevo Orden Jurídico Internacional', Seminario sobre el Nuevo Orden Internacional, Bogotá, Colombia, October.

Perry, G. (1977a) 'Relaciones Económicas de Colombia con Países Socialistas', *Coyuntura Económica*, FEDESARROLLO, August.

—— (1977b) 'El Nuevo Orden Comercial Internacional', *Coyuntura Económica*, FEDESARROLLO, December.

Shonfield, A., *et al.* (1976) *International Economic Relations of the Western World* (New York: Oxford University Press).

Singh, S. (1976) 'The International Dialogue on Commodities', *Resources Policy*, June.

Stewart, F. (1976) 'The Direction of International Trade: Gains and Losses for the Third World', in Helleiner (ed.) (1976).

Tinbergen, J., *et al.* (1976) *The Rio Report: Reshaping the International Order* (New York: Dutton).

UNCTAD (1977) 'Evolución y Tendencias Recientes del Comercio de Manufacturas y Semimanufacturas', TD/B/C.2/75, New York, May.

Vaitsos, C. (1973) 'Transferencia de Recursos y Preservación de Rentas Monopolísticas', *Revista de Planeación y Desarrollo*, vol. 111, no. 2.

—— (1976) 'Power, Knowledge and Developing Countries', in Helleiner (ed.) (1970).

Vernon, R. (1966) 'International Investment and International Trade in the Product Cycle', *Quarterly Journal of Economics*, May.

—— (1973) *Sovereignty at Bay* (Harmondsworth: Penguin).

Walter, I. (1971) 'Non Tariff Barriers and the Export Performance of Developing Economies', *American Economic Review*, May.

Wolter, F. (1976) 'Adjusting to Imports from Developing Countries: The Evidence from a Human Capital-rich Resource Poor Country', Symposium KIEL, December.

11 World Markets for Manufactures and Industrialisation in Developing Countries: a Comment

NORBERTO GONZÁLEZ

I am in broad agreement with Guillermo Perry. My comments follow a line similar to his, and primarily indicate points which I think should receive greater emphasis or attention.

First of all, I think a clearer distinction should be drawn between two kinds of protection in developed countries. One is the protection which has been in existence for years, of the kind dealt with in Tables 10.4 and 10.5 in Perry's study. The other is the escalation of protection which has occurred recently in those countries, consisting in a very steep rise in certain sectors. Both aspects are very important. The first is well covered in Perry's study. The second is mentioned but, in my opinion, deserves greater attention, especially bearing in mind that in the last year there have been cases of sharply increased protection in the case of leather manufactures, textiles, electronics, iron and steel and other groups of products. According to official GATT data, the amount of world trade affected by these protectionist measures, recently or about to be adopted, varies between $30 billion and $50 billion. All these goods are of great immediate export interest to the developing countries, and the Latin American countries in particular.

The prospects of dynamic growth of the exports of developing countries which prevailed until not long ago have given way to uncertainty and anxiety; and the rise in protection is a major factor, although not the only cause. I think the true nature of this escalation needs to be studied. There are grounds for thinking that this is not purely a short-term development, but rather the result of policies resulting from 'stagflation', which is a prolonged problem, and of the large-scale penetration of international manufacturing markets by the Third World for the first time in history. Some developed countries are trying to carry out policies to adjust their industrial structure. On the one hand they wish to place greater emphasis on technologically more demanding sectors, while leaving to the developing countries part of the field of the industries producing non-durable and durable consumer goods and some capital and intermediate goods; on the other hand, the pressures brought to bear by internal groups, together with concern for their own balance-of-payments and employment problems, lead these countries to adopt defensive measures which protect their inefficient activities and hinder the growth of industries in which many Third World countries are perfectly well equipped. This is a structural phenomenon: the end of one stage and the beginning of another in the international division of labour. I think that a thorough study of these structural trends in the world economy, and of Latin America's new role and the policies it should follow are of great importance for the region. Last year CEPAL proposed that a case-by-case approach should be adopted in studying a number of sectors to see what is happening in the developing and developed countries, and the implications, as concerns production, employment, trade and trade policy. The idea would be to carry out an exercise resembling sectoral programming for selected sectors (textiles, leather, electronics, motor-vehicles, and so forth) in order to see to what extent it would be possible to shift part of each of these industries from the North to the South without unnecessarily disrupting the developed countries in the short term, in response to the new possibilities open to many Third World nations as a result of their semi-industrialised economic status.

In addition, in the face of the protectionist trends clearly visible in traditional industrial sectors, careful thought must be given to the most appropriate strategy to be followed from the standpoint of the structure of manufacturing exports; for example, one type of reaction could be the diversification of exports to include not only products of industries facing an escalation of protectionism, but also others which do not face such protection, for the time being at least – for example, products of a variety of engineering industries. I think that these topics, as regards the role of Latin America in terms of a new division of labour, the possibilities and problems of industrial redeployment in the developed countries, protectionism and recession should receive far greater attention.

With regard to transnationals, in recent years there have been interesting developments in terms of new forms of operation by these corporations in both the developing and the socialist countries. Traditionally, these corporations had set up subsidiaries, in the capital and management of which they had at the least an absolute majority. Decisions on the transfer of technology and exports were taken almost exclusively by the transnational itself. This *modus operandi* is giving way to new forms. As a result either of legislation or of case-by-case negotiations, or sometimes both at once, many developing countries, including some Latin American ones, are ensuring that the transnational corporations behave in new ways, by using the bargaining power stemming from their own domestic markets. In exchange for allowing them to start producing for the domestic market, they impose the obligation to secure a certain level of exports, purchase technology separately from ownership of the corporation and sometimes likewise purchase separately the different components of the technology, encourage the transnational to enter into partnership with local public and private capital, etc. This issue has been dealt with in Guillermo Perry's chapter, but I think special emphasis should be placed on the examination of these new trends, the ways in which the transnationals operate in developing and socialist countries and the policies which these countries, particularly in Latin America, are following to secure these new kinds of behaviour. An analytical inventory of the different cases would be very interesting.

Speaking of bargaining power, I would like to point out in passing that the possession of a large market with a limited degree of protection, although significant enough to allow some advantage to enterprises producing within it, can give the developing countries enough bargaining power to obtain specific conditions from the transnationals, in exchange for allowing them to start production for their market.

Another point which would be worth studying in connection with transnationals, is the growing competition between European, Japanese and United States corporations. It would seem that European firms are attempting to penetrate areas which were traditionally the exclusive preserve of North American corporations. The same is true of United States corporations trying to win markets previously dominated by European or Japanese firms. It would be interesting to study whether, as part of their penetration strategy, the transnationals attempting to win new markets are in practice prepared to offer the developing countries more favourable conditions than the corporations already installed in the country.

I also think that a distinction should be drawn between subcontracting as dealt with in this study and forms of co-production and specialisation which frequently occur in the case of developed countries working together and which are beginning to occur in their relations with some Third World countries. Subcontracting, as dealt with in this chapter, consists in setting up in a developing country a labour-intensive production process which calls for little investment and has very little or no effects in terms of backward or forward linkages. In contrast, under co-production agreements the production of the various components, parts or pieces of a single final good, which is assembled in one or several countries, is located in different countries. These arrangements also occur in Latin America. I think it would be important to distinguish between these different kinds of arrangements and include in the work programme a study of the new developments taking place from the standpoint of their effects on the countries of our region.

As concerns trade with the countries associated to the Council of Mutual Economic Assistance (CMEA), I would like to point out that in recent years some Latin American countries have increased this trade quite spectacularly. Argentina recorded exports to these countries to the tune of almost $600 million in 1977, starting from a very low level. The value of Brazilian exports was also considerable: $900 million in 1976, $860 million in 1977. Broadly speaking, however, Latin American exports to CMEA member countries consist mainly of raw materials or products with very little processing; this is not true in the case of Cuba, where a large proportion of total exports consist of manufactures.

There are also problems due to heavy trade surpluses which may limit the future growth of this trade. A study of the sectors in which exports of the socialist countries are competitive, and the new forms of co-operation which are arising (e.g. payments in machinery), would be also very interesting. Section 2b of Perry's chapter provides interesting data on the proportion of total exports by the United States and the United Kingdom accounted for by transactions among affiliates of transnationals. I would like to point out that data is also available on the percentage represented by intra-firm transactions not only within total trade, but also for the total amount exported by transnationals both for the United States and for some Latin American countries. Of course these proportions are much higher than those given in Chapter 10, Section 2b, and help to give a more exact idea of the great relative weight of this intra-firm trade. Data also exists comparing the production of affiliates abroad with exports of transnationals from their countries of origin.

I think that the relationship between the behaviour of the transnationals and comparative advantages could be made a little clearer than is the case. On the one hand, it is reasonable to think that the corporations have a certain economic rationale in their behaviour and tend to produce wherever it is cheapest to do so. On the other, imperfections of markets operating in conditions of oligopoly or oligopsony makes it possible to fix prices which often have very little to do with production costs; the case of intra-firm transactions is a clear but by no means unique example. I would like to repeat that I share the opinion of Guillermo Perry; my comment is only aimed at securing greater clarity in the treatment of this subject.

12 Foreign Trade, Industrialisation and Development Policies

RICARDO FFRENCH-DAVIS

In this chapter we shall examine a number of elements essential for the understanding and design of efficient foreign trade policies which can contribute to a balanced internal development in LDCs. Emphasis will be placed upon areas in which conventional knowledge is least relevant, and research in LDCs is most limited.

Over the last two decades significant progress has been made in the theoretical understanding of the variables which have an influence on the structure of trade and on the effects of foreign trade policies. Outstanding advances have been made in the areas of natural resources (Vanek, 1959), human capital (Keesing, 1966), technology (Vernon, 1966), the internal market (Linder, 1961), the behaviour of TNCs (Vernon, 1978), and the concept and measurement of effective protection (Balassa, 1971; Corden, 1971). As regards internal disequilibria, a major contribution has come from research on the relationship between distortions in the labour market and trade (Bhagwati, 1968; Krueger, 1976; Magee, 1976). Nevertheless, the dominant position in the neo-classical literature is that distortions should be attacked through internal subsidies and taxes; obstacles or incentives to trade are seen as a sub-optimal alternative, while direct forms of intervention are ignored or rejected out of hand. With the exception of the terms-of-trade optimising tariff and of 'non-economic' arguments in favour of tariffs, this approach leads to trade free of state intervention; however, such an approach does not free LDCs from the oligopolistic practices of the TNCs, the instability of external markets, or the structural disequilibria of the domestic economies. Consideration of these aspects leads to policy proposals very different from those offered by orthodox economists.

157

Along with those theoretical developments, knowledge on the working of international markets and Third World economies has increased. Among studies on the first of these areas are those of institutions such as UNCTAD and GATT, and of a number of authors who have examined the imperfections and the heterogeneity of international markets (Baldwin, 1970; Bhagwati, 1976; Helleiner, 1978; Vaitsos, 1974). From these analyses it follows that a significant proportion of the markets faced by LDCs operate differently from what the competitive model suggests, and that crucial implications for the design of economic policy can follow.

With regard to domestic markets, dynamic disequilibria (polarisation phenomena and destabilising movements) and the relationship between savings and foreign exchange gaps (the two gap model) have been taken up in the literature on economic development (Hirschman, 1958, 1973; Little, Scitovsky and Scott, 1970; Pinto, 1970; Chenery and Strout, 1966). Over the last decade knowledge on labour markets and technology, and on the behaviour of TNCs and the new forms of dependence in Latin American countries has grown, too (PREALC, 1975; Katz, 1976; Fajnzylber, 1971, 1976; Cardoso and Faletto, 1969; Helleiner, 1973; Sunkel, 1971).

The theoretical and empirical progress has been made mostly in the developed countries nevertheless, and has not been incorporated systematically into international trade theory or into the design and implementation of policy.

This chapter concentrates upon the analysis of criteria for determining the profile of protection of national production (Section 1), the relationship between import substitution and export promotion (Section 2), the role of policy tools other than the tariff, the specific problems which arise in the presence of TNCs, public enterprises, and the instability of foreign markets (Section 3), the implications of the processes of adjustment (Section 4), and the role of the state in planning the development of the external sector (Section 5).

1 PROTECTION CRITERIA FOR NATIONAL PRODUCTION

Most neoclassical literature on tariff policy is framed in a 'first best' world, where tariffs are not an optimum policy.[1] Evidently, a tariff has limitations with respect to an ideal alternative. However, the option of utilising tariffs as an active policy instrument should be compared with other viable alternatives and not with a non-existent ideal. The design of each specific economic policy on the assumption that it will operate in an optimal context, when the real world is in fact very different, tends to perpetuate underdevelopment rather than to overcome it.

The efficiency of a given economic policy is conditioned by the feasibility of using alternative policies, and by the structural characteristics and degree of development of the national economy. The greater the disequilibria and the distortions in the LDCs' markets, and the greater the difficulty of superseding them by alternative devices, the greater will be the role that tariff policy can play.[2] In consequence, empirical and theoretical analysis as well as the design of economic policies should be pursued in the framework of the by now old theory of the 'second best'.

As a result of the bias in the conclusions derived from the conventional approach, little attention has been paid in the literature to the theoretical and empirical study of the role which an active tariff policy can play in economic development. In what follows we illustrate the kind of objectives which might be pursued by means of such a policy, and discuss some of the problems of design and implementation which arise.

(a) Effects of the tariff

Tariffs may discriminate between imports in terms of their use, their origin, or the characteristics of the processes by which they are produced, and between import substitution and export promotion. Nevertheless, regulation of the tariff of a given good does not permit *direct* discrimination between alternative technologies for the production of that good. Furthermore, it generates effects upon consumption which are the contrary of those upon production. It is on these two grounds that conventional international trade theory generally rejects tariffs. The argument for using them stresses their capacity to promote changes in the structure of production, to regulate the transmission of external instability and of consumption patterns, and to generate fiscal revenues.

(i) Effects upon the structure of production Tariff discrimination on the basis of processes of production has been scarcely used in practice, although it constitutes the most solid basis of support for tariff protection. A number of aspects of this issue might be considered.

However, the pioneering efforts which have been made in this field (JUNAC, 1973) have led us to select some arguments which reflect problems that can be attacked by means of a tariff, and are common to the majority of LDCs. These are illustrated by three characteristics of productive activities: the capital-labour intensity, the extent to which the activity is in its 'infancy' and its capacity to increase its productivity by 'learning by doing', and the externalities generated by the given activity for the rest of the economy. Different productive activities present varying patterns as far as these aspects are concerned; at the same time, the level of development, factor endowment, stage of industrialisation and the sort of market distortions prevailing in each LDC, bear upon the types of activity which should be promoted.

To the extent that changes in relative prices induced by a tariff alter the structure of production, effective protection for labour-intensive processes will tend to increase the demand for labour, provided there are no pervasive effects on the demand for labour-intensive non-tradables. Incentives should be higher for activities intensive in the 'dynamically' most abundant type of labour. Furthermore, the existence of 'acquirable' comparative advantages supports a recommendation to protect particular import-substituting industries and new export industries on the grounds of their 'infancy'. Finally, each activity tends to provoke indirect effects upon the rest of the economy, many of which take on the character of externalities. One variable in this category is the capacity of some activities to generate technological knowledge of which other firms may take advantage: this is what might be called 'diffusible technology' (JUNAC, 1976).

(ii) Effects upon consumption It is commonly argued that tariffs prejudice consumers, since they face a price which differs from the international price. However, accepting the neoclassical assumptions and the absence of distributive problems, the weight of this distortion is negligible (Vanek, 1971). A less coherent version of the argument claims that the consumer faces prices higher than those prevailing internationally, when the fact is that the tariff changes relative prices; therefore some consumers lose and others gain, depending upon their demand pattern. The implications for social welfare depend, once the effects on efficiency on the production side have been considered (and there are, clearly, interrelationships which make it difficult to separate the two sides), on the equity of income distribution, the social groups which consume the protected good most intensively, the effect on the level of employment of the factors which each consumer owns (Uri,

1973), and the degree of information, independence and rationality with which consumers take their decisions (McEwan and Weisskopf, 1974, Part III).

(iii) Redundancy and the effects upon efficiency   The tariff may also affect the efficiency of a given set of factors (Leibenstein, 1966; Corden, 1974, Chapter 8), or encourage changes in the stock of resources (Vanek, 1971).

Where conditions diverge from the model of competitive equilibrium, the level of the tariff in a given activity tends to affect its productivity, and in particular its evolution through time if tariffs become redundant. As the tariff rises, imports fall and internal production increases (gradually if costs are increasing, abruptly if they are constant or falling). When imports are completely eliminated, the tariff becomes redundant (has no effect) from the point of view of trade flows. Nevertheless, an even higher tariff allows the domestic producer to charge prices above his marginal or *average* costs, depending on the case, instead of encouraging production. At the same time, redundant protection allows the sector which benefits from it to neglect the continued introduction of technological and administrative improvements: this gives rise to what has been described as 'x-efficiency' (Leibenstein, 1966). The first argument (monopolistic over-pricing) is static, and the second is dynamic.[3] In the case of potential exportables, although tariff redundancy does not promote import substitution, it may alter the conditions in which the domestic market is supplied, as well as export possibilities, by allowing price discrimination if the domestic market is not competitive.

In summary, in a competitive internal market tariff redundancy has no effect. However, where such markets are not competitive it encourages monopolistic behaviour, and discourages the efficiency of production. On the positive side, redundancy can facilitate the development of exports, reduce the transmission of external instability to the internal market, and contribute to restrict the magnitude of 'product differentiation'.

(b) Tariffs or subsidies?

There are four elements which bear upon the validity of the traditional neoclassical conclusions which lead to a preference for subsidies over tariffs. These are: (i) budget constraints, (ii) administrative constraints, (iii) distortions in consumption, and (iv) technological constraints (Ffrench-Davis, 1979, Chapter VII).

First, a subsidy involves government expenditure, while tariffs, if they are not prohibitive, provide fiscal revenue. This constitutes an indirect positive effect in countries where the government finds it difficult to balance its budget. In consequence, the orthodox recommendation of generalised subsidies to compensate distortions in commodities or factors markets may not be feasible, as a result of fiscal or budget constraints.[4]

Second, LDCs tend to have a poor administrative organisation. To design an efficient tariff system certainly requires organisational capacity. So, however, does a system of subsidies. Furthermore, all countries commonly possess customs posts, if only for reasons of national security. As a consequence there exists, even in a free trade regime, the germ of an institution which can operate a tariff system. It should be easier therefore to apply a tariff system than to set up subsidies. This is, then, an *administrative constraint*.

Third, a tariff which promotes import substitution also restricts the consumption or utilisation of a given good. To the extent that demand is dependent upon supply, and that the distribution of income is not that which is desired, the changes in relative prices and the redistributive effects which the tariff generates might eventually become progressive and reduce *distortions in consumption*.

Finally, it is important to establish the extent to which the allocative effects generated on the supply of goods by 'optimal' selective tariffs or subsidies differ one from another. As regards the comparison with subsidies on production, the relevant parameters are the elasticities of supply and demand: for example, a low elasticity of demand means that both instruments will have similar effects. As for the comparison with subsidies on factors, the key parameters are the elasticity of substitution between factors in each activity, and the labour/capital coefficients in different economic activities. In a case of incomplete import substitution, if there were no possibility of substitution between factors, the tariff would have the same effect upon production as an equivalent subsidy on labour. The technological constraint implies that there would only be inter-industrial or macroeconomic substitution between these factors; as a result, the 'optimal' selective tariff allows the economy to operate along the optimal social supply curve. In contrast, if each economic activity were carried out with identical production functions and technical coefficients, tariff policy would prove ineffective as an employment-producing mechanism: only intra-industrial or microeconomic substitution could take place.

Actually, factor intensity differs significantly from one good (or group of goods) to another (García and Mezzera, 1976; JUNAC, 1976; Teitel, 1975);[5] in contrast, given the technology available to LDCs, substitution between factors is relatively limited within each activity. Consequently, the potential changes in the structure of domestic production induced by an actively reallocative tariff policy acquire significance.

(c) Priorities for further research

In contrast to the free trade bias of conventional theory, the market performance of LDCs indicates that there are sound reasons for applying an active tariff policy, with selectively differentiated rates. Knowledge of how to design a system of 'optimal' selective tariffs is, however, deficient.

Some research areas that deserve priority are: (i) the empirical weight of the variables which enter into the choice of tariffs or subsidies as protection mechanisms; (ii) the distortions that a tariff might compensate more effectively, and the bearing of the economic context upon this; and (iii) the practical problems of implementation.[6]

The first set of issues concerns the four constraints and distortions outlined in Section 1b. In particular, from the point of view of feasibility, it is important to evaluate the significance of the *budget constraint*, and to examine the conditions in which the fiscal contribution of tariff policy becomes optimal: the tariff treatment of importables not produced internally is crucial in this connection. From the point of view of the ability of the tariff to achieve the allocative objectives demanded of it, we need a better knowledge of the characteristics of different processes of production. As far as employment is concerned, substantial progress has been made in relation to factor intensity and to reversals. However, as to the criteria for determining the significance of infant industries in macroeconomic terms and of the diffusion of technology, the available studies are very limited, despite the practical importance of each variable. Finally, the notorious weakness of the theory of consumption makes necessary a drastic revision of traditional orthodoxy. Research carried out in this field is clearly of interest to numerous branches of economics; in the field of international economics, competition via product differentiation rather than prices has profound implications for the efficiency of production and social welfare derived from different patterns of consumption.

The criteria for defining the level and the profile of tariff protection in LDCs should be empirically determined; since there are distortions and disequilibria common to many of them, differences between countries would be reflected not in the criteria employed, but in the weight given by tariff policy to each distortion or disequilibrium. More specifically, the degree of development of the national economy bears on criteria such as infant industry and technological diffusion; the situation of the labour market (for example, forms of segmentation and heterogeneity) may lead, furthermore, to different definitions of the employment criterion from one country to another. Finally, an important case for LDCs is that of the specific problems arising out of the design of a common tariff policy in processes of economic integration (JUNAC, 1973).

The practical application of an 'optimal' tariff policy demands a number of critical decisions during the implementation phase. An area in which significant problems arise is that of the degree of disaggregation of the tariff universe and the criteria employed to group items. The way in which tariff redundancy is treated is also relevant, on account of its impact upon income distribution, technological innovation, and the transmission of instability and of patterns of differentiated consumption from abroad. The last two elements mentioned make it advisable to maintain a certain degree of tariff redundancy, in the sectors in which a significant degree of domestic competition already exists.

2 EXPORT PROMOTION AND IMPORT SUBSTITUTION

The foregoing analysis has focused upon import substitution, which has many elements in common with export promotion. Both processes help to close a balance of payments deficit, attenuate a recession, and affect the level and composition of factors' demand. Finally, import substitution can constitute the initial stage of new exports of manufactures, for which the national market serves as a support base; this is particularly important for infant activities and for those which are not based upon rich natural resources.

Nevertheless, the two policies are frequently presented as antagonistic. There are two reasons for this situation, one theoretical in origin, and one arising out of practical experience (Bhagwati, 1978, Chapter 7; ECLA, 1974). In traditional theory – especially in the neoclassical models of 2 × 2 × 2, and competitive markets – an increase in exports implies a contraction in import substitution; and many economists implicitly think in terms of that model. But, furthermore, substitution policies have often been applied in ways that have given rise to excessive protection, which isolates the national market from foreign markets, and actually discriminates against exports.

Apart from differences between export promotion and import substitution which relate to the nature of the economic policies involved, there are intrinsic differences between both processes. The major one is that import substitution rests upon the internal market, while export promotion depends upon the international market. Thus one is regulated by the national authorities, while each segment of the other is controlled by the authorities of different countries, and/or by TNCs. Furthermore, there is a significant gap between the *cif* import price and the *fob* export price. And lastly, exports count potentially with a wider market than import substitutes, a factor which is crucial for activities in which economies of scale are important.

(a) The role of exports

Export promotion involves actions of two kinds, one oriented toward the exterior, and one toward the national economy. The first type concerns the exploitation of economies of scale and improving the terms of trade. If these objectives are to be achieved, access to the international market must be swifter and more stable, and this often requires a process of organisation of marketing, and of negotiation with countries, TNCs, and associated countries, such as in common markets. These can provide export markets with levels of development relatively similar to those prevailing domestically, and may allow an intermediate stage of learning and maturation prior to attempts to penetrate more difficult markets.

With respect to action aimed at the national market, an active state policy at the level of production is required, along with incentives promoting exportable value added capable of contributing efficiently to integrated national development and the pursuit of strategic objectives.

Advances recorded in the industrialisation of a number of countries, and the growing importance of economies of scale, point to the need to seek wider markets if the process is to continue efficiently. Apart from the economic arguments examined in the previous section, the theoretical literature has popularised the hypothesis that LDCs seek industrialisation as an objective *per se* (Cooper and Massell, 1965). Nevertheless, in many cases, this is not so much a non-economic bias, as an 'intuition' on the part of public officials that greater industrialisation will contribute in a number of ways to a deeper development. It is difficult to distinguish between these two elements, but it is obvious that the greater the extent to which the contribution made by the sector becomes visible in objective terms, the more efficient industrialisation policy may become.

The economic arguments in favour of an ISI policy remain valid with respect to exports. Naturally, activities which enjoy economies of scale and relatively dynamic demand will be able to respond more intensively to export incentives. Furthermore, the specific nature which import substitution policies have tended to exhibit, in the presence of indivisibilities and economies of scale, has brought about excess capacity in several sectoral branches. As a result, an export promotion strategy can utilise that excess capacity as one of its points of departure (Schydlowsky, 1976).

The conventional recommendation that efficient resource allocation requires that the cost of generating a unit of foreign exchange through exports should equal that of liberating one such unit through the substitution of imports is so general that it admits, in broad terms, two interpretations with very dissimilar implications for the design of economic policies.

One interpretation leads to the unilateral elimination by LDCs of the controls applied to trade. In the absence of generalised liberalisation it is frequently recommended that exports should be exempted from customs duties for their imports of capital goods and inputs. This policy reduces the negative effective protection of exports, but at the same time works against import substitution, by depriving it of the demand for intermediate goods derived from the production of exportables. Thus the exoneration from customs duties constitutes a 'distorting compensation'.

The second interpretation takes into account the various sources of discrimination to which LDC exports are subject, in particular those which originate in the instability of international markets and in the disequilibria and distortions of domestic markets. It permits the design of an export promotion policy consistent with import substitution and the integration of both into a global strategy. Policies of this kind can be called 'optimal equalising compensation'.

In practice, numerous LDCs have embarked upon export promotion policies characterised by the proliferation of incentives of all kinds, including distorting compensatory mechanisms. The resulting lack of selectivity can bring with it an inefficient diversion of resources towards exports, by promoting them to excess, or in a distorting manner.

(b) Bases for differentiating between the protection of importables and exportables

The profile or structure of import tariffs should tend to coincide with that of export subsidies. There are nevertheless certain characteristics of LDCs which suggest that export incentives should be lower than tariffs covering the same items.

Import substitution protection is financed by the consumer, without entailing a fiscal cost. In contrast export incentives have to be paid out by the government if they are to take place, with the corresponding impact upon the budget constraint.

Furthermore, an excessive tariff is not always utilised by the protected producers, and may therefore be redundant. A subsidy to the exporter, on the other hand, will always be used, with the corresponding impact upon public expenditure and eventually upon the internal price of the given product.

In the third place, policies of marketing and access to foreign markets tend to play a leading role in export promotion. Their design and implementation have a cost for the public institutions concerned, which should be computed among the incentives received by the export sector.

The presence of these three factors – financial constraints, tariff redundancy, and benefits granted through policies regarding negotiation and market access – leads to optimal selective tariffs larger than optimal equalising-compensation for exports.

A special case arises in a process of economic integration which suppresses internal tariffs and establishes a common external tariff. The definition of the margins of preference for import substitution at the level of the regional market also establishes the protection which intra-regional exports will enjoy. As a consequence, the common external tariff sets the structure of nominal protection for regional import substitution and export promotion simultaneously.

The elements analysed here provide a basis for rationalising systems of protection for national economic activity. The objective, then, is to design an export promotion policy which recognises the natural differences between selling in domestic and in foreign markets, but which applies norms common to those used to protect import substitution. Thus the argument as developed here supports deliberate discrimination between different commodity groups, on the basis that divergences between the social and market values of production are not uniform across all activities. On the other hand, a given good should receive similar treatment whatever the market to which it is directed, saving heterogeneity between internal and external markets, and fiscal budget constraints.

(c) Priorities for further research

We shall distinguish three areas, related to: (i) criteria for promotion commonly used in LDCs; (ii) the relationships between monetary incentives for import substitution and export promotion; and (iii) access to external markets.

Since the mid-1960s numerous LDCs have introduced vigorous export promotion policies. They have rested upon customs exemptions and other distorting compensatory devices (Bhagwati, 1978; Díaz-Alejandro, 1976; Ffrench-Davis, 1979, Chapter VIII), and on subsidies directed to compensating for the real costs faced abroad (such as transport costs, and restrictions applied by importing countries). Information on the mechanisms employed has been accumulating; however, little is known still of the effects of these forms of promotion upon the development of the rest of the national economy.

As for optimal equalising-compensation policies, there is a need to investigate the weight of the variables which suggest that these should provide less money compensation than that received by import substituting activities. Additionally, the distributive effects and their bearing upon the design of incentives should be more fully explored, both as regards their internal repercussions and the impact of exports by TNCs, building on the recent contributions by a number of authors (Díaz-Alejandro, 1976; Fajnzylber, 1971; Helleiner, 1973; Morgenstern and Muller, 1976; Tironi, 1978); these are also relevant to the case of import substitution

As regards access to external markets, there are, in addition to the ground covered by Perry in this volume, two elements related to national action which have scarcely been examined. The first concerns the characteristics needed in co-operation schemes among LDCs, if they are to promote reciprocal trade on a stable and equitable basis (UNCTAD, 1973). The second relates to research on the *marketing life cycle* of LDCs' exportables, using elements of the technological life cycle (Vernon,

1966), and support by the domestic market argument (Linder, 1961), especially in relation to the role played by integration schemes as a trampoline for exports to the rest of the world of products with high value added.

3 NON-TARIFF MECHANISMS

The level and structure of Latin America's international trade have been controlled by a wide range of mechanisms. Most of the countries have had frequent recourse to import tariffs and tariff exemptions, multiple exchange rates, prior deposits on imports, exchange controls, free zones, prohibitions, quotas, and drawbacks for the regulation of foreign trade (Friss, 1969; Kiss, 1973; Díaz-Alejandro, 1976; Ffrench-Davis, 1979, Chapter IX). Among other instruments which affect foreign trade, use has been made of state purchasing power, preferential loans, systems of accelerated depreciation, and tax incentives for the production of import substitutes and exportables. In the two foregoing sections the analysis concentrated on import tariffs and export incentives. Nevertheless, these two instruments and the exchange rate are not enough in themselves to regulate trade in the circumstances common in LDCs.

In this section we examine the problem of achieving the desired profiles of protection in a framework of multiple internal disequilibria, transnational corporations with maximisation objectives which differ from those of national firms, a central government and public enterprises that exert considerable influence in trade flows, and international markets suffering from economic cycles and price instability.

(a) Non-tariff instruments

Research on non-tariff devices has been sporadic, and investigation of the role they might play in LDCs has been less prominent still. The theoretical literature has principally concentrated upon the comparison of tariffs and quotas in a stable external framework, and upon taxes applied at the frontier and different taxation systems for internal transactions. Systematic analyses are exceptional (Baldwin, 1970). Nevertheless, some international institutions – such as GATT and UNCTAD – have devoted increasing attention to these instruments, owing to their importance in industrialised countries as obstacles to LDC exports.

We may distinguish three categories of non-tariff instruments, on the basis of the way in which they regulate trade: (i) those which directly affect the tariff-inclusive cost of imported goods or the income received by the exporter; (ii) quantitative controls; and (iii) regulations of a qualitative nature, consisting of controls intended to ensure the full efficacy of the levels of protection planned.

(i) Mechanisms which operate via price or quantity   Among the mechanisms which affect directly the cost or income, free zones and systems based upon the assembly of imported parts have become increasingly significant. In the free zones, which represent a mechanism to exempt tradables from tariffs and sometimes internal taxes, production and/or marketing operations take place in areas isolated from the domestic market, with regulations and price relations which differ from those in the rest of the country. This therefore tends to promote economic dualism, developing 'enclaves' rather than activities integrated into national industry. The 'assembly' industries provide an extreme example of this segmentation, promoted by industrialised countries by means of preferential customs treatment for imports from LDCs based on components exported by the industrialised countries themselves (see Chapter 10 in this volume). Other incentives in favour of exports which have gained ground are authorisations to apply special charges to costs (Gal-Edd, 1971), and preferential credits (UNCTAD-GATT, 1974).

Many of the promotion devices mentioned are not particularly suitable for LDCs, but tend to be internationally acceptable. As a result, the countries which apply them do not suffer retaliation on grounds of unfair competition (Balassa and Sharpston, 1976).

With respect to quantitative restrictions, it should be pointed out that export quotas may not only originate in the producing country, but also can be imposed by the importing country. For example, the international textile agreement provides for quantitative restrictions in importing and exporting countries. Similarly, there are quotas which result from the external suppliers 'voluntarily' restricting the volume of their exports (Bhagwati, 1976) under the threat of imposition of counter-vailing tariffs or quotas by the importing country.

(ii) Qualitative mechanisms   These are the mechanisms which have received least attention in the specialised literature. They are directed to ensuring the full efficacy of trade policies that affect *directly* the relative

prices of traded goods. Qualitative mechanisms are not intended to modify directly the volume of trade or the prices at which it takes place. They include controls upon remittances of foreign currency, import or export applications, and a requirement to obtain the approval of the body directing foreign trade (also known as licensing or prior registration) before clearing customs; official prices for customs purposes; regimes regulating foreign trade of public enterprises and TNCs; quality control, and mechanisms to protect the life and health of individuals, the natural environment, cultural endowment, and national security.

Controls on trade and capital movements are intended to ensure that remittances and reimbursements are equivalent to the price of the goods traded, and coincide with the values utilised to calculate customs duties (Bhagwati, 1969a).

The overstatement of import prices, for example, is encouraged by the maintenance of an artificially low exchange rate. This can be countered by means of an efficient exchange-rate policy for LDCs. Even so, this is not sufficient to prevent fraud, as false declarations reduce the total liability in taxes or duties. Furthermore, during processes of social change fraudulent declarations are motivated by capital flights sought by economic groups.

Administrative controls may be applied at different stages of the process of exchange: at the outset, with prior approval of applications, before customs clearance, and, finally, when foreign currency is bought or sold. The different stages are mutually supportive, as information gathered at each helps to evaluate the performance of the others. If these regulations are to be effective, access to currency markets must also be controlled. In fact, the checking of prices declared by the importer cannot prevent capital flight if free movement of capital is maintained. The controls may be costly and bureaucratic, or efficient in terms of time and cost, and thus the way in which they are designed is of crucial importance.

(b) Trading activities of transnational corporations

First, income transfers are frequently produced by the manipulation of the prices of goods and services exchanged between subsidiaries located in different countries but belonging to the same parent company, with the purpose of minimising payments of taxes and tariffs (Vaitsos, 1974; Lall, 1976).

Second, TNC's subsidiaries may also acquire imported inputs from the supplier of other subsidiaries throughout the world, even if the cost ex-customs is larger than that of a national product of similar quality. This may respond not only to a bias in favour of imports, but also because of economies of scale achieved by the parent company through the centralisation of purchases of inputs and/or the exploitation of idle capacity in other subsidiaries. In these circumstances, the marginal costs for TNCs are lower than average costs, and hence it may be convenient for the subsidiary in question to purchase abroad despite the fact that the 'normal' import price is higher than the internal price (Ffrench-Davis, 1974).

Thus, consideration should be given to the establishment of selective controls going beyond checking the prices declared, allowing potential national suppliers information regarding the purchasing policies of subsidiaries, and leading to imports being made only when the ex-customs price is lower than the cost of similar domestic substitutes.

(c) Purchases by state enterprises

In many LDCs the public sector has considerable purchasing power. Paradoxically, several countries which have undertaken ambitious processes of import substitution have granted their public enterprises implicit or explicit exemptions from import duties, thus failing to exploit the contribution which public sector purchasing policy can make to the viability or efficiency of national industrial activities. As a result, the norms which regulate the market behaviour of public enterprises are of considerable significance. We shall return to this point in Section 5.

(d) The problem of instability

The theoretical literature on international economics tends to operate on the assumption of stable external markets. In such a situation, the opening of a country allows the elimination of the instability of internal prices of tradables.[7] In fact, however, international markets, constituted as they are of the excess supply and demand of each nation for tradables, are relatively unstable and heterogeneous.

External instability poses for each country the need to choose between allowing it to be transmitted to the domestic economy or adopting mechanisms to neutralise its effect. If the first option is chosen, the transmission of fluctuations affects domestic price indexes, if the given commodities are of some significance, such as foodstuffs for mass consumption; if prices are rigid downward, it tends to have an inflationary ratchet effect (Ffrench-Davis, 1968). On the production side, instability implies a fluctuating demand for exportables and for import substitutes; where capital markets are imperfect, factors of production immobile and profit maximisation horizons short, price fluctuations induce an inefficient allocation of resources, and are a cause of structural unemployment. Among the mechanisms available to combat external price instability are specific tariffs, reference prices and compensatory transfers. The latter may take the form of permanent transfers, such as taxes or subsidies, or temporary transfers, such as obligatory credits or debts. Before these mechanisms can be applied, it is essential to distinguish between long-term trends in international prices and reversible or short-term fluctuations. Given that there will be uncertainty in every case as to the precise trend, and that any stabilising mechanism will involve administrative costs, it is necessary to establish how far the policy will stop from full stabilisation.

(e) An efficient set of instruments

Even when an abstract analysis leads to a recommendation for the use of a single selective instrument to protect import substitutes (effective tariffs) and exports (effective subsidies), the simultaneous use of various instruments may be convenient in practice. For example, multiple instruments may be advisable if it is difficult to apply a single selective instrument with the intensity and flexibility desired. The difficulties involved may be institutional obstacles, political constraints or psychological considerations: examples might include legal obstacles to customs duties, the time needed to change existing norms due to conflicts between executive and legislative branches, and the belief that a dispersion of restrictions across various instruments generates lower inflationary expectations. These are difficulties which can be overcome in the long term, but only if it proves possible to live through the short-term first.

Furthermore, situations frequently arise in which the partial application of other non-tariff instruments is advisable. This depends upon the nature of the external sector and of the parallel objectives pursued. Special situations would include unpredictable balance of payments crises, budget deficits, and commitment to redistributive policies.

Finally, even when nothing prevents the introduction of tariffs and subsidies on trade goods, it will probably be convenient to set up a complementary system of selective qualitative regulations, among them control of access to foreign exchange markets, of prices declared by importers and exporters, and of operations of TNCs subsidiaries, the use of the purchasing power of public institutions as a means of promoting industrialisation, quality controls, and measures aimed at preventing the transmission of the instability of international markets to the domestic economy.

(f) Priorities for further research

Numerous studies have examined the substitutability between tariffs and other means of regulating trade; others have examined instability, and different aspects of the behaviour of TNCs. In contrast, little research has been devoted to ways in which the problems arising out of the presence of instability and of TNCs might be faced, or to the role of non-tariff instruments in situations which orthodox theory considers special cases, but which in reality are common. Of these 'special' cases, we shall refer briefly to emergencies, external instability, and the presence of TNCs.

Given the frequency of balance of payments crises, high priority should be allotted to the systematic study of the mechanisms most appropriate for coping with them with the minimum disturbance to the rest of the economy. The set of instruments which might satisfy that purpose has been described in part in the previous sub-section.

It is difficult to cope efficiently with instability in external prices in such a way that short-term fluctuations are avoided while the allocation of national resources is allowed to respond to trends in international markets. The operation of any of these mechanisms requires a definition of the 'normal' price or of the trend, as well as information regarding national prices. Both elements present difficulties, which can be overcome in two ways: first, by limiting the system to the most important products only; and, second, by defining a range of prices beyond which compensatory mechanisms will enter into operation, rather than a unique 'normal' price. Scarce research has been done on criteria for defining optimal ranges for price fluctuations permitted in internal markets and the coverage of stabilisation mechanisms, in terms of quantity and types of goods, in a framework of limited administrative capacity and uncertainty regarding trends in international markets.

With regard to TNCs, one priority for research concerns the theoretical and empirical analysis of the mechanisms appropriate to control their foreign trade transactions, and the aspects most relevant to negotiations between these companies and national governments.

4 THE PROCESS OF ADJUSTMENT

The costs entailed in the transition to a new state of equilibrium received notoriously scant attention in the orthodox trade theory. Hence the traditional recommendations with regard to tariff policy, economic integration or foreign capital movements minimise the significance of adjustment problems, distributive consequences and disequilibrating movements they may provoke.

(a) The costs of the transition

If sufficient attention is not devoted to the adjustment process when economic policies are designed, the forgone income due to the temporary under-utilisation of productive resources may outweigh the eventual positive effects of a policy which supposedly leads to an optimal position in the long term.

The cost of the adjustment process tends to increase with the heterogeneity of the economy and the instability it faces. The heterogeneity of social and economic structure makes slower and more difficult the transfer of resources from recessive activities to those in expansion, making adjustments to sudden changes in markets or in national policies costly. Instability also implies difficulty in identifying the appropriate signals for guiding the reallocation of resources. In heterogeneous economies measures should be considered which avoid unstable signals and promote gradual planned adjustments in foreign trade, along with direct action upon the structures of demand and/or production in order to complement indirect policies, especially in the case of acute disequilibria.

The cost of abrupt changes is brought about not only by the under-utilisation of productive potential, but also by internal distributive effects which tend to be regressive, given the differing capacity to react of each group. At the international level, the position of the countries of the centre tends to be intrinsically stronger because of their greater economic capacity and adaptability, and of the various defence mechanisms to which they resort in order to confront external changes.

Finally, the process of adjustment itself may be unstable, in the sense that it does not lead to a new equilibrium, or that it sets in motion disequilibrating movements. For example, capital does not always flow to regions where it is scarce. And this cannot be explained simply in terms of political instability, as the phenomenon can be observed not only internationally, but also within individual countries, in which growing regional disequilibria can be seen (Barzanti, 1965). The utilisation of excessively short maximisation horizons, the existence of dynamic external economies, and the limited information available to suppliers and buyers give rise to disequilibrating movements.

(b) Priorities for further research

The problem of adjustment has been present in two significant contexts in the real world: in relation to instability, and in relation to the processes of liberalisation of foreign trade. We have discussed the former in Section 3, and the research priority is to distinguish between trends and fluctuations, and to design adequate mechanisms of internal stabilisation.

In the case of the processes of liberalisation, political and technical issues arise. With regard to the former, the proponents of an abrupt removal of barriers assert that liberalisation in any other way is impossible. In this connection there are two points on which greater knowledge would be useful for future policy making: (i) the size of the adjustment cost incurred by an abrupt removal of barriers, the degree to which it is increased if liberalisation is combined with recessionary domestic policies, and its comparability with the present value of the eventual benefits of liberalisation; and (ii) the extent to which an abrupt removal of barriers proves permanent, or is reversed after a short period on account of the social and political problems it provokes.

With respect to the more technical implications, an area of research priority relates to the criteria for determining the optimal path of a change in tariff policy. In addition to (i) determining the target profile correctly, which has generally not been done in cases where the removal of barriers has been the simple-minded commitment to free trade, it is important (ii) to examine the effects produced by different stages of liberalisation, (iii) to identify the capacity to reallocate resources and the obstacles it faces, and (iv) to analyse the government actions which facilitate the reorganisation of the structure of production.[8]

5 THE ROLE OF THE STATE AND THE EXTERNAL SECTOR

The limited consideration of the role played by the state in the national economy constitutes another weak aspect of conventional theory, despite the fact that in several LDCs state intervention has been of great significance. Some of the most relevant issues relate to the role of the state as a negotiator of improved access to external markets and with TNCs, as leader of economic activity in markets in which comparative advantages are relatively diffuse, and the organisation of public bodies fulfilling the double role of dynamising investment and serving as a national alternative to the leading role which TNCs would otherwise assume.

(a) Access to external markets

If international markets are imperfect, and knowledge regarding new export markets is scarce and costly, a policy of negotiation and organisation by the state provides a mechanism capable of improving the volume, stability and price obtained for non-traditional exports from LDCs.

In general terms there are two forces in international markets which act in favour of perfecting them: the reduction of tariff restrictions in industrialised countries, and the appearance of new TNCs in competition with those already in existence; and two forces which increase the extent to which they are segmented: the growing importance of intra-trade between the subsidiaries of TNCs and the enlarged role of non-tariff restrictions in industrialised countries.

The instability and lack of competition in some markets brings up the need to undertake action, directed at modifying the conditions of access faced by non-traditional exports from LDCs. The possibilities for action cover a wide range, the nature of which depends upon the characteristics of the external market in question.

The alternatives include measures such as joint action between groups of countries to regulate the functioning of TNCs and co-ordinate relationships with them (Wionczek, 1971; Tironi, 1977), the creation of MNCs owned by LDCs, or the possibility of signing agreements which provide better access to markets in industrialised countries in exchange for guaranteed access to the raw materials possessed by LDCs. Finally, the search for new export markets within LDCs is a vein which has scarcely been explored, despite its long presence in government thinking and in the literature (Prebisch, 1964; Bhagwati, 1969).

The systematic expansion of reciprocal trade between LDCs might be achieved in two ways, by processes of economic integration or by specialisation agreements.

Economic integration constitutes a generalised negotiation directed at a reciprocal opening of markets between member countries, which may rest exclusively upon the liberation of reciprocal trade, or may extend to the regional planning of investment.

The regional planning of investment – including specialisation or production agreements – represents a more ambitious form of integration, which can complement the harmonisation of commercial policies. Its essential characteristic consists of the allocation to each member country of advantages in the development of particular economic activities. In this way the decision as to where production should take place is taken out of the market place. The schemes have been proposed with two key purposes in mind. First they comprise one of the mechanisms for assuring the equitable distribution of benefits between member countries, avoiding the tendency of the market to produce a geographic polarisation of industrial production (Robson, (ed.), 1971; UNCTAD, 1973). Second, they are intended to plan the investments which will take advantage of the economies of scale arising out of the enlarged market and to afford potential producers, public or private, a clearer picture of 'acquirable' comparative advantages, to which we turn now.

(b) Planning

There are at least two arguments for direct state involvement in economic activity, as a complement to the role of decentralised units (firms and consumers). These concern the wide range of markets and products which might be the subject of negotiations abroad, and the practical difficulty of identifying comparative advantages.

As a result of the direct character of actions related to the removal of obstacles to access to external markets, and the variety of products and markets which might come under consideration, these policies must be selective. Selection may be made in terms of (i) the zones in which efforts to improve means of transport will be concentrated, (ii) the regions to which the search for information and the diffusion of exportable supplies will be directed preferentially, and (iii) the countries, TNCs and products upon which the negotiating capacity will be concentrated. An additional point concerns the allocation of responsibility for marketing exports: the most appropriate organisational formula will depend upon the nature of the external markets, the type of product, and, of course, the ideological orientation of the government.

In economies undergoing a process of change, the apprehension of comparative advantages cannot be relatively defined and known, except in the cases of goods whose advantages are based upon (i) rich natural resources, climate, or geographic location, (ii) some acquired characteristic (captive technology, exceptionally skilled labour), (iii) the significant weight of labour supply. These cases are far from covering all possible productive activities; there are many projects where costs and benefits depend to a significant extent upon external economies or economies of specialisation, and upon the size of the markets at their disposal. In these conditions it is probable that the comparative advantages will be diffuse, and the market mechanism alone unable to give a single optimal answer (Ffrench-Davis, 1977).

At a more subjective level, it appears that private investors tend to overestimate the significance of existing externalities. This phenomenon may have its origins in narrow 'economic horizons', the lack of information available to the investor, and the resulting influence of the past on the image of the future (Arrow, 1974), factors which also tend to discourage infant industries.

(c) Public enterprises

Productive activities must be implemented through one of the multiple modalities which might be adopted by public or private, multinational or transnational companies.

In LDCs, with limited capital markets, narrow horizons, dynamic external economies and diffuse comparative advantages, it is difficult for national private firms to play the leading role in industrial development. If this is the case, in the absence of public enterprises, the role remains vacant or is taken on by TNCs. In consequence, the anti-state bias which proliferates in the conventional literature tends to limit the possibilities for dynamic and autonomous development.

An aspect of public enterprises which merits attention concerns mechanisms and norms which assure their efficient functioning. Direct and indirect norms may be established to improve their contribution to industrial development. Indirect actions may include: (i) subjecting them to normal customs treatment; (ii) avoiding tax rebates to importing companies; and (iii) adopting regulatory norms of such a nature that these institutions take tariffs into consideration when framing their purchasing policies. As for direct action, the central body directing the process of industrialisation may actively promote the development of activities supplying intermediate and capital goods, using public sector demand as a support base. Their decisions should naturally be subjected to norms of social efficiency, in the sense that they satisfy the specific objectives for which they were created, and the general objectives of national development strategy.

The literature on criteria and mechanisms for the regulation of public enterprises in LDCs and on the experience of specific cases is particularly scanty (Sheahan, 1976).

(d) Priorities for further research

The role of the market and of the state merits preferential attention in LDCs. The theme covers the criteria for defining the sphere of action of each, and the forms of intervention (direct or indirect) to be adopted by the state. It is undeniable that, beyond ideological options, technical elements enter into play, and that under the guise of technical 'purity' orthodox theory harbours a sizeable ideological content.

In the area of international trade, the issue of the role of the market *vis-à-vis* that of the state is present in analyses relating to criteria for defining profiles of protection, types of disequilibria in internal markets and the incidence of tariff redundancy, the relationship between export promotion and import substitution, the alternative approaches to the problems posed by TNCs, political and institutional obstacles and external instability, the function of public enterprises as dynamising agents for autonomous development, and the regulation of their behaviour, and the significance of the characteristics of the process of adjustment in inflexible and heterogenous economies.

NOTES

1 Excellent comprehensive accounts appear in Bhagwati (1968), Corden (1974) and Johnson (1965).
2 Some distortions (such as external economies or dynamic externalities) disappear only with development; others are connected with foreign countries or decision makers (such as oligopolistic or unstable foreign markets), while others still can only be partially removed (as is the case in many instances with unemployment).

3 Made-to-measure tariffs, on the basis of the costs of national production, may also generate the same negative dynamic effects (Corden, 1974, pp. 224–31).
4 This point is generally ignored in the literature. Exceptions to this are Vanek (1971), Corden (1974, Chapters 3, 4) and Balassa (1977, pp. 18–19).
5 Empirical data from the Andean countries indicate, for example, that in the industrial sector (ISIC classification, to three digits) the activity which uses labour most intensively absorbs ten or twenty times more labour per unit of value added or of capital, respectively, than the activity at the other end of the scale of factor proportions (Garcia and Mezzera, 1976).
6 These priorities suggest a change in emphasis from empirical research on effective protection in a supposedly optimal framework, to criteria for defining a system of effective protection which would be 'optimal' in the sub-optimal framework prevailing in LDCs.
7 It is assumed usually that no shifts take place between importables and exportables, and that the substitutability between domestic and foreign tradables is very high.
8 This is the aspect which has attracted detailed examination, in relation to the problems of adjustment affecting developed countries. See Baldwin and Mutti (1973).

REFERENCES

Arrow, K. (1974) 'Limited Knowledge and Economic Analysis', *American Economic Review*, March.
Balassa, B. (ed.) (1971) *The Structure of Protection in Developing Countries* (Baltimore: Johns Hopkins Press).
Balassa, B. (1977) *Policy Reform in Developing Countries* (New York: Pergamon).
—— and Sharpston, M. (1976) 'Export Subsidies by Developing Countries: Issues of Policy', Working paper, no 238, (Washington, DC: World Bank).
Baldwin, R. (1970) *Non-tariff Distortions of International Trade* (London: Allen & Unwin).
—— and Mutti, J. (1973) 'Policy Issues in Adjustment Assistance: The United States', in Hughes (ed.) (1973).
Barzanti, S. (1965) *The Underdeveloped Areas within the Common Markets* (Princeton University Press).
Bhagwati, J. (1968) 'The Theory and Practice of Commercial Policy: Departures from Unified Exchange Rates', Special Papers in International Economics, no. 8 (Princeton University Press).
—— (1969a) 'Fiscal Policies, the Faking of Foreign Trade Declarations, and the Balance of Payments', in Bhagwati, *Trade, Tariffs and Growth*, (Cambridge, Massachusetts: MIT).

—— (1969b) 'Trade Liberalization among LDCs: Trade Theory and GATT Rules', in Bhagwati, *Trade, Tariffs, and Growth*.

—— (1976) 'Market Disruption, Export Market Disruption, Compensation and GATT reform', *World Development*, December.

—— (1978) *Anatomy and Consequences of Exchange Control Regimes*, National Bureau of Economic Research (New York: Ballinger).

Cardoso, F. and Faletto, E. (1969) *Dependencia y Desarrollo en América Latina* (Mexico City: Siglo XXI).

Chenery, H., and Strout, A. (1966) 'Foreign Assistance and Economic Development', *American Economic Review*, September.

Cooper, C. H., and Massell, B. (1965) 'Towards a General Theory of Customs Unions for Developing Countries', *Journal of Political Economy*, October.

Corden, M. (1971) *The Theory of Protection* (Oxford: Clarendon Press).

—— (1974) *Trade Policy and Economic Welfare* (London: Oxford University Press).

Díaz-Alejandro, C. (1975) 'Trade Policies and Economic Development', in Kenen (ed.) (1975).

—— (1976) *Trade Regimes and Economic Development: Colombia*, (New York: National Bureau of Economic Research).

ECLA (1974) 'Algunas Conclusiones Relativas a la Integración, la Industrialización y el Desarrollo de América Latina', *Boletin Económico de América Latina*, vol. XIX, nos 1, 2.

—— (1977) 'En torno a las Ideas de la Cepal: Problemas de la Industrialización en América Latina', *Cuadernos de la Cepal* no. 14, Santiago.

Emmanuel, A. (1972) *Unequal Exchange* (New York: Monthly Review Press).

Fajnzylber, F. (1971) 'La Empresa Internacional en la Industrialización de América Latina', in Stanzick and Godoy (eds) *Inversiones Extranjeras y Transferencia de Tecnología en América Latina* (Santiago: ILDIS-FLACSO).

—— (1976) 'Oligopolio, Empresas Transnacionales y Estilos de Desarrollo', *El Trimestre Económico*, no. 171, July–September.

Ffrench-Davis, R. (1968) 'Export Quotas under Market Instability', *American Journal of Agricultural Economics*, September.

—— (1974) 'Integración de la Gran Minería a la economía nacional: El Rol de las Politicas Económicas', in Ffrench-Davis and Tironi (eds) *El Cobre en el Desarrollo Nacional* (Santiago: Ediciones Nueva Universidad).

—— (1977) 'Distribución de Beneficios y Eficiencia en la Integración

Económica', *Estudios CIEPLAN*, no. 18, Santiago, October.

—— (1979) *Economía Internacional: Teorías y Políticas para el Desarrollo*, (Mexico City: Fondo de Cultura Económica).

——(ed.) (1980) *Lecturas Sobre Intercambio y Desarrollo*, (Mexico City: Fondo de Cultura Económica).

Friss, I. (ed.) (1969) *Reform of the Economic Mechanism in Hungary* (Budapest: Academy of Sciences).

Gal-Edd, I. (1971) 'Tax Incentives for Export', *Journal of World Trade Law*, May–June.

García, E. and Mezzera, J. (1976) 'Los Instrumentos de Integración y la Creación de Empleos en el Grupo Andino', Santiagó: PREALC.

Helleiner, G. (1973) 'Manufactured Exports from Less Developed Countries and Multinational Firms', *Economic Journal*, March.

—— (1978) 'World Markets and Developing Countries', Overseas Development Council, May.

Hirschman, A. (1958) *The Strategy of Economic Development* (New Haven, Connecticut: Yale University Press).

—— (1973) *Desarrollo y América Latina*, Lecture no. 5 (Mexico City: Fondo de Cultura Económica).

Hughes, H. (ed.) (1973) *Prospects for Partnership: Industrialization and Trade Policies in the 1970s* (Washington, DC: World Bank).

Johnson, H. (1965) 'Optimal Trade Invervention in the Presence of Domestic Distortions', in Baldwin *et al.*, *Trade, Growth, and the Balance of Payments* (Amsterdam: North Holland).

JUNAC (1973) 'Orientaciones para la Elaboración del Arancel Externo Común', Lima, October.

—— (1976) 'El Proceso de Elaboración del Arancel Externo Común', J/PE/63, Lima, March.

Katz, J. (1976) *Importación de Tecnología, Aprendizaje e Industrialización Dependiente* (Mexico City: Fondo de Cultura Económica).

Keesing, D. (1966) 'Labor Skills and Comparative Advantage', *American Economic Review*, May.

Kenen, P. (ed.) (1975) *International Trade and Finance: Frontiers for Research* (Cambridge University Press).

Kiss, T. (ed.) (1973) *The Market of Socialist Economic Integration* (Budapest: Academy of Sciences).

Krueger, A. (1976) 'Growth, Distortions, and Patterns of Trade among Many Countries' *Princeton Studies in International Finance*, no. 4, February.

Lall, S. (1976) 'Developing Countries and Multinational Corporations', *Commonwealth Economic Papers*, no. 5, London.

184   *Latin America and the New International Economic Order*

Leibenstein, H. (1966) 'Allocative Efficiency versus X-efficiency', *American Economic Review*, June.
Linder, S. (1961) *An Essay on Trade and Transformation* (Stockholm: Almqvist & Wicksell).
Little, I., Scitovsky, T., and Scott, M. (1970) *Industry and Trade in Some Developing Countries* (London: Oxford University Press).
Magee, S. (1976) *International Trade and Distortions in Factor Markets* (New York: Dekker).
McEwan, A. and Weisskopf, T. (eds) (1970) *The Economic Problem: A Book of Readings in Political Economy* (New York: Prentice-Hall).
Morgenstern, R. and Muller, R. (1976) 'Multinational versus Local Corporations in LDCs: An Econometric Analysis of Export Performance in Latin America', *Southern Economic Journal*, January.
Pinto, A. (1970) 'Naturaleza e Implicaciones de la Heterogeneidad Estructural en América Latina', *El Trimestre Económico*, no. 145, January–March.
PREALC (1975) *El Problema del Empleo en América Latina y el Caribe: Situación, Perspectivas y Políticas*, Santiago.
Prebisch, R. (1964) *Nueva Politica Commercial para el Desarrollo* (Mexico City: Fondo de Cultura Económica).
Robson, P. (ed.) (1971) *Economic Integration* (Harmondsworth: Penguin).
Schydlowsky, D. (1976) 'Capital Utilization, Growth, Employment and Price Estabilization' (Boston University: Center for Latin American Development Studies).
Sheahan, J. (1976) 'Public Enterprise in Developing Countries', in W. Shepard (ed.), *Public Enterprise* (Mass.: Lexington).
Sunkel, O. (1971) 'Capitalismo Transnacional y Desintegración Nacional', *El Trimestre Económico*, no. 150, April–June.
Teitel, S. (1975) 'Acerca de la Hipótesis de Invariabilidad en el Ordenamiento de las Industrias de Acuerdo con la Intensidad en la Utilización de los Factores', *El Trimestre Económico*, no. 166, April–June.
Tironi, E. (1977) 'Políticas Frente al Capital Extranjero en la Integración Andina', *Estudios CIEPLAN*, no. 11, Santiago, June.
—— (1978) 'Teoría de los Costos y Beneficios de la Inversión Extranjera en Procesos de Integración', *Notas Técnicas*, no. 9, CIEPLAN.
UNCTAD (1973) 'La Distribución de Beneficios y Costos en la Integración entre Países en Desarrollo', *Problemas Actuales de la Integración Económica*, TD/9/394 (New York: United Nations).

—— GATT (1974) *Financiación de las Exportaciones*, (Geneva: International Trade Center).

Uri, P. (1973) 'The Role of the Multinational Corporation', in Hughes (ed.) (1973).

Urquidi, V., and Thorp, R. (eds) (1973) *Latin America in the International Economy* (London: Macmillan).

Vaitsos, C. (1974) *Intercountry Income Distribution and Transnational Enterprises* (Oxford: Clarendon Press).

Vanek, J. (1959) 'The Natural Resource Content of Foreign Trade, 1870–1955, and the Relative Abundance of Natural Resources in the United States', *Review of Economics and Statistics*, May.

—— (1971) 'Tariffs, Economic Welfare and Development Potential', *The Economic Journal*, December.

Vernon, R. (1966) 'International Investment and International Trade in the Product Cycle', *Quarterly Journal of Economics*, May.

—— (1978) *Multinational Enterprise Project*, Annual Progress Report (Cambridge, Massachusetts: Harvard Business School).

Wionczek, M. (1971) 'Hacia el Establecimiento de un trato Común de la Inversión Extranjera en el Mercado Común Andino', *El Trimestre Económico*, no. 150, April–June.

13 Foreign Trade, Industrialisation and Development Policies: a Comment

PEDRO MALAN

My comments will be divided into three parts. The first part is related to Ffrench-Davis's basic stand with respect to the underlying 'theories' we have grown accustomed to see utilised to analyse – and often criticise – foreign trade regimes in developing countries. The second part deals briefly with some specific points in his essay, those about which, in Ffrench-Davis's judgement, 'conventional knowledge is least relevant, and research in LDCs is most limited'. The third part is a rather brief comment on Ffrench-Davis's research priorities in this wide, shadowy and changing area.

1 THEORETICAL ISSUES

There is now an impressive body of literature on the normative theory and practice of trade policies and the principles of government intervention which goes all the way from the abstractions of pure barter theory to specific policy prescriptions, and has evolved to a careful analysis of the relationships between 'domestic distortions' and trade restrictions.

The conclusions of these latter developments are unmistakeably clear: restrictions on foreign trade should never serve as first-best compensation for domestic distortions in product and/or factor markets. These distortions could – and should – be directly offset by an appropriate use of taxes and subsidies – on production, consumption or factor use – for otherwise, 'welfare' could be easily reduced by mispriced scarce resources and excess supplies or excess demands in both commodity and factor markets.

The standard two commodities (both tradables) trade model – a real model where full employment always obtains – has been widely used to clarify the relevant issues and policy prescriptions. Distortions were identified as departures from the marginal conditions assuring Pareto optimality: equality among the foreign rate of transformation, the domestic rate of transformation in production and the domestic rate of substitution in consumption.

These results, and their extensions, do require a careful scrutiny of the conceptual problems involved in some key elements of the implicit model, specifically (a) the use of the community indifference map, (b) the significance and classification of 'distortions', and (c) the so-called non-economic objectives of government intervention. With respect to (a), the distribution of income and the individual tastes that determine the demand for the two tradable commodities of the standard model are assumed to be summarised by a family of well-behaved (convex) indifference curves. Since 'welfare' is associated with the *currently* available flow of goods and services, this map of community indifference curves represents ordinary welfare levels as well as community preferences, only on the assumption that a *given* income distribution is maintained by an independent policy; that is, that a social welfare function is being consistently – *and costlessly* – applied.

This is a rather stringent hypothesis since, as we know, the so-called community indifference map may be very unstable. Whenever international prices change, each country's product mix will change and its income distribution will be altered through changes in factor prices; as a result, community indifference curves will change shape and position.

Be that as it may, the fact is that, whenever the traditional definition of social welfare (the currently available flow of goods and services) is utilised, the only arguments for trade intervention allowed by theory are those resulting in *optimal* intervention in the form of tariffs due to monopoly power in international trade and/or those leading to *optimal* intervention in the form of domestic tax-cum-subsidies on consumption, production or factor use.

However, when non-traditional social welfare functions are utilised, such as those emphasising conflicts between present and future consumption or those that consider so-called non-economic objectives, the theory has no more clear-cut answers, except to continue to insist that, in principle and broadly speaking, a movement towards 'freer' trade is the best solution.

The classification of these departures from the first-best assumptions of the theory, whether behavioural (non-utility or non-profit maximisation by decision-making units), environmental (state-imposed or not), or technological, ought to be seen as what they really are: the expression of underdeveloped economies' imbalances and institutional inadequacies and often the result of development efforts attempted without great confidence in the capacity of the price mechanism to induce non-marginal transfers of real resources – one of the basic purposes of government intervention in most semi-industrialised countries.

In short, elegant, formally rigorous and logically derived as they were, the conclusions of the pure theory are indeed a poor guide to policy discussions in actual less-developed economies where 'distortions' are very often merely names for some very real characteristics of their economic sectors. In fact LDCs are 'dominated' by market fragmentation or segmentation (especially for factors) and there are no 'costless' government policies to correct them.

The *pure theory* approach to government intervention, therefore, is not of much help in understanding the *rationale* underlying *actual* trade intervention and the reason why the foreign exchange market has frequently been a privileged locus for this intervention.

There is another strand in the literature, not so theoretically inclined, but which also influences Anglo-Saxon tinkering with foreign trade regimes in LDCs. I have in mind the inability of conventional *macroeconomic* theory to understand and interpret analytically the fact that growth is often foreign-exchange constrained in semi-industrialised economies undergoing a process of rapid change. Indeed, except for the so-called two-gap literature (admittedly a very special and rather crude class of models), for the main theoretical tradition in the 'theory' of balance of payment adjustment there is no analytical meaning in the idea of a foreign exchange constraint on any growth process. Since, for most of the profession, growth (given the productivity of capital) depends upon the rate of domestic savings, a foreign exchange shortage is simply a sign of an overvalued exchange rate, unwarranted government interventions in foreign trade or simply inconsistencies between the targets of income and export growth.

This view had three major implications. First, it led to a strong critique of overvalued currencies (and of inflation, since usually currencies become overvalued as a result of permissive attitudes towards inflation), of the export tax implicit in any differential between export and imports rate, and of any anti-export biases involved in government policies such as an excessive concern with diverting exportables to domestic consumption. The first criticism is justified, but the other two are incorrect generalisations.

Second, it led to a strong criticism of the most frequently attempted solution of the problem: import substitution, industrialisation implemented through import duties, quantitative restrictions, multiple exchange rates and other *ad-hoc* devices, all justified by some variant of the infant industry argument. As expected, the larger and more diversified countries went farther in this process than economies restricted by the size of their domestic markets, incurring high inefficiency costs and – according to some observers – potentially aggravating the problem they were meant to solve.

Third, it led to a downplaying of historically specific situations such as the changing external *demand* conditions facing a developing country and the productive structure of the country whose supply of exportables was supposedly being held back through policy-created obstacles.

2 CONVENTIONAL WISDOM AND LDCS

Ricardo Ffrench-Davis's excellent essay could be seen as a discussion – and critique – of the conventional wisdom implied in the two major strands of Anglo-Saxon literature just mentioned. The merit of his paper is that he does so not in *general* terms, but rather by selecting specific issues for further discussion, thereby making clear the shortcomings of the conventional approaches.

The issues discussed by Ffrench-Davis are the following: (a) criteria for (tariff) protection; (b) export promotion and import substitution; (c) non-tariff instruments of trade regulation; (d) the role of the state in foreign trade and; (e) the adjustment process.

In commenting on each of these issues, one sees Ffrench-Davis's 'long struggle to escape' from the orthodox straitjackets and stipulations of the conventional views referred to in Section 1 above. One may question specific points of the discussion, such as, in connection with (a) above, Ffrench-Davis's hopes for an 'efficient' selective system of tariff protection which would take into account the changing character of the productive structure of the economy, the rate of diffusion of technological progress, labour absorption and infant economic activities. The discussion is stimulating but the conclusions are probably still too general.

With respect to the discussion on export promotion and import substitution, Ffrench-Davis notes that the recommendation for efficient allocation of resources, equality – at the margin – between the domestic resource cost of generating a unit of foreign exchange through export and saving it through import-substitution, is too general a formula for actual policy-making in LDCs. He rightly points out that lack of selectivity 'can bring an inefficient diversion of resources towards exports', the incentives to which have a fiscal cost which must be taken into account and which is not present in protection for import substitution activities (the cost of which is borne by the domestic consumers). His suggestions, after a good discussion, fall into the wide ground between the two extremes of 'free-trade and arbitrary protectionism'.

The section on 'non-tariff instruments of trade regulation' is a long and useful discussion about the plethora of *ad-hoc* measures which semi-industrialised economies growing under adverse external conditions resort to.

The section on the adjustment process then addresses itself to the crucial problem of the day in Latin America – and elsewhere: namely, the burden and *distribution* of the cost of domestic adjustments due to instability in the world economy. As is well known, the higher the degree of integration with the world economy through trade *and finance* and the more heterogeneous and inflexible an economy, the higher the cost of adjustment and the price to be paid when there are 'mistakes' in economic policy-making. Since the early 1970s, for semi-industrialised countries, this adjustment problem has been one of the most serious issues in the agenda. Unfortunately, this is the least developed section in Ffrench-Davis's chapter, although all the subjects discussed in the other sections ultimately have a bearing on it.

Finally, the section on the role of the state starts with an observation about the important and increasingly recognised phenomenon that orthodox theory *does not* give any role to the public sector and to public enterprises when discussing foreign trade policies. There are obvious reasons for that, and much remains to be done in the area. The author raises some interesting points about what is likely to be an important topic for future research (at least in Latin America): namely, the criteria, mechanisms and experiences of regulation of public enterprises, especially with respect to trade – and, I would quickly add, international borrowing.

Undoubtedly, Ffrench-Davis has provided us with a number of stimulating thoughts and reflections on crucial issues which will remain on the agenda for many years to come.

3 RESEARCH PRIORITIES

The research priorities presented by Ffrench-Davis at the end of each section follow quite naturally from the discussion in the chapter. The author suggests that there is a lot to be done in connection with: (a) *theoretical* efforts to elaborate a 'relevant and rigorous conceptual framework as an alternative to the orthodox theory', (b) empirical studies examining 'the specific characteristics of the policy instruments available as well as of the structural domestic conditions under which they are used'; and (c) comparative analysis of national experiences. At the abstract level few would disagree, with the possible exception of the first item. However, the major underlying issue behind the whole array of themes raised in the chapter is the old question of the role of state intervention *vis-à-vis* the role of market forces. Here, one could subscribe to Ffrench-Davis's sensible remark: 'It is undeniable that, beyond ideological options, technical elements enter into play, and that under the guise of technical "purity" orthodox theory harbours a sizeable ideological content.'

14 Technological Change and Development in Latin America

JORGE KATZ

Development theory has never satisfactorily incorporated the issue of technological change. For many years this was treated as a variable exogenous to the economic system. It is only recently that there has been a recognition of the possibility that the nature and pace of the technological change which is incorporated by a given society are endogenously conditioned by the overall functioning of the economy.

For economic theory to evolve in this direction it has been necessary to make a gradual but significant move away from the framework of the neo-classical theory, which assumes that technological change reaches each firm free of cost. The new direction taken by theorists in recent years is mainly concerned with the study of the micro-economic determinants of technological behaviour.

Unlike the traditional models, in which technological change is defined as a 'major' shift of the production function as a whole, the new theoretical models use the concept of 'minor' and 'localised' changes, to include practically any *non-routine* modification of the engineering rules followed by a particular production unit.

Within this analytical framework, it is possible to explore the microeconomic behaviour of the entrepreneur as he faces the periodic dilemma of whether or not to allocate resources to the 'production' of new technological know-how with one (or more) of the following objectives in mind: (*a*) to cut production costs by saving on capital, labour, energy or raw materials; (*b*) to improve the quality of the finished product; (*c*) to diversify production; or (*d*) to remove bottle-necks which prevent increases in the physical volume of production obtained with the existing capacity.

One can see that it is no longer just the relative price of factors or the relative weight of capital and labour in total costs which determines particular strategies for expenditure on technology. The following must also be taken into account: (*a*) the productivity and cost of the various possible strategies for 'technological research'; and (*b*) the scale of production on which the entrepreneur operates. Taken together, these variables will decide both the overall magnitude of the technological effort made and the internal allocation of resources within the various options open.

In other words, current research is moving towards the study of those factors which determine the profitability of the alternative technological strategies available to a given firm at any given point in time, irrespective of whether or not the technological development of the firms is original within the global economic context, whether it shifts the production function as a whole or whether it is merely a 'localised' improvement affecting one particular technique.

So far, what is available to us in terms of the theoretical development of this new approach to the study of technological progress refers to the industrialised countries, where it is reasonable to assume that there exists a systematic flow of technological and scientific creativity which is subsequently absorbed by the different sectors of production.

In contrast, the problem of technology for the so-called 'less developed countries' (LDCs) has remained practically unexplored, lacking both a systematic programme of empirical research and an interpretation theory. The object of this programme should be primarily to throw some light on the technological situation in developing nations. Although these countries are not on the frontier of science and technology, and do not produce a flow of new technological knowledge on the same scale as the industrialised countries, they are none the less following their own path of technological modernisation, the particular features of which remain as yet unknown.

The construction of such a theory of technological change for the LDCs is not an easy task. One of the basic difficulties is the heterogeneity of the so called 'developing countries'. In Latin America, for example, it is obvious that three countries – Argentina, Brazil and Mexico – represent, as far as technology is concerned, a very different case from others in the region. These countries have travelled far enough along the road of industrial modernisation and technological maturity to separate them clearly from the rest. Together with other factors, this growing technological maturity is gradually giving rise to a number of new types of economic relations in Latin America, such as: (*a*) the export of manufactured goods of significant technological complexity (which range from vehicles and machinery to antibiotics, including iron and steel products, chemicals, electronic goods, etc.); (*b*) the sale of technology under licence, complete 'turn-key' plants, etc.; (*c*) direct investment; and (*d*) technical assistance in the development of basic infrastructure, such as atomic energy and transport facilities. Seen as a whole these new technological and commercial manifestations reveal an incipient form of 'internationalisation' within the region, which was virtually unknown in Latin America until recently.

It is, therefore, urgent to examine this issue more closely and to understand its technological foundations, since the gradual strengthening of the international position of a few developing countries will certainly be the rule and not the exception in years to come. A new situation seems to be arising in Latin America and the rest of the world and, in our view, the transfer of technology within the region and the creation of technological know-how locally are both central elements of this development.

The pages which follow are an attempt to reflect on the themes outlined above. They bring together some of the results obtained in different studies on innovatory activity, carried out within the framework of the IDB/ECLA Programme of Technological and Scientific Research, in different branches of the manufacturing sector of five Latin American countries: Argentina, Brazil, Mexico, Peru and Colombia.

1   STAGES OF DEVELOPMENT, TECHNOLOGICAL CHANGE AND DOMESTIC RESEARCH AND DEVELOPMENT

It is as well to begin by distinguishing at least two different typologies as regards the process of modernisation and technological change within the overall context of the 'developing countries'.

On the one hand, we have the case of countries at an intermediate stage of development, which the literature in recent years has taken to calling 'recently industrialised' (Hirschman, 1968). On the other hand, we have the case of most of the underdeveloped countries – several in Latin America and the majority of the African and Asian countries – in which the process of modernisation and technological change is the exception rather than the rule. The bulk of society in the latter group can be characterised as belonging to a stage of evolution several decades behind both, the industrialised world and the developed sectors of those countries in the first group.

Within Latin America, the cases of Argentina, Brazil and Mexico – despite the profound differences which separate them in other ways – can be seen as typical examples of 'recent industrialisation'. Outside the region, cases such as Spain and Greece come to mind, or Eastern European countries like Yugoslavia and Poland.

Unlike the situation in the more developed countries, much of the process of modernisation and technological change which takes place in the 'developing' world consists of the imitation of events which have occurred previously in more advanced societies. Often, the incorporation of these technological developments requires the allocation of susbsidies, to national or foreign capital, and is based on the transfer of technological designs which have originated abroad. In general, the opening up of new branches of industry presupposes the entry of transnational corporations, engineering firms and financing agencies from the industrialised world.

There are very few differences among the various LDCs at the stage of purchasing technological designs from the relatively more advanced countries. Given that most industrial technology comes from outside, and has to be acquired in relatively imperfect markets, the LDCs retain only a few prerogatives such as: (*a*) selecting from the gamut of technology available; and (*b*) negotiating the terms of the transfers within a framework where differences in the bargaining power of the contracting parties is a predominant factor.

For many years most of the Latin American literature on technology assumed that the region's problem could be reduced to the acquisition of more or less suitable foreign technology. We now know that this view of the situation is grossly over-simplified, and that a large number of relevant problems only begin at this point. Moreover, the main differences between the 'recently industrialised' countries and the other nations of the underdeveloped world arise precisely at the stage following the purchase of foreign technology, and are directly linked to the existence or absence of domestic technological capacity. This capacity serves to complement the original imported technological designs by means of 'adaptation' or 'improvement'.[1]

It is our view that at the present time, Argentina, Brazil and Mexico have a substantial number of sufficiently highly-trained professional and technical personnel to 'produce' an internal flow of technological knowledge in addition to the technology which is imported. The availability of such engineering and technical manpower in the rest of the countries in the region is more in doubt. Hence, the degree of 'adaptation' of imported technological designs eventually achieved is significantly less. This point is of particular importance to understand the situation, so it would seem necessary, in the first place, to examine the complementarity between the importing of technology and domestic research and development, in order to explore, subsequently, how this relates to the degree of industrial, educational and technical development achieved within a given society.

(a) Imports of technology and domestic research and development

For many years, conventional reasoning assumed that there was a relationship of substitution (that is, an inverse relationship) between importing technology and creating it locally. We now know, as the Japanese case shows very clearly, that this assumption is a gross simplification. While for the economist the design of a product or the specifications of a process are fixed technical data which may only very occasionally be modified as a result of discontinuous improvements in the technological knowledge available, the industrial engineer is accustomed to the idea that every engineering design evolves and improves in time as a result of the particular circumstances in which it is used in a specific context. In other words, he knows that there are no two plants (or product designs) in the world which are exactly the same. If this is true in a static sense, it must be more so in the case of a dynamic process which admits the improvement and adaptation of technological design over time. The virtual impossibility of perfect reproduction is even greater when we are concerned with processes which have to function in different physical environments and levels of sophistication of demand, different scales of plants, conditions of supply and quality of basic inputs. Finally, the skills of the industrial work-force may be also completely different from what was envisaged when the technology was originally developed.

There are many factors which may render a particular technological design 'inadequate' in a given environment and make 'adjustments' or 'adaptation' necessary (Teitel, 1976). Some of these are strictly of an engineering nature, and have to do with bottle-necks in the original design; this is relatively similar to Rosenberg's (1976) concept of 'compulsory sequences', which are the physical signs of this 'inadequacy'.

Other signs of 'inadequacy' are more associated with economic variables; these may have to do as much with microeconomic factors relating to an individual plant as with macroeconomic factors affecting whole branches of industry, or even the entire manufacturing sector. Whatever the source of the 'inadequacy' of imported technology, it remains true that this generates a certain demand for new technological knowledge in the area of adaptation, to allow a relatively more efficient use of imported technology.

(b) Domestic research and development and skilled human resources

The fact that every 'inadequacy' potentially creates an endogenous demand for technological know-how to complement imported technology is not sufficient reason to assume that the demand will be satisfied or, if it is, that this will be achieved on the basis of domestic research and development (R & D).

Seen in its broadest terms, the regional picture in this respect presents us with two distinct 'educational models'. While Argentina provides a typical example of autonomous growth in the supply of skilled labour and professionals, the situation of Brazil and Mexico, among others, should be seen as one in which the educational system is geared to supply the demands of the productive sector. The first of these 'models' gathered momentum early in this century as a consequence of an autonomous political and institutional process which included the establishment of compulsory primary education in the 1920s, and a rapid development of technical and professional training in the 1940s and immediately after the war. This process was not a consequence of import substitution and industrial expansion, but the expression of an autonomous goal of the political system. The practical eradication of illiteracy and the establishment of a sector of technical and higher education of considerable proportions are, without doubt, two of the main factors which explain the relatively abundant supply of skilled labour to be found underlying Argentinian industrialisation in the post-war period.

The development of the educational sector as a response to the demands of the productive sector constitutes an entirely different model.

Experiences such as those of Brazil or Mexico show expansion of the educational system to be a belated phenomenon, which occurred after the end of the Second World War; it was particularly concerned with higher education but showed little interest in the primary level. In such cases, expansion of the educational sector was a response to the requirements of industrialisation rather than an autonomous development. Even though on average the level of skill of the industrial work-force in these countries is lower than that achieved in Argentina, the evidence available suggests that this model has had significant success in creating the technical and professional resources necessary for industrial expansion.

In summary, then, although every form of 'inadequacy' in imported technology potentially creates a demand for endogenous technological know-how geared to adaptation and improvement, such a demand may or may not be satisfied, depending on the availability of skilled human resources to undertake the task of 'producing' locally the incremental technological know-how which all adaptation or improvement requires.

The shortage of skilled manpower is a structural feature, which can be altered only in the long term, since the setting-up and maintaining of professional and technical schools requires an investment programme which takes decades to mature. It is therefore reasonable to assume that it will be difficult, as far as the immediate future is concerned, to narrow the technological gap which exists between Argentina, Brazil and Mexico on the one hand, and the rest of the region on the other.

2 THE NATURE AND SCALE OF DOMESTIC R & D IN LATIN AMERICA

We argued in the previous section that one of the main structural features which differentiates Brazil, Mexico and Argentina from other countries in the region as regards technology is the recent emergence – and gradual consolidation – of a sector creating domestic technological know-how to complement the flow of imported technology. This sector may be located in departments of process and/or product engineering and in groups providing technical assistance on the production side of large and medium-sized national firms and in local subsidiaries of transnational conglomerates, as well as in corporations in the public sector.

Until now, this structural feature of the recent-industrialisation model has received little attention, as regards either empirical study or its theoretical dimensions. There is a lack of information on domestic innovation in countries which are at an intermediate stage of development, which would enable us on the one hand to throw some light on the main determinants of entrepreneurial behaviour in this field and, on the other, to incorporate these determinants into a broader analytical framework, which might enable us to trace the pattern of growth and of foreign trade in these countries.

In this section we will look briefly into the nature, the determinants and the pace of domestic innovation, while in the next section we will examine the relation between domestic innovation and patterns of foreign trade and comparative advantage.

Let us look firstly at the empirical evidence available, even though it is relatively scanty. Two studies of the Argentine manufacturing sector (Katz, 1976a; INTI, 1974) give figures for expenditure on R & D which, up to the end of the 1960s, fluctuated at around US$30 million per annum. This figure represents an approximate average of between 0·3 and 0·4 per cent of annual sales of the firms considered. More recent work has produced very similar figures (Maxwell, 1978; Katz, 1978; Ramírez Gómez, 1976), which are perhaps marginally higher in the chemical and pharmaceutical industry (Katz, 1976b) or electronic goods (Petrecolla *et al.*, 1974).

A recent study of the situation in Mexico by CONACYT estimates expenditure on R & D in the Mexican manufacturing sector to be around US$12 million, which is approximately equivalent to 0·1 per cent of the value of the production of the establishments concerned.

The situation in Brazil confirms the previous findings, at the same time showing a spectacular increase in expenditure on R & D by the public sector in that country.

These figures are not very big in absolute terms, but they cast a certain amount of doubt on the *a priori* assumption that domestic technological endeavour practically does not exist. In the three countries mentioned, it is reasonable to suppose that the 100–200 major industrial concerns spend on R & D, on average, around US$150 000 a year per firm, a figure which would certainly enable them to employ an experimental-research and technological-development team which, again on average, could represent as many as six or eight professionals.

The existence of this flow of expenditure on domestic technology raises a number of questions: firstly, what sort of technological R & D is being carried out locally, and what is its purpose? Secondly, which micro- and macroeconomic facts or circumstances stimulate or hinder domestic efforts in R & D? Thirdly, what direct effects does local R & D have on the productive enterprises which engage in it, and what are the different externalities which it creates? And, fourthly, what can be said of the advisability of this type of domestic technological enterprise from a macroeconomic point of view?

(a) Type of technological R & D carried out

The first question is closely related to the definition of technological change itself. In one of the most thorough studies on the creation of technology at plant level, Hollander (1965) defines technological change as any modification in a production technique put into effect by a specific plant with the object of reducing the unit cost of production.

The virtue of this definition is that it takes 'technological change' to be *any* modification in the operating routine of a plant, irrespective of whether it is 'major' or 'minor', or of whether it is new or not at the level of the industry or of the society. Its main limitation, however, is that it only takes into account modifications in technical performance which are related to cuts in the unit cost of production, and it leaves out other possible effects of technological enterprise, such as improvements in quality, diversification of output or substitution of raw materials and imported spare parts with near equivalents or national production.

A number of the studies carried out within the framework of the IDB/ECLA Programme of Research into Science and Technology show that cost reduction has not always been the main concern of the technological R & D carried out by the firms. Rather, the launching of new products (Fidel and Lucangeli, 1978; Fidel, Lucangeli and Sheperd, 1976; Vitelli, 1976) and the improved utilisation of installed capacity (Maxwell, 1976; Katz, 1978) seem to have been goals equally important as or more important than cost reduction. This seems to have been the case particularly in those cases where it was possible to detect low market pressure or competition not based specifically on prices but on quality, product differentiation, etc.

When these results are examined from the point of view of accepted theory (which, as we have seen, is based on the assumption that the main objective of technological R & D is to reduce costs), it is difficult to escape the impression that the theory still lacks the sensitivity to capture and describe the technological situation of many of the industrial markets in Latin America. Until now, for historical reasons, these markets have been more concentrated and more protected than those of the USA or Europe and, as a result, have been much less concerned with efforts to cut production costs. Their situation has favoured technological strategies based on product differentiation and oligopolistic competition.

In synthesis, the type of technological R & D detected by various studies on the creation of technology in Latin America reflects a number of objectives of which the lowering of production costs is only one, and not necessarily the most important. In a less competitive world than that of the industrialised countries, the pursuit of operational efficiency may well assume less significance than other alternative strategies.

(b) Micro- and macroeconomic variables which stimulate or impede technological R & D

Of all the microeconomic factors which influence the nature and scale of domestic R & D (tending towards a relative saving of one factor in particular), the following are especially relevant: (i) the conditions of the original design (Sercovich, 1978; Rosenberg, 1976); (ii) the nature of the product (Vitelli, 1976; Fidel, Lucangeli and Shepherd, 1976; Katz, 1978); (iii) the morphological features of the market in question (Maxwell, 1978; Katz, 1978); (iv) the relationship with the foreign suppliers of the technology (whether a head office, a licensing firm or a firm supplying machinery); (v) the quality and technical capacity of the engineers employed.[2]

Taken together, these microeconomic factors will have an influence on: (i) the initial choice of technology; (ii) its suitability to the local circumstances and the extent to which the (particular) design chosen proves to be optimal; (iii) the orientation and productivity of the different innovatory programmes to be undertaken after the inauguration of the plant.

At the same time, a number of studies show how macroeconomic variables influence the nature and amount of technological know-how created locally; these include: the exchange rate, the rate of interest, the cost of skilled labour (Fidel and Lucangeli, 1978; Canitrot, 1977), the rate of growth and fluctuations in the economy, and the degree of uncertainty which characterises it. Together with microeconomic variables previously mentioned, these factors condition both the rhythm of investment – and, through this, the rate of technological change 'incorporated' in new plants – and the opportunity cost of decisions to continue operating machinery of an older technological generation, but repaired and 'improved' as a result of local innovatory activity. The results of our studies suggest that firms do, in fact, produce a technological response to the constraints and bottle-necks created by the technology originally chosen, just as they do in the face of changes over a period of time in the circumstances in which they operate (for example, the prevailing degree of market competition, the cost and availability of raw materials, and the relative cost of labour and capital).

(c) Technological R & D and economic performance

There are a number of consequences which follow from a flow of 'minor' inventive activity (or 'sub-innovation'). Two of these are particularly important from the point of view of their influence on long-term economic growth.

The first one is the impact which local R & D has on the aggregate productivity of all the factors used by a firm. The second, which derives in part from the first, concerns the effect which an increase in productivity has on the gap separating a particular industrial establishment from the 'average standard' prevailing at the international level in a particular manufacturing sector. We shall argue here that both increases in productivity and adaptive forms of technological change are necessary elements (though certainly not sufficient) to bring a particular firm up to international standards of competition and eventually enable it to participate in foreign markets both within the region and beyond.

(i) Domestic R & D and growth in productivity

A number of studies carried out over the past few years have confirmed the tremendous importance of 'minor' technological change as a source of substantial increases in manufacturing productivity. Perhaps the most detailed of these studies is that of Hollander (1965), which examines a number of rayon-producing plants run by the Du Pont corporation in the United States, and concludes that the contribution of 'minor' technological change towards increased efficiency over a period of time has been of great importance. Other authors, although their analyses are not as detailed as Hollander's, essentially confirm this finding.

A number of different research projects carried out in Latin America provide a relatively similar picture: Petrecolla, *et al*, (1974) with reference to the Argentine electronics industry; Ramírez Gómez with a study of the electricity sector in Colombia (1976); and Katz, both within the framework of a cross section study, which covered the 200 largest manufacturing companies in Argentina (1976a), as well as within a microeconomic framework (1978), similar to Hollander's. All these studies show that, even in countries where industrialisation has been retarded, the flow of domestic technological innovation, most of which is 'minor', has a significant impact on the evolution of manufacturing productivity.

In summary, the statistical relationship between expenditure on technology and increases in overall productivity, which the literature on 'sources of growth' has demonstrated in the case of industrially developed countries during the 1960s, does not seem to be particularly confined to these societies. Wherever the presence of skilled human resources at the level of the manufacturing plant makes it possible to generate new technological know-how locally, it is reasonable to expect that, after a certain period of time and by a process of accumulation, the flow of local technology will become the main 'explanation' for the growth observed in manufacturing productivity.

(ii) Domestic technological effort and export capacity

We have already seen that the development of local technology by firms operating on the basis of an imported design is frequently a response to the need to adapt this design to local market conditions. This need for adaptation depends on: (*a*) the type and cost of raw materials available on the domestic market; (*b*) the relative factor prices; (*c*) the scale of plant set up; (*d*) the geographic and climatic conditions under which the product and/or process involved are used locally[3]; (*e*) the particular requirements of the local consumer as regards quality and specifications, etc.[4]; (*f*) the nature of the by-products and waste materials derived from the finished product itself as from the process involved; or (*g*) differences in the institutional and legal framework, in the field of labour relations and in the structure of the local market.

Once the various shortcomings of the imported technological design have been overcome, by means of 'minor' local innovation, it follows intuitively, that the technological 'package' available must necessarily be different from what was originally obtained abroad. Either in its 'embodied' form (the end product, or the machinery used to produce it, etc.) or in an 'unembodied' form (in terms of engineering procedure, operating manuals, etc.), the 'new' technological package should be more suitable to local conditions than the original design.

In these circumstances, it is hardly surprising that the 'new' technological package should find a ready market in the rest of the world where geographic and climatic conditions, institutional framework, size, and the type and price of factors and raw materials available are comparable to those in the markets which created the original need for adapting the technology. In other words, the technological effort of innovation eventually gives rise to the emergence of a 'new' product or process capable of generating profit when it is marketed in third countries. This may occur through the direct export of products with new technology incorporated; direct investment programmes; the granting of licences to third parties; or the sale of entire plants.

In recent years, the following have acquired increasing importance: (i) exports of manufactured goods, including some of relatively complex technology, which have required a considerable degree of local innovation, as in the case of vehicles, tractors, antibiotics, electrical and mechanical equipment and agricultural machinery; (ii) the sale by contract of 'turn-key' plants; and (iii) direct investment by local entrepreneurs in other countries within the region.[5]

Some of these topics have been studied over the past few years, but almost all of them require more sustained research. We know, for example, that local subsidiaries of transnational corporations control a significant share of the export of sophisticated manufactures within the region, but do not have as great a share of the increasing flow of exports of pure technology[6]; this appears to be more closely associated with medium-sized companies, national engineering firms and financial arrangements made through national banks. The empirical evidence of Argentina[7], Brazil and Mexico[8], suggest the possibility that these three countries are now beginning, belatedly, to produce their own cycles of direct foreign investment and export of sophisticated manufactures and pure technology. It is also known that the export of sophisticated manufactures and turn-key plants is not confined to the Latin American countries mentioned here, but is also becoming increasingly important in Korea, Singapore and Taiwan.

(d) Domestic technological effort and the allocation of resources

Previous sections of this paper have enabled us to establish, on the basis of material collected for various studies in the IDB/ECLA Programme, that: (i) There is an important source of domestic technological endeavour in R & D carried out by manufacturing plants in Latin America; (ii) this technological undertaking has a number of different objectives aside from cost reduction; (iii) only a small fraction of the local technological R & D is aimed at reducing the unit cost of production; (iv) domestic technological innovation has a significant impact on the aggregate productivity of the sum of factors used at the manufacturing plant; (v) there is an increasing capacity for exporting technologically complex manufactures and an incipient (but clear) tendency towards the export of technology in the form of 'turn-key' plants, technical assistance contracts, the provision of basic engineering for works of infrastructure.

In spite of the intrinsic interest of these findings, they cannot be taken to establish with certainty whether we are witnessing a flow of domestic technological endeavour which, seen from a social (rather than private) perspective, may be regarded as an efficient allocation of resources. To put it another way, it is not clear whether this technological endeavour means that, in the long run, society is maximising the rate of growth in *per capita* output. It could well be that, through domestic technological activities and 'minor' innovations, a particular country may be keeping industrial plants in operation artificially in industries in which that country does not have 'dynamic' comparative advantages. The operation of such industries could be maintained, through the protection against imported substitutes or by other equivalent means of subsidising the local producer. The drafting of 'optimal' policies in this field is clearly linked both to the internal rate of technological learning *vis-à-vis* the rate of technical change which the respective branch or sector of activity achieves internationally, and to the real possibility of operating a selective and flexible system which avoids both excessive protection and indiscriminate access, irrespective of the specific technological history of the branch or sector in a given social context.

Thus, we are dealing with a case of 'infant industry', which requires a certain degree of protection for its support and growth. The initial degree of protection and the way it develops in time, should be a function of the initial relative disadvantage and of the effectiveness of domestic technological capacity. The latter should enable relative productivity to increase gradually, making it possible at some point to do away with protective measures and to incorporate the industry concerned into the category of those in which the country has 'acquired' comparative advantage. The time factor becomes an important element in analysing the cost which society has to pay for this learning process.

All this implies the advisability of operating a flexible and selective system, clearly related to the industrial and technological history of a given society, as well as the need for differential treatment to industries as a function of the origin of their technologies, and extent of their diffusion and assimilation to local conditions. Given that there is no single 'technological path' available, but rather a number of alternative technological strategies, any analysis should also include a comparative study of these in order to evaluate the benefits which might have been gained through strategies other than the one adopted.

3 FINAL REMARKS

A theory of technological change which will contribute to an understanding of the situation of the relatively less-developed countries, as well as efficient technology policies, must go beyond the field covered by the creation of domestic industrial technology, and explore the technical, economic and institutional dimensions of topics such as purchase of foreign technological knowledge and scientific and technological research in fields not strictly related to industry.

(a) The acquisition of foreign technology

In spite of the growing importance of the domestic creation of technology, there is little doubt that most of the industrial technology in use today, and most of what is incorporated annually into the different sectors of production, comes from abroad. It is acquired either by licensing, by TNC's direct investment programmes, or through other similar channels. The oligopolistic nature of the international markets in which such acquisition takes place, as well as the concentration of monopolistic rents resulting from the different bargaining strength of the contracting parties, have been emphasised often enough. The enormous difficulties faced by the operation of the price mechanism in this field make it necessary for the state to take appropriate steps to intervene.

In recent years some countries have moved in this direction, but failures have been more striking that successes. It is only reasonable to conclude that, besides an administrative apparatus to regulate contracts for the purchase of technology, what is also called for in this area is a more active intervention by the state in the fulfilment of two roles which have been given little emphasis until now: (i) as a 'talent scout' in the field of world-wide technology and (ii) as a centralised buyer of technology in world markets.

These two lines of approach would be justified, both from the point of view of resource of allocation (because a centralized search of technology would avoid the duplication of efforts and reduce expenses) and from the point of view of strengthening the bargaining position of countries purchasing technology.

(b) Creation of domestic technological know-how outside industry

In most countries there are, or have been, tax policies specifically designed to encourage spending on research and development. However, a close look at the policies instruments used reveals a very poor understanding of the phenomenon.

Any project for the creation of technology implies a set of derived effects, either in terms of the relative saving of factors (capital and labour) or in terms of the use or saving of foreign exchange. This points to the need, on the part of those responsible for implementing official policies, to establish a 'portfolio' of R & D projects in line with the 'national interest', however this is defined.

It is obvious, however, that there is an enormous range of very important scientific and technological problems which will not be taken up by the private sector, either because of their low profitability or because of the considerable time required for maturation. This means that a government policy on the creation of domestic technological know-how would necessarily go beyond the granting of subsidies to the private sector, and set out a clear agenda of those areas of research to be taken up directly by the public sector itself, or by private institutes financed out of government funds.

Almost two-thirds of the cost of R & D carried out by countries like the USA, Great Britain, France or Australia is financed out of government spending. There is a somewhat greater variation as regards the direct pursuit of research programmes, since in the USA only 15 % of overall expenditure goes on studies carried out by the public sector itself, while in France and Great Britain the figure is around 30%, and it accounts for almost two-thirds of the total in Australia.

Until now, the Latin American states have shown little inclination to act as planning agents for R & D programmes carried out by the private sector, but confine themselves to a passive involvement through indirect fiscal measures. Equally, as regards research carried out by the public sector itself, there has been no attempt to outline specific policies on scientific and technological development other than to confirm in retrospect decisions already taken by the scientific and academic community with regard to research work and the allocation of funds.

It is our opinion that both these areas call for a significant restructuring of public policy and much more decisive intervention by the state apparatus. This implies the adoption of more dynamic and managerial attitudes on the part of government, rather than confining itself to assessing the research proposals of entrepreneurs and academics.

Practically every country in the region is still confronted with deep-rooted problems of public health, nutrition, environmental pollution, housing, transport, lack of opportunities for leisure activies, animal and plant health and high risk factors in industry – to mention only a few of the fields in which the task of promoting further understanding and formulating new working hypotheses requires urgent attention. We believe that the social return on investment in research into many of these areas must necessarily exceed its private profitability. Some of the issues mentioned above should be given high priority on the research agenda of the public sector itself, since it would be unreasonable to expect them to be dealt with by the private sector, even with the aid of reasonable subsidies.

(c) A new regional economic order

Finally the previous pages have suggested the possibility that a new regional scenario may be in the process of formation, and it is possible to predict that the major countries in the region will play a predominant role as suppliers of technologically sophisticated manufactures as well as of technology itself through licence and direct investment.

The novelty of these topics in Latin America is clearly reflected in the lack of a juridical and institutional framework capable of effectively regulating the flows of goods, capital and technology within the area. There is an obvious danger that the relatively developed countries will tend to reproduce the oligopolistic patterns of behaviour which they, at one time, were confronted with as buyers of technology on the world market.

As an example, there are only six countries in Latin America at present which belong to the group of signatories of the Paris Convention on Marks and Patents. This treaty has been strongly criticised in recent years on the ground that it affords one-sided protection in favour of countries which export technology. It is obviously unthinkable that such a framework should provide a legal basis for the increasing traffic of goods, capital and technology within the region, and it is therefore important to start taking steps at the regional level to find mechanisms more attuned to the present economic condition of Latin America.

NOTES

1 A number of studies of Japan show the complementary relationship between the importing of technology and the domestic creation of technological know-how. The success of several different industries on the international market has been attributed to their proven capacity for importing and improving technology already available in the USA or Europe.
2 We observed significant differences in the quality and degree of technical training of R & D personnel, even between firms competing on the same market. While Ford Argentina, for example, employed over 200 people in its product engineering department, for other companies in the car-manufacturing sector local innovation remained a very marginal activity. Similar examples can be found in practically every branch of industry.
3 The car manufacturing and tractor production industries are typical examples in which the physical infrastructure of the country and the nature of the rural environment and its exploitation (large expanses of flat, unbroken terrain) have led most of the industrial concerns which operate on the Argentine market to introduce significant modifications and adaptations in technological designs originating in the USA or Europe.
4 Consumer durables from the electronics industry and car manufacturing are frequently quoted as examples of industries in which the domestic consumer does not demand the same level of sophistication as one would expect in more developed societies. In such cases, domestic technological enterprise may well attempt to reduce the level of sophistication of imported technological design.
5 There are a number of introductory monographs on this topic, but this line of research should be pursued further. See Diaz-Alejandro (1977). E. White, in a research at the Instituto para la Integración de América Latina (INTAL) identifies some fifty cases of interest throughout the region.
6 Of thirty-five 'turn-key' plants exported by companies based in Argentina, only six were built by subsidiaries of transnational corporations.
7 Data collected by the author for the period 1933–77, identified exports of turn-key plants or engineering works with a value of US$340 millions. The list of thirty-four exports includes items as diverse as a hospital, an airport, a vegetable oil factory and a citrus-fruit processing plant.
8 As regards Mexico, from January 1973 to June 1975, exports in the form of technology and special services rose to US$137 million, a very promising figure in view of the vigorous growth in this field since then. One plant alone, sold to Argentina in 1976 to produce newsprint, was a project involving US$200 million. Mexico has been successful in the sale of plants produced as a result of – amongst others – four basic technological developments of its own: (i) the H and L (Hojalata y Lámina) technique for direct reduction in the iron and steel industry, which has already been incorporated – or is about to be – in iron and steel production in Venezuela, Brazil, Iraq, Iran, Indonesia and Zambia; (ii) the PEMEX technology developed by *Petróleos Mexicanos* (PEMEX) for the extraction of metals from crude oil (used in Columbia and

Jamaica), and a system for oil-refining which is to be marketed by one of the largest firms of consultants in the petro-chemical field, UOP Inc.; (iii) the Cortina method, developed by *I.C. Construction* for the pre-cast reinforced concrete, already being used in Columbia and Venezuela; (iv) the Ousi process from *Bufete Industrial* for making newsprint from sugar-cane bagasse.

REFERENCES

Canitrot, A. (1977) 'Un esquema para evaluar el significado de las variables macroeconómicas en el análisis de incorporación de tecnologías', *Monograph* no. 12, IDB/ECLA Programme (Buenos Aires) September.

David, P. (1975) *Technological Choice, Innovation and Economic Growth* (Cambridge Universtiy Press)

Díaz-Alejandro, C. (1977) 'Foreign direct investment by Latin Americans', *Center Paper* no. 258 (Economic Growth Center (Yale University).

Fidel, J. and Lucangeli, J. (1978) 'Costos y beneficios de distintas opciones tecnológicas en el marco de un oligopolio diferenciado. La industria del cigarrillo', *Monograph* no. 18, IDB/ECLA Programme (Buenos Aires) July.

Fidel, J., Lucangeli, J. and Sheperd, P. (1976) 'Perfil y comportamiento de la industria del cigarrillo en la Argentina', *Monograph* no. 7, IDB/ECLA Programme (Buenos Aires) December.

Freeman, C. (1977) 'Technical change and unemployment'. Paper presented to the conference on 'Science, technology and public policy', University of New South Wales, December, *mimeo.*

Griliches, Z. (1973) Commentary on W. F. Moeller, 'The origins of the basic inventions underlying Du Pont's major product and process innovations, 1920–50', in Nelson (1962). Also 'Research expenditure and growth accounting', in *Science and technology in economic growth* (London: Macmillan).

Hirschman, A. (1968) 'The political economy of import substituting industrialization', *Quarterly Journal of Economics*, February.

Hollander, S. (1965) *The Sources of Increased Efficiency: a Study of Dupont Rayon Plants* (Cambridge, Massachusettes: MIT Press).

—— (1966) *The sources of efficiency growth*, Chap. IV (MIT Press).

INTI (1974) *Aspectos económicos de la importación de tecnología en la Argentina* (Buenos Aires: Instituto Nacional de Tecnología Industrial) November.

Katz, J. (1976a) 'Creación de tecnología en el sector manufactuero argentino', *Monograph* no. 2, IDB/ECLA Programme (Buenos Aires).

—— (1976b) *Importación de Tecnología, Aprendizaje e Industrialización dependiente* (Mexico: Fondo de Cultura Económica).

—— (1978) 'Productividad, tecnología y esfuerzos locales de investigación y desarrollo', *Monograph* no. 13, IDB/ECLA Programme (Buenos Aires) March.

Maxwell, P. (1978) 'Estrategia tecnológica óptima en un contexto económico difícil', *Monograph* no. 16, IDB/ECLA Programme (Buenos Aires) March.

Nelson, R. (1962), ed. *The rate and direction of inventive activity* (Princeton: NBER).

—— and Winter, S. (1977) 'In search of useful theory of innovation', *Research Policy*.

Nordhaus, W. (1973) 'Some skeptical thoughts on the theory of induced innovations', *Quarterly Journal of Economics*.

Petrecolla, A. *et al.* (1974) *Industria Electrónica y Progreso Técnico en un contexto de Industrialización* (Buenos Aires: Editorial del Instituto di Tella).

Ramírez Gómez, M. (1976) 'Cambio tecnológico en la industria de generación de energía eléctrica de Colombia', *Monograph* no. 8, IDB/ECLA Programme (Buenos Aires) December.

Rosenberg, N. (1976) *Perspectives on Technology* (Cambridge University Press).

Sercovich, F. (1978) 'Ingeniería de diseño y cambio tecnológico endógeno', *Monograph* no. 19, IDB/ECLA Programme (Buenos Aires) June.

Teitel, S. (1976) 'Acerca del concepto de tecnología apropiada para los países menos industrializados', *Trimestre económico*, no. 171, July–September.

Vitelli, G. (1976) 'Competencia, oligopolio y cambio tecnológico en la industria de la construcción. El caso argentino', *Monograph* no. 3, IDB/ECLA Programme (Buenos Aires) December.

15 Technological Change and Development in Latin America: a Comment

PATRICIO MELLER

In the sixties, the current belief in the benefits for LDCs from the use of modern technology developed in the industrialised world seemed beyond question: the technology was available and LDCs had to bear none of the costs of generating it. Nowadays this assumption is being questioned, as LDCs have discovered conflicting implications involved in the use of modern technology (Helleiner, 1977): (i) it is a fact that modern technology plays a crucial role in economic development; but (ii) the technology created by the industrialised countries is not appropriate to the resource endowment of LDCs; (iii) modern technology is not as free of cost as had been thought, as there is a significant flow of foreign exchange involved in acquiring it; (iv) modern technology can produce patterns of growth which may lead to serious problems with the absorption of manpower and concentration in income distribution; and (v) modern technology may constitute a new form of colonialism, which would discourage technological research in LDCs and condemn them to dependence *ad infinitum* upon imported technology developed in the industrialised world.

From a practical and empirical point of view, while it is true that there is modern technology available for use by LDCs, it can be seen that there is in reality an enormous technological gap between LDCs and the industrialised countries, and within LDCs themselves. The traditional framework used to examine the problem of modern technology in LDCs distinguishes three stages: (*a*) generation, (*b*) transfer, and (*c*) adaptation and/or innovation.

1 THE GENERATION OF TECHNOLOGY

Some 98 % of the world's technological research is carried out by the industrialised nations and is obviously designed to solve their own problems (Bergsten, 1973). This immediately suggests that modern technology is biased towards the needs and demands of the industrialised world. This raises the following basic question: who should be responsible for generating technology appropriate to the needs of LDCs – the institutes presently carrying out technological research in the industrialised countries, who enjoy considerable acquired comparative advantages, or the practically non-existent technological research institutes in LDCs? Moreover, how can the technological research institutes in the industrialised world be induced to create technology appropriate to LDCs? And, on the other hand, would the research priorities laid down by these research institutes be the same as those pursued by research institutes in LDCs? The answer to this question would in most cases be negative: it is obvious that the development of a synthetic substitute for petroleum would be a low priority project in Venezuela, while the opposite would be the case in Japan. Moreover, not all LDCs necessarily have the same priorities as regards research.

2 THE TRANSFER OF TECHNOLOGY

It is said that one of the principal roles of TNCs is to act as the main channel for the transfer of modern technology (Helleiner, 1977). Until recently, LDCs have attached very little importance to the type of technology used by TNCs, and in fact it was only in the 1970's that a discussion arose, almost exclusively in the academic world, as to the possibility of the adaptation or non-adaptation of the technology used by TNCs in LDCs.

From the point of view of LDCs, one of the crucial questions is whether there are effective mechanisms other than TNCs; can technological packages be had without the TNCs, and in which sectors? It is here that the specific characteristics of the market for technology become apparent; this market is one in which information is limited and imperfect, and this gives monopolistic power to those who create the technology.

In view of the oligopolistic characteristics of the market for technology, it would be to the advantage of LDCs to press for changes on two fronts: (*a*) as regards the supply of technology, increased competition among TNCs, limits to restrictive practices and changes in international agreements on patents for the transfer and development of technology; and (*b*) as regards the demand for technology, the creation of institutions to inform entrepreneurs of the type of technology available and the best means of negotiating with the companies who sell technology.

In this process of perfecting knowledge in the market for technology, there are obviously economies of scale, which is something LDCs should take advantage of, both between and within countries; although this is obvious at the theoretical level, is it really possible to put it into practice, bearing in mind the infinite variety of productive processes in existence?

3 ADAPTATION AND INNOVATION IN TECHNOLOGY

If it can be assumed that the modern technology created in the industrialised countries is not appropriate to the needs of LDCs, it will be necessary to create incentives for a certain degree of adaptation of this technology in LDCs; what incentives would be best suited to this end? How can one apply the argument for infant industry to the technological research institutes in LDCs for them to develop the necessary capacity for innovation? What is meant by appropriate technology from the LDCs' point of view? Traditional theory has emphasised almost exclusively the relative capital intensity of modern technology, but has neglected other characteristics which render it inappropriate for LDCs, such as the scale of production, the use of local inputs and the nature of consumption patterns. On the other hand, it could be that how to use the technology is as important as finding what is appropriate; some technology may be capital intensive, but its use could be intensive in labour use through shift work, the accelerated use of machinery, etc. (Sen, 1975).

In the literature on technology and LDCs, emphasis has been given to (*a*) reducing the price of imported technology and (*b*) inducing changes in the technology appropriate to the relative resource endowment available in LDCs. Nowadays the main problem is taken to be that of developing the capacity for creating technology in LDCs; how can this be done, and how can it be financed? This is what Katz focuses attention upon.

Katz's work attempts to go beyond the level of generalisation already outlined and presents research at the microeconomic level to identify the determining factors of innovating behaviour on the part of Latin

American entrepreneurs (in Argentina, Brazil, and Mexico). The following are some of the more important results of Katz's work which challenge a number of the general beliefs outlined previously: (*a*) within the manufacturing sector there are resources being channelled into research projects to create technology appropriate to the prevailing conditions in Latin American countries; (*b*) the technology coming out of the industrialised countries is adaptable to conditions in the local economics. Moreover, Katz suggests that the technology of the industrialised countries and of LDCs are not substitutes for each other, but may be complementary. From this it may be inferred that the general debate on technology in LDCs should consider specifically the formation of human capacity for generating adaptable technology within the different countries; (*c*) finally, a very interesting aspect of Katz's study is that he shows that some Latin American countries are exporting technology. What attracts the attention is that this technology, created in some Latin American countries and exported to others in the region, generates some similar negative structural features which previously characterised the technology imported from the industrialised countries: increasing foreign participation, growing concentration and oligopolisation, deterioration in patterns of income distribution, etc. In other words, it would seem that one should not expect technological innovation, even when it is produced in LDCs, to contribute spontaneously to solve the problems of unemployment and income distribution in developing countries.

REFERENCES

Bergsten, F. (1973), ed. *The Future of the International Economic Order: An Agenda for Research*, (Massachusetts: D. C. Heath & Co.)

Helleiner, G. (1977) 'International Technology Issues: Southern Needs and Northern Responses', in J. Bhagwati, ed., *The New International Economic Order: The North-South Debate*, (Cambridge, Massachusetts: MIT Press)

Sen, A. (1975) *Employment, Technology, and Development*, (Oxford: Clarendon Press).

16 International Economic Co-operation: A View from Latin America

ENRIQUE V. IGLESIAS

The aim of this chapter is to help draw some conclusions about the central objective of this book, which is to promote research on the new international economic order by identifying the major issues involved.

My purpose here is not to undertake a detailed analysis of the problem for Latin America; most readers are probably already quite familiar with it, not only from the technical standpoint but also as concerns the present state of the negotiations on the question. I shall therefore limit myself to a number of comments which are the fruit of my personal and professional experience in this field, in an attempt to convey not so much a set of specific ideas as a series of concerns about the way in which the concept of international co-operation is developing.

1 EVOLUTION OF THE CONCEPT OF CO-OPERATION

Those who have watched this concept evolve over many years cannot but recognise that at the international level great changes have taken place in the way co-operation is defined.

One of the first attempts at a coherent statement of what international co-operation should be was made by CEPAL through the set of proposals put forward at the economic conference held in Quitandinha in 1954. After that first attempt, the concept has evolved from being one centred on a preoccupation with security during the Cold War, to the growing recognition of the mutual interests of developing and industrialised countries.

At first, international co-operation was basically aimed towards stimulating the economic reconstruction of a very important segment of the Western capitalist world, the European countries devastated by the war: this was the main objective of the International Bank for Reconstruction and Development in its initial stages.

Later on, in the 1950s, the concept of co-operation with the developing countries gained ground, responding to clearly political factors. First, it was brought to the fore by the Cold War, in which economic co-operation was seen as an instrument in the competition for winning friends and forging political alliances. In addition, it began to be understood that the rapid decolonisation process then taking place, with the ostensible support of the United States, had to receive some kind of international support if the new nations were to be numbered within the orbit of the Western world. Underlying that concept of international co-operation was the political interest of the centres in gaining the upper hand in the struggle between the two major blocs on which world public attention was focused. In that context, North-South relations were a mere appendix to the central conflict between the Eastern bloc and the Western world.

The concept of co-operation was not merely underpinned by these political motivations, but also had a number of implicit values. First of all, the purpose of economic co-operation was to create or reconstruct economic systems similar to those of the donor states. There was no attempt to find solutions better suited to the characteristics and needs of the recipient countries, nor any interest in the type of economic and social organisation actually desired by the people involved. Co-operation was designed to implant in the developing countries the values and structures existing in the industrial societies, which provided the resources channelled through co-operation programmes so that the peripheral countries could be integrated into the international economy. In addition, an extremely quantitative approach prevailed, in which co-operation was reduced to the problem of the transfer of financial and technical resources with a view to reducing the gap between North and South.

Since then, this concept has changed in at least three important ways. First, there is a new political awareness in the world, including the industrialised countries, of the need for collaboration by the entire international community to solve the global problems of the planet. This new attitude is arising not only as a result of the repudiation by the conscience of mankind of the persistence of inequality and poverty in a wealthy world, but also because of the recognition of the growing interdependence of all peoples of the world.

Second, there is clearly a new balance of power in the world, including that between the countries of the North and those of the South. The latter have considerably increased their bargaining power in recent years. The part played by OPEC in this process, by showing the other developing countries what could be achieved by more concerted action, is well known. What is equally important is that the non-oil-exporting countries also understood the importance of this message by maintaining solidarity with the members of OPEC.

Finally, international co-operation has become much more complex in scope and coverage. It takes place in a much wider framework ranging from issues about population, the environment, the role of women in development, human settlements, sea resources and the arms race. This expansion of the number of problems considered stems from the fact that the idea of interdependence, long a purely rhetorical concept, has recently begun to acquire real meaning. There is now a much more enlightened collective awareness of the importance of the interdependence existing in the international economic setting.

The United Nations played an important role in these three changes of the concept of co-operation. It made a decisive contribution to creating the new political awareness about the moral issues involved. It provided the multilateral framework needed for the negotiations stemming from the OPEC initiatives. It has worked unflaggingly to demonstrate that the global problems affecting mankind should be solved in an integrated manner in a true spirit of international co-operation.

It is interesting to note that, for a number of reasons, in recent years international co-operation has followed two parallel paths which have had few mutual links and at times have even been antagonistic: the integrated approach which arose in the United Nations, and the economic and financial approaches which have evolved outside the system or through its financial and monetary agencies.

Over the last twenty years, both the problems addressed and the institutional structure on which international relations are based have proliferated tremendously. The four UNCTAD meetings, the special sessions of the United Nations General Assembly, the Conference on International Co-operation and Development, the Conference on the Law of the Sea, the World Conferences on the environment, population, food, employment, industrialisation and various other issues, the meetings of the non-aligned countries, and the resolutions adopted at these meetings, such as the Declaration and Programme of Action on the New International Economic Order and the Charter of Economic

Rights and Duties of States, have enriched this international dialogue with a wealth of ideas and lines of action. Although they have also given rise to a wealth of rhetoric, which often hides the true problems which exist in this field, it cannot be denied that these actions have increased the less developed countries' bargaining positions.

This approach has led to the appearance in the developed countries of many groups committed to the solution of these problems, which have renewed the thinking about North-South relations and fostered the creation of new forms of organisation to allow a constructive dialogue between the two groups of countries.

At the same time, negotiations have been taking place in the places where power really lies, such as the International Monetary Fund, the World Bank and GATT, where the more pressing problems of financing, trade and the reform of the international monetary system are discussed. The two processes have very few links between them and often even appear antagonistic. Beyond these apparent contradictions, the industrialised countries retain a basic coherence, making rhetorical concessions in the 'softer' forums and negotiating on the real problems in those 'harder' forums whose structure still ensures the predominance of the major centres, and in which the decisions of immediate interest are adopted.

Basically, interdependence continues to be managed through the 'hard' forums, whereas the 'softer' ones continue to play a rhetorical role. Nevertheless, the latter's work is not at all to be despised, since it has helped significantly to create an awareness which favours the improvement of North-South relations, and to accumulate the intellectual knowledge which is of tremendous importance for the analysis and solution of the problems besetting them.

2 TOWARDS A NEW INTERNATIONAL ECONOMIC ORDER

The fact that the concept of international co-operation has become more politicized in recent years has been expressed in the commitment of the developing countries to the struggle for the establishment of the new international economic order.

The programme of the new international economic order basically stems from political motives, and it should not be studied primarily from a technical standpoint. At heart, it is a long list of demands summarising the political grievances of the Third World in the face of the present international imbalance. It would be far from accurate to claim that it constitutes a systematic programme. The United Nations has only recently begun to study the coherence of the different targets put forward in the various world forums in recent years, an extremely painstaking task since it is not easy to harmonise so heterogeneous a series of initiatives or proposals by a group of countries whose situations and interests are often very divergent, as is the case of the Third World.

This heterogeneity, both of the characteristics of different developing countries and of their specific demands, means that the concept of the new international economic order is fertile ground for confusion. Often the leaders and specialists think they are talking about one and the same issue when in fact they are referring to different questions. It is therefore worth while attempting to specify exactly what the concept means for the countries of the North and for the countries of the South.

In the North there is one set of positions, which I would describe as radical, in which the new international economic order is viewed as an instrument which should make it possible to carry out a thorough transformation of the present structure of international relations on the basis of a critical analysis of their own industrial or post-industrial societies. I think this radical line of thought has had a great deal of influence and has become one of the main factors for change in the relations between the industrialised nations of the North and the developing countries of the South. For these changes are to a large extent due to the emergence of intellectual and political groups acutely aware of the need to forge new life styles in their own societies and to make way for new forms of international relations, particularly with the developing countries. Thus some countries of the North (of specific groups within them) have become sincere, loyal and effective friends of the developing countries, and one of the main agents of change in North–South relations.

Side by side with these radical currents, in the countries of the North there continues to grow what I would call 'reformist thinking', i.e. one which, starting from an acceptance of the *status quo*, particularly in the field of international relations, would like to improve it and eliminate existing discriminatory factors through the adoption of new international rules of the game. It is important to distinguish clearly between these two points of view so as to avoid distorting them.

Exactly the same is true in the South. There are groups and currents of opinions which uphold a radical philosophy and are committed to an all-embracing questioning of the present forms of the international division of labour. These groups range from those which merely emphasise individual and collective self-reliance as the core of the new international economic order to those which go to the extreme of proposing a radical delinking of the developing countries from the international economic system, as the only way of breaking the traditional dependent relationship between the two groups of countries and restructuring North-South relations on a suitable basis.

At the same time, in the Group of 77 more moderate currents of opinion exist, and even predominate. These currents, which I would describe as reformist, are perhaps those which have best managed to specify their viewpoints on the desired direction of the transformation of the relations between the developing and the industrialised countries, through an organic set of proposals on the changes to be made in North-South relations. It is upon these proposals that much of the recent negotiating activity has concentrated.

3 THE HISTORICAL MOTIVATIONS AND CONDITIONING FACTORS OF THE NIEO

The programme of the new international economic order cannot be characterised merely by bringing together a common platform of the old issues which governed relations between the developing and the industrialised nations.

The question needs to be placed in its historical and political setting, since it is impossible to discuss this new international economic order without beginning by clarifying three of the current features of international relations which I consider fundamental: first, the transformation of the centres; second, the great changes in the periphery; and, finally, the still more profound changes which have taken place in the international economic setting.

The analysis of the transformation of the centres in recent years is one of the great challenges still facing thinkers and researchers. We are all aware of the striking growth of the industrial centres over the last thirty years, a period which constitutes one of the more brilliant stages in the evolution of mankind, at least from the standpoint of concrete economic variables and objective indicators of well-being. The international order which emerged from Bretton Woods worked quite well from the standpoint of the centres.

The events of recent years are well known but it is still worth recalling them.

In the first place, there is the increasing interdependence among the centres, above all through the internationalisation of their industry, technology and finance. This growing interdependence has enabled the industrial economies to achieve an ever-larger share of international trade and capital movements.

Second, this process took place at the cost of a progressive relative marginalisation of the periphery. The progress in the centres was based on increasingly close relations among their economies, whose counterpart was a decreasing share for the developing countries in international trade.

Third, the greater interrelations among the industrial economies was accompanied by the appearance of new poles of economic growth, which made the power structure of the centres more complex. At the end of the Second World War the international economy was dominated by the United States, which had to meet the reconstruction needs of the war-ravaged countries. Later, the United States' predominance in the world economy was reduced as the European Economic Community and Japan emerged as new economic powers.

Fourth, new actors have appeared on the world stage, including the transnational corporations, which are characterised by their long-term approach, global action and flexibility. Other important new actors are the international financial banks, which operate outside the control of monetary authorities and handle vast financial resources with extraordinary ease.

Fifth, the changes in the centres include an increasingly strong link between the external cycle and the internal performance of their economies, and a growing dependence of each with respect to the others in tackling their domestic economic problems.

In addition, mention must be made of the change taking place in the periphery, where even more spectacular progress has been achieved. The growth rates, degree of diversification and even technical level of the economies of some developing countries have easily surpassed the most optimistic expectations of two decades ago.

However, this progress has not equally benefited all the developing world. To speak today of the Group of 77 or of the uniformity of the Third World may be too much of a generalisation. In fact, four or five different categories of Third World countries may be distinguished. They include the continent-nations characterised by their high degree of self-reliance, such as China; the countries with special prospects because of their large size; the oil-exporting countries; the middle-income countries; and the least developed countries, which form what has been called the Fourth World.

Of these, it is perhaps the intermediate countries, with their own problems and opportunities, which offer the most interesting experience. They are basically interested in expanding their exports of manufactures and winning access to the markets of the industrialised countries; in continuing to operate with private financial sources and in speeding up their incorporation in world capital markets; in increasing the flow of advanced technology from the centres; and in exploring new forms of partnership with the transnational corporations which will be more beneficial than past arrangements.

If the Paris dialogue ended in failure, as is well known, I think this is largely due to the fact that the time was not then ripe for a suitable harmonisation of the above-mentioned differences in interests. I think that the Brandt Commission has a fresh opportunity of doing this. But we must bear in mind that its limitations are also great, and that its prospects ultimately depend on what the governments wish to do in their respective negotiating forums. I believe that multilateral negotiations must continue, and that it is necessary to go on paying the price of the dose of rhetoric which inevitably filters into those negotiations, since they help to create awareness, build up knowledge and smooth the way for understanding among countries with divergent interests in the main issues of North-South relations. At the same time, however, I think it would be very dangerous to allow oneself to be carried away by the illusion that such negotiations are basically technocratic. They are in fact essentially political, and their results depend on the power of the parties involved; what is at stake is a power relationship. I think it would be dangerous to depoliticise this dialogue, because then the negotiations would cease to deal with realities and become cloistered in an almost exclusively rhetorical atmosphere. It will be necessary to continue insisting on an integrated approach to those problems through multilateral channels, but it will be also necessary to begin dialogues on specific questions in forums in which the countries directly interested can participate. What is more important, this second kind of negotiation will have to be based on the identification of common interests, so that they redound to the benefit of all parties concerned.

Finally, the international setting has also changed profoundly. The scenario of growth and stability envisaged in the 1950s and 1960s no longer fits the facts. Recession, instability and uncertainty have become chronic at the world level. The combination of recession and unemployment prevailing in the central economies, together with their disturbing inflationary processes, call into question the theoretical framework within which those problems have been interpreted hitherto. The differences among the industrialised countries from the standpoint of the rate and dynamism of their economic recovery further complicate the management of the international economy and understanding among those countries, which forces them to look to economic summits at which the leaders of the great world economic power centres meet. The prospects for the developing countries in general, and for the Latin American ones in particular, depends to a considerable extent on the agreements and guidelines adopted at those levels.

4 LATIN AMERICA'S PLACE IN THE NORTH–SOUTH DIALOGUE

What is Latin America's position in this setting? We are all aware of the economic transformation undergone by the region over the last thirty years. The changes exceeded the most optimistic predictions made at the beginning of the period and present a positive picture from the standpoint of the indicators used to measure the progress of countries in conventional terms: gross product, industrialisation, growth of exports, agricultural modernisation or technological progress. But this is not the case when one looks at the social indicators of the process.

We are also aware that a very important process of internationalisation of the Latin American economies has taken place. Until recently, the region's participation in the international economy took place fundamentally through conventional trade and foreign aid channels. Today it mostly takes place through financial, technological and business channels. Latin America has thus become incorporated in the international economic setting in a way which is not only new, but also much more solid and complex.

The transformation of the productive capacity of Latin America and its new forms of international linkage during recent years explain the surprising defensive capacity demonstrated by the regional economy in the face of difficulties stemming from a turbulent international economy. If we had been told some years ago that at a time when the OECD countries were registering sub-zero growth rates the Latin American economies would be capable of maintaining positive growth rates, we would not have believed it. However, the fact is that the Latin American countries did continue to grow in the difficult years 1974 and 1975 in the midst of very unfavourable external circumstances. This was possible thanks to the greater complexity and diversification acquired by the region's industrialisation process, and to the fact that the region had established new types of external linkage which enabled it to find alternatives to attenuate the negative impact of international economic events in that period.

Side by side with these positive developments, serious problems remain which cannot be overlooked, and which we in CEPAL have repeatedly emphasised and denounced. I am referring to the enormous ambivalence resulting from the successes shown by the economic indicators and the state of affairs shown by social statistics on the distribution of the economic progress achieved and on social justice.

Together with these issues, there are others directly linked with the region's international problems. The first lies in the structural differences among the countries of the region. It is increasingly difficult to produce global figures for Latin America. The specificity of each country and the heterogeneity visible when one considers the region as a whole are every day greater. When analysing any problem, previously it sufficed to exclude Venezuela, placing a footnote at the bottom of statistical tables. Today however, for one reason or another almost every country is an exception. Hence the difficulty of producing averages or establishing categories with any interpretative value for a major group of countries of the region.

A second problem is that, as seen by the states when looking at their international linkages, Latin American solidarity occupies a very insignificant place. The countries' capacity for joint action is at present extremely weak. In contrast, there are clear trends in favour of bilateralism and more emphasis is placed on the analysis of each country's relations with other specific countries rather than on its insertion in the region as a whole. The undermining of Latin American solidarity is one of the reasons why the region seems so impassive – if not altogether blind or even hostile – towards the international debate which has taken place in recent years on North–South relations. Whence the paradox that a region of the world able to conceive a world order along UNCTAD lines (which in the last analysis was a Latin American conception, one of its main creators being precisely Dr Raúl Prebisch) has today not merely lost weight in forums such as UNCTAD, but seems deliberately to attempt to pass unnoticed in these discussions. This is largely due to a growing feeling of discomfort stemming from Latin America's status as a region of intermediate development, which places it between the two categories of countries – those of the industrialised world and those of the less developed countries – into neither of which it properly fits.

The fact is that the debate about the international economic order has come upon us at a time of great regional disarray and of profound confusion about our role *vis-à-vis* the rest of the world.

On the one hand there is the so-called 'economic integration crisis'. Of course this is not so much a real as a formal crisis, since the interrelations among the Latin American economies have not ceased to grow stronger in recent years and there is much stronger and more varied complementarity among them. But it is also true that there are ideological positions in many of the governments of the region which are not very favourable towards or are even against making headway in integration processes and formal regional collaboration. Above all, many governments adopt this attitude to co-operation not only because their philosophical positions are against it, but also because of the very real fact that they feel afraid of entering into long-term commitments without knowing what costs they may have in the future as a result of changes in the international picture. Consequently, a number of countries do not wish to subject themselves to collective discipline – and thus restrict their individual defensive capacity against external shocks acquired during the adverse period they have recently had to pass through – in a period of high international uncertainty. This is one reason why regional solidarity has sharply diminished, as various recent events demonstrate.

A third problem is what role Latin America should play in the framework of international economic relations and in the new international division of labour, bearing in mind the stage it has already achieved in its development process in comparison with other Third World regions.

In connection with our insertion in the international setting, for some time attention has been drawn to the asymmetry which characterises the region's external trade. This is a problem which is going to continue for some time, bearing in mind that, despite the success in expanding manufacturing exports in recent years, these do not yet represent 20 per cent of the total; the remaining 80 per cent consists of raw materials. Latin America will therefore continue to depend heavily on its exports of primary commodities, and will continue to possess the vulnerability inherent in that position. Thus the region, while having its own traits, continues to share many of the concerns of the other developing countries, and should continue to be interested in many of the issues of the NIEO. At the same time, however, Latin America will have an increasing concern for the growth of its exports of manufactures and their access to the markets of the industrialised countries, and will continue to view the protectionism in the centres as one of the most serious obstacles to its development process. The countries of the region will continue to be concerned about problems of external financing; but there are no grounds whatsoever for believing that official financing can continue to grow in relative terms and, above all, that it can satisfy the enormous capital needs which will continue to exist. Consequently, access to the private markets will be a fundamental condition for our future growth capacity. It is therefore also the case that the transnational enterprises will continue operating in the region, and that they will play an important role in its growth. The problem with these corporations will be to find more suitable forms of partnership which respect the legitimate interests and sovereignty of the countries and do not entail undesirable political or economic interference.

5 THE INTERNATIONAL, REGIONAL AND NATIONAL LEVELS

I therefore believe that there should be a three-tiered response to the challenge of Latin America's new position in the international setting: first, at the level of international agreements; second, at the level of regional co-operation; and third, with regard to the lessons to be learnt from the present international situation for national development strategies.

With regard to Latin America's position in the international context, there is a broad field for reflection. I think that in this area it should develop a flexible strategy: Latin America is part of the Third World, and it would be contrary to its political and economic interests for the region to attempt to divorce itself from it. The great challenge is to find forms of harmonising its particular interests with those of the other developing countries. A strategy which could cool its relations with the rest of the Third World and cut it off from the Group of 77 could further weaken the already feeble bargaining power of the Third World. In addition, it could bring very serious complications both within Latin America and in its relations with the rest of the world. It should be recalled that in Latin America there are still countries which quite objectively belong to the group of less developed nations. Other more developed countries are members of OPEC or have strong links with Africa. It would be difficult to imagine a strategy which could not be brought into line with the position of the developing countries as a whole, and which would help to solve problems which, while not having the same priority in Latin America, affect it as much as the rest of the Third World.

But it is time to think that Latin America must attach increasing importance to a number of specific issues, such as exports of manufactures, access to international capital markets or negotiations with foreign investors and transnational corporations. These are problems of great importance in the region due to the development level it has reached.

This underscores the need to formulate a Latin American international strategy to clarify the confusion at present besetting it, and enable it to define a position within the international context in keeping with its specific priorities and interests. The fact is that the present lack of definition is causing Latin America severe harm. At present it is not playing the role which it could in the North–South dialogue. What is more serious, the intellectual analysis required for such a definition of policy has not even been undertaken in the Latin American countries. Thus a fertile field is available for reflection on the part of Latin American intellectuals, not only within international organisations, but also in academic circles.

A second need stemming from this context is that of rethinking regional co-operation. I think that if there is a lesson to be learnt from the present difficult international situation, it is the urgent need to reflect upon the new role which regional co-operation has to play. In other words, Latin America needs to take advantage of the potential of mutual collaboration to attenuate the effects of the external economic cycle and to provide an additional boost to regional development. It is very significant that during a recessive phase in international trade, as occurred in 1974 and 1975, reciprocal trade among the Latin American countries continued to increase. These considerations may provide fresh arguments for defending and rethinking the role of regional co-operation as a defensive weapon against the major fluctuations in the world economy and a stimulus for the growth of the Latin American economies.

A third aspect consists of the role of national development strategies in relation to the forms which Latin America's international position can adopt. In this connection a number of issues are becoming outdated in the Latin American countries. One of these is the famous argument over the advantages of inward-looking growth processes as opposed to the new forms or outward-looking development with which an increasing number of countries are experimenting; or in other words, over protectionism versus free trade. A number of sterile ideological dichotomies are becoming obsolete – and points of agreement are emerging – as the countries tend to find a sound balance between the use of the domestic market and the encouragement of export activities. The experience Latin American countries have acquired allows them to weigh up whatever excesses are committed in one direction or another. Finally, the recent experiments in 'opening up' the Latin American economies to the external markets should be assessed in the light of the protectionist tendencies prevailing in the centres and of an international recession. Thus, serious thought must be given to the risks involved in launching out, with practically no external protection, into the stormy waters of the world economy today. An analysis of the protectionist trends in the centres – their causes and latest forms – as well as the desirable level of protection in Latin American countries are among the most important research topics for anyone engaged in the study of Latin America's international economic relations.

6 IMPORTANT RESEARCH TOPICS IN NORTH-SOUTH RELATIONS

This leads us to make a number of comments on some of the topics which we feel should receive priority in the study of North-South relations, in the light of the results to which the negotiations in this field have led. But first of all it must be recognised that those results have been rather mediocre.

If we take the case of commodities, we find that in practice there is a continuing deadlock. The Geneva negotiations on the organisation of the common fund have made no headway. Serious doubts remain not only on the part of those who have to assume major responsibility for financing it, but also – and this is much more serious – on the part of the countries of the periphery themselves, among whom serious divisions have arisen that have even endangered the unity of the Group of 77.

While the question of financing is progressing slightly more rapidly, particularly as regards the proposals made in the Paris talks for the cancellation of the debt of the least developed countries, the intermediate developing countries continue to have specific points of concern about any financial agreement representing a blanket solution which could affect their external credit. This is understandable since they are countries which depend heavily on private financial markets, and which feel that any kind of global action which affects the fulfilment of their international commitments could threaten their presence in world financial circles. Hence the danger that these countries would view with great suspicion any measure of a global nature which could be viewed as a threat to their possibilities of access to private international sources of financing. In fact, the cancellation of the debt of the poorest countries may be the only point on which there is a certain amount of consensus in the international community.

As concerns transnational corporations, some progress has been made towards drafting a code of conduct, but the negotiations have come to a standstill on a crucial point, namely, whether or not it should be binding. If an entirely voluntary instrument – a kind of moral code – is adopted, the problem will remain unsolved, since the attitude of many developing countries to transnational corporations has hardened and the awareness of the problems involved has increased in the industrial countries, too.

These considerations also hold, broadly speaking, for the code on the transfer of technology being negotiated in UNCTAD.

A discussion of the issue of individual and collective self-reliance would go beyond the space available here. This is a very complex issue which has not yet been dealt with in sufficient detail. But let it be said quite clearly, this is an area of unquestionable importance for the future of the Third World, and one which should receive full intellectual and political support.

Perhaps a comment should also be made on the question of basic needs, another of the points which seriously threaten to divide the Third World, but also one which attracts great attention in the industrialised nations. Some developing countries, such as India and the Latin American countries, have expressed great reservations on this question, not because the satisfaction of the basic needs of the population is not a central objective, but because they consider that in fact this objective is being used by some central countries as an escapist formula, a trick designed to reduce international co-operation to the level of mere charity instead of using it to foster the structural changes required in international economic relations and to bring about the major transformation which must take place in the developing nations themselves in order to satisfy their needs in a self-reliant manner. Hence some developing countries are seriously questioning this approach as the focus of their relations with the industrialised world.

7 FINAL REMARKS

The first comment called for in rounding off this analysis concerns what negotiations can be undertaken at this point in international economic affairs. It is a fact that the recession affecting the central countries will continue restricting the prospects of the developing world. This limitation works in two ways. First, the world economic recession directly affects the developing economies by reducing demand for their export products and by restricting the flow of direct investment and financial aid. Second, to the extent that the recession countinues, the industrialised countries will be less disposed to tackle the internal reforms needed to make way for a new international division of labour in line with comparative production costs in the centres and in the periphery, which would contribute to the war on inflation in the centres and to boosting the productive capacity of the South. Consequently, the limits of the possible are at present very narrow, and the political will in the central countries to undertake the structural changes needed for a profound reorganisation of North-South relations is very weak. The upsurge of protectionism in the centres – one alternative to the introduction of such reforms – is a direct manifestation of this lack of political will.

In addition, I have the impression that these limits will be even narrower as the North-South dialogue concentrates on financing and raw materials, two areas which tend to call for solutions based on the transfer of resources from the central countries to the periphery rather than mutually beneficial action. Hence the enormous interest of the fact that the international community has begun to stress how important the economic dynamism of the South is for the North, and how the steady growth of the import and export capacity of the Third World would stimulate economic activity in the industrial countries. I think that this understanding of the role of the South as an instrument for reactivating the international economy is of major importance today: it should help to provide a new basis for its relations with the North and in the discovery of constructive and mutually advantageous solutions.

The other problem is how to negotiate, an area where it appears that we are bound by obsolete arrangements. We have been overtaken by three kinds of events. First, by the number of parties involved; negotiating with 40 countries is not the same thing as negotiating with 150. Second, by the complexity of the problems; the time is past when a few figures could be thought to provide a panacea for the evils of underdevelopment, and we now live in a time when challenges have grown qualitatively more complex and more closely interdependent. Finally, negotiations have become more difficult as a result of internal diversifications in the centre and the periphery. Various currents have emerged in the former regarding the needs and claims of the periphery which further complicate the difficulties arising from the heterogeneity of the developing countries themselves.

The proposals on the restructuring of the negotiating machinery spring from two schools of thought. One is that of the United Nations, which insists on presenting an integrated approach to the problems, discussing them in global forums and maximising the results of the corresponding negotiations. Currently, however, an experiment is being undertaken in shifting the focus of these negotiations from UNCTAD in Geneva to New York on the grounds that these questions should be discussed to some extent in a political forum of the highest possible level. The other, mainly from the Northern countries, favours a thematic approach, replacing these great international forums with a discussion of each topic in specialised bodies, in which only the countries directly interested would participate, while the inherently global problems which interest the whole international community would be the object of broader collective agreements.

I think that relations between the centres and the periphery will continue to grow in importance in the future. The old theories of dependence must be revised and improved in the light of constantly changing reality. Knowledge of the changes taking place in the centres and their effects on the periphery are an increasingly inescapable challenge for our intellectuals and academic institutions, because I think that the major changes will come from the North and not from the South, particularly for the middle-income countries. A thorough knowledge of what is happening and what will happen in the central countries and of the changes which will take place in the international setting will allow us to anticipate more accurately the new forms which the developing countries' dependence on the industrialised countries will take. It will also make it possible to visualise the new conditions in which they could optimise their participation in the international system.

At the same time, a greater effort must be made to analyse the effects that the changes which have taken place in the international economy will have on the development strategies of the peripheral countries. This is another rich field for research and one in which CEPAL is very interested, since it is impossible to anticipate the future growth trends of the Latin American economies without having a clear idea of their future external strategies.

Finally, a topic about which I am personally concerned is that of the state, particularly the new Latin American state. I think that this is a very important issue, since the changing national and international scenarios for our countries in the coming years will force them to experiment with highly imaginative, flexible strategies, for which purpose they will have to redefine thoroughly the functions of the state.

17 International Economic Co-operation: a Comment

DUDLEY SEERS

Dr Iglesias has written a wide-ranging essay touching on many aspects of international economic co-operation, but in a way that is far from superficial – indeed on some issues his comments have a depth and frankness that senior UN officials rarely allow themselves. I would like, however, to suggest some implications that perhaps even he cannot draw.

I start with some doubts about one or two rather optimistic passages in his essay. Is there now 'a more enlightened [world] collective conscience'? Has 'a constructive dialogue' become more possible? Certainly, as he says, OPEC now provides diplomatic and financial support to the rest of 'the South'. Moreover, some quarters in the industrialised countries, show a greater sensitivity to overseas problems. There has, indeed, been 'an impressive proliferation' in the number of international institutions' and particularly of world conferences concerned with major issues (the Law of the Sea, population, employment, food, etc.) and many new items are on the agenda of international discussion, such as the role of women in development.

Yet he himself draws attention to the prevalence of mere 'rhetoric' and the lack of genuine progress on commodity policy, international finance, control of transnational corporations and the transfer of technology. He points to the apparently never-ending world recession and the new wave of protectionism in the industrialised countries; realistically he stresses the lack of genuine solidarity among the governments of 'the South'. Even more serious are the deepening struggle for sources of energy and other basic inputs and the growing military conflicts accompanied by mounting expenditure on arms.

Increased discussion does not count for much in the face of these rising tensions.

Some of his remarks in fact throw doubt on whether the 'North-South' framework for this discussion is useful analytically or even diplomatically. He draws attention to the growing diversification in both 'the North' and 'the South', and at one point mentions the lesser role of Latin America in international discussions, which he attributes in part to 'a growing feeling of discomfort stemming from Latin America's status as a region of intermediate development which places it between the two categories of countries – those of the industrialised world and those of the less developed countries – into neither of which it properly fits'.

But if he is correct here – as I believe he is – can one usefully continue to talk of 'the South' or 'the Third World'?

He speaks of the need to formulate a Latin American international strategy, corresponding to its own interests and priorities. But I wonder whether there are now sufficient interests and priorities in common. In the 1950s, when Raúl Prebisch did successfully appeal to Latin American regional sentiment, there were, in addition to the historical roots and cultural heritage: (a) common trade interests derived from the fact that all countries in the region were 'less developed' and heavily dependent on exports of primary commodities; and (b) a degree of political unity, in that ideological divergence was subordinated to the desire to contain very strong pressures from the United States, which dominated the region economically and politically; every government gave support at that time to CEPAL as an institution, to Prebisch himself and to his 'doctrine', in the teeth of US hostility.

A quarter of a century later, (a) as he says, some Latin American countries have both become less dependent on trade and greatly diversified their exports; and (b) what perhaps he cannot say, there is a greater ideological range, from (say) Chile to Cuba, and the geographical diversification of trade and political contacts has meant that resistance to influences from the United States no longer unifies the region.

The logic of his argument seems to me to imply areas of Latin American research additional to those he lists.

We need a classification of economies going beyond the old simplistic amalgamation of Latin America, Africa and Asia into a single category – which reflects the conventional neglect of taxonomy in the social sciences. Dr Iglesias does indeed suggest one tentative solution, dividing 'the Third World' into four or five distinct groups: the self-sufficient; other very large countries; oil exporters; those with intermediate incomes; and the 'least developed'. I am sure he is on the right track, but, in practice, it may not be very easy to use a classification based, as this is, on three criteria – size, resources and income – which are not closely correlated. Some very large countries, Pakistan for example, are by most criteria among the 'least developed' and some oil exporters (e.g. Iran) only have an intermediate level of incomes. Moreover, some European countries of 'intermediate income', such as Portugal and Greece, share many of the structural and international problems of Latin America. Perhaps one needs to experiment with different criteria for different purposes – e.g. resources (including industrial capital) when discussing trade policy; size, for assessing possibilities of self-reliant planning. A taxonomic investigation of this kind could be extended to meet another need he mentions, a useful classification of the countries of Latin America itself.

Dr Iglesias cites the need for research on protectionism in the industrial countries. Perhaps one should take a step beyond this and envisage Latin American centres of regional studies. Protectionism cannot really be understood without an appreciation of the different economic contexts – indeed of the changing socio-political structures – in the industrial countries, which in fact he sees as extremely important for Latin America. To my knowledge, there is no scholar in Latin America dedicated full-time to the study of Japan (hardly, indeed, anyone who could give an informed account of the specific nature of Japanese protectionism – and it is very specific!). When foreign affairs departments in Latin America require material to establish a position on Japanese trade and political initiatives, or a diplomat or business executive needs briefing on Japan, or a social scientist needs analyses of Japanese society for a world model, they have to turn to the research centres of North America or Western Europe – where the material is naturally coloured by different perceptions of the world and different political priorities. The rationale for establishing centres of Latin American Studies in North America and Western Europe could be applied in Latin America in reverse. There are embryonic centres of studies of the United States (in Mexico and Colombia), and a few Latin American economists have read a good deal about the Soviet Union or studied in Britain or France. But there is no real institutional specialisation appropriate to the needs of Latin American policy-makers or social scientists. Does not Latin America need four centres (which would have, in the first place at least, to serve the region as a whole and which, therefore, would need to be located in different countries) specialising in North America, Western Europe, the Socialist countries and Japan? to which should be added, for somewhat different purposes, three others, the Middle East, Asia and Africa.

Dr Iglesias mentions the need for work on the role of the state. Within this area, there seem to be some priorities relevant to the theme of this conference. One is research on the association between foreign economic policies and political systems. To be specific, under what conditions, if any, does foreign exchange liberalisation imply military dictatorships? There are also other important areas (such as the role, class origins and political affiliations of the state bureaucracy), but these would take us outside the scope of our agenda.

He refers in several places to the growing influence of the transnational corporations. It would be useful to study how deep their penetration is now in Latin America and what form it takes, and especially how much this is inhibiting or encouraging the growth of indigenous technological capacity and bargaining capability. Is the rapid industrial growth of Brazil, for example, increasing or reducing imports of technology (and related equipment)?

Although we were invited to discuss research needs in international *economic* policy, these priority areas I have suggested, based on Dr Iglesias's analysis, all raise issues beyond the merely economic. Just as in the field of domestic policy, it is difficult to separate the 'economic' factors from the political and cultural, and analyses which try to do so are usually seriously misleading. Economic policy, therefore, does not need merely economic research.

18 Research Priorities in International Economics: a Latin American Perspective

CARLOS F. DÍAZ-ALEJANDRO AND RICARDO FFRENCH-DAVIS

In these notes we outline a group of research areas in the field of international economics which have a high priority for LDCs, and for Latin America in particular. Naturally, we do not intend to cover the whole range of possible research projects. It has thus been necessary to establish priorities, although the area marked out here remains relatively extensive.

In order to establish priorities, it is necessary to take into consideration who is doing the research and with what end in view. On the first point, we limit ourselves here to academic research institutions concerned with the problems facing LDCs. As to the end in view, we address ourselves here, in the main, to the search for economic policies which satisfy criteria of efficiency, equity and self-reliancy.

The different essays and comments in this volume have drawn attention to topics of importance for Third World countries, and on which present knowledge is limited or inadequate. Three major research categories can be identified from the material presented. At a theoretical level, there is a need for the elaboration of more relevant theoretical frameworks than those at present available; empirical studies are needed on the implications of different domestic structural conditions and of the specific characteristics of the policy tools used in different historical circumstances and their functioning in alternative conditions; finally, comparative analysis of different national experiences are required. The three areas for research are interlinked, particularly as regards the design of economic policies and their adaptation to the specific conditions in individual LDCs.

In the theoretical field, the need is to develop those aspects which have most bearing upon the design and implementation of foreign trade policies. The lack of 'theoretical' research in LDCs has tended to result in practice in the inadequacy of many empirical studies when it comes to interpreting reality and contributing to the design of more efficient economic policies, as they are limited to the repetition of conventional approaches elaborated and popularised in rich countries.

There is broad scope for the incorporation into the theory of international trade of advances made in other areas of economics and in related disciplines such as sociology and political science.

Furthermore, there is a need to explore the theoretical implications of some distinctive features of Third World countries. Among these are the heterogeneity of social and economic structures, unemployment and underemployment, the concentration of political and economic power, the asymmetry of power in foreign relations, and the prominence of transnational corporations and of public enterprises. Taken together, these characteristics suggest the need for a revision of international trade theory if recommendations for economic policies are to be relevant to the internal and external context of different LDCs.

Finally, the priorities to be established will depend upon the objectives pursued. Two in particular have been present in the essays collected here; they are the search for greater internal equality and for a pattern of development which does not merely imitate that of the more powerful nations. Within this context the state plays a crucial role, and this makes it essential to devote more attention to studying the conditions in which it can perform its functions efficiently.

Fruitful advances in the theoretical field will depend upon further empirical research in two directions. First, regarding case studies of individual countries, with attention focused on problems such as the simultaneous existence of numerous sources of disequilibria and distortions in markets, and to the impact of alternative public policies upon employment, the distribution of power and income, and upon a self-sustained development in the future. The second line of research should aim at enriching the national studies with comparative analyses which allow the identification of the influence of the specific characteristics of each country, of the external situation they face, and of the chronological sequence of the different actions carried out.

In what follows we describe briefly five areas of research which we consider of the highest priority, in terms of their practical importance for many LDCs and of the insufficiency or inadequacy of current knowledge.

1 MODES OF 'OPENING' THE ECONOMY TO WORLD MARKETS

The opening of the economy to world markets constitutes the main characteristic of the development strategy of a number of Third World nations. Some of them have seen it as a natural sequence of 'inward-oriented development' policies adopted in the past. Others, in contrast, have sought to turn sharply away from their previous experiences.

The attempts to open the economy promised or carried out in recent years in some Latin American countries have taken on forms different from those of previous experiences, and some of the processes involved have been markedly more intense and systematic than in the past.

The wide range of issues involved in the processes of opening the economy can be grouped into five areas of high priority. They are: (i) the coverage of the process; (ii) the structural and conjunctural conditions in which it takes place; (iii) the degree of stability and permanence of the process; (iv) the nature of the period of transition towards a new equilibrium; and (v) the role of foreign capital in the process.

The coverage of the process of opening the economy may vary considerably. It may cover all markets related to the foreign sector – those of goods, services, finance, direct investment and foreign exchange – or it may take in only a segment of one of those markets, as for example a group of import substituting goods or the promotion of exports of manufactures. Naturally, the implications of different options also vary widely. The time at which processes of opening the economy take place and the conditions prevailing in domestic and relevant world markets are also of significance, as are the degree of selectivity of the process and the sequence of different actions. One aspect of selectivity is the option of carrying out the process unilaterally or in the company of other countries: for example, selectivity can be expressed in the adoption of different degrees of openness to different groups of countries, with the adoption of a mixed scheme of greater openness towards countries with a similar level of development, and participation with them in an integration scheme. The role of state activity is also significant: the range of variants runs from an attitude of non-participation and total reliance on the market, to an active state with a role in the process of opening the economy and in the allocation of resources.

The influence of the conjuncture at which the opening of the economy occurs is also significant. A number of liberalisation processes have been carried out as part of an anti-inflationary policy; in many cases this has meant depressed effective demand, along with high unemployment and low investment levels. We should also mention the question of the stability or permanence of the process. A basic problem is the question of why so many of these processes have been partially or wholly reversed; apparently, this is related to the manner in which the opening is carried out, and with the prevailing political and economic conditions. In this sense much can be learnt from historical experiences in the political and the technical fields, and analysis of them might avoid excessive liberalisation and subsequent reimposition of arbitrary restrictions.

A further point relating to the stability or permanence of the process concerns the decision as to how far the process of opening should go, and the examination of what happens during the period of transition or adjustment, especially as this may be long. It is thus necessary to evaluate the final target as well as the process of adjustment, in attempts to open up each of the different markets related with the external sector. One should examine the consequences of different sequences of actions and levels of intensity upon different entrepreneurial groups, and upon employment (where it is necessary to go further than using the simplified Heckscher-Ohlin-Samuelson model as a theoretical framework).

It is also important to analyse the impact upon migration. One of the hopes expressed by some who have advocated extreme policies of trade liberalisation is that the process of opening up the economy will halt or reverse the flow of migration from the countryside. In more general terms, some of the questions raised with regard to the effects upon labour of opening the economy are how it affects the nature and the intensity of internal migration, what the impact is upon large and small firms, how it conditions trade union activities, what implications particular processes of liberalisation carry for social and cultural conditions, and what are the repercussions of the adjustment path upon the absorption of technology and the capacity to develop it locally.

The aspects mentioned here vary greatly from one context to another. The speed of the adjustment process undoubtedly has a substantial effect: for example, a rapid import liberalisation may transform entrepreneurs engaged in production into importers; at the same time, the impact upon the structure of consumption and saving is also relevant. With regard to the last two points – the effects upon technology and upon consumption and saving – two relevant issues which have not been sufficiently explored are the existence of product differentiation and what has been called 'x-efficiency'. Very different conclusions will be reached regarding the way in which markets are expected to behave if the theoretical analysis takes these elements explicitly into consideration.

Finally, also in the field of the new forms of opening the economy, it would be desirable to carry out national case studies of several processes now taking place. Although they have been in operation for relatively short periods of time, it should still be possible to learn from the few years of experience accumulated. It would probably be worth looking again at experiences studied in the past, and re-examining them in the light of the new conditions which have emerged in the international environment and, in the national economies, seeking to analyse more thoroughly the institutional framework, the policy instruments employed and the socio-political context in which they were introduced.

A different group of topics concerns the role of foreign capital in the processes of opening the economy. Little attention has been devoted to this subject, particularly with regard to financial capital movements. Nevertheless, even with respect to transnational corporations, there has been insufficient analysis of the implications of different ways of treating direct foreign investment, such as for example the manner in which particular national policy instruments affect the behaviour of TNCs in different situations. On the financial side, including foreign debt, much could be learnt from a study of the different forms in which economies have opened to financial capital, the various consequences of each of them in specific cases, and the influence of the nature of domestic markets. For example, the impact will differ in accordance with the role played by the state, the degree of development of national capital markets, and the foreign exchange policy applied. Points of interest in this area are the influence of the form of liberalisation not only upon the stability of the balance of payments, but also upon the development or underdevelopment of the domestic capital market, the discrimination arising between different types of large and small or national and foreign firms, and the manner in which the present and future degrees of freedom of national policies in other areas of the economy are restricted.

2 EXPORT PROMOTION AND DEVELOPMENT

From the 1960s onwards export promotion policies have been adopted in a number of LDCs. At this stage of progress of research in different areas it is possible to identify three areas in which more detailed national case studies and a comparative analysis of representative experiences would be fruitful.

The three groups of issues which seem to have highest priority are: (i) the forms in which export promotion affects the domestic economy; (ii) access to external markets; and (iii) the effects of different methods of promotion.

With regard to the effect of export promotion upon the domestic economy, a key issue concerns the manner in which the two variables interact. Export promotion can take place either integrated or unintegrated with the non-export sector; for example, it can substitute or complement import substitution. Some of the repercussions on the national economy relate to the effects of a particular export promotion strategy upon the utilisation of natural resources and of labour, and the generation of demand for intermediate or capital goods. In another area, one might explore the effect of export promotion upon income distribution and the capacity to carry out an autonomous national economic policy. The diversity of effects depend, naturally, upon the strategy of promotion adopted and the characteristics of the economy to which they are applied.

One aspect which is regularly debated concerns the extent to which (and the conditions in which) export promotion can become the 'motor of development'. It becomes necessary to examine the manner in which the impulse from export promotion is transmitted to the domestic economy; there can be no doubt that the direct effects upon resource utilisation mentioned in the previous paragraph are insufficient to generate a self-sustained growth. There are therefore indirect and dynamic effects which should be examined, such as the impact of different export promotion strategies upon saving and consumption, upon investment opportunities, upon the incorporation of new technologies and upon the behaviour of entrepreneurs. In this sense, it is important to examine the conditions in which export promotion can initiate a process of development which can later be led by other forces, and/or the conditions in which it performs only the role of a link in a chain of mutually supporting effects.

Beyond the 'easy' stage of export promotion, which provides an outlet for surplus production and thus contributes to the expansion of growth, we are at present able to say very little about the nature of the interrelations between export promotion and national development.

A second area in which many questions are raised is that of the problem of access to external markets. How have those countries which have been successful with export promotion penetrated foreign markets? What is the role of TNCs, public enterprises and different marketing organisations?

Another aspect of access to external markets is the contribution which can be made by co-operation among LDCs: processes of economic integration seem to have contributed to the expansion of non-traditional exports and to industrialisation in several countries of the region, and to have attenuated the impact of the critical period through which the international economy passed in the years 1975–6. However, little attention has been devoted to the relationship between exports to member countries and those to the rest of the world, the extent to which the former complement the latter, and the way in which they affect the capacity to negotiate with third parties.

Finally, the analysis of the instruments and mechanisms utilised plays a role that is crucial in many ways. The type of promotion strategy employed has very different effects upon particular groups of entrepreneurs or workers, rural and urban sectors, and modern and traditional activities. Two additional points of importance relate to the nature of the import substitution policies which accompany export promotion, and the influence of the international environment on the choice of export promotion mechanisms.

The various export promotion experiences carried out by semi-industrialised countries in the last fifteen years exhibit great heterogeneity; thus, a more detailed analysis of a number of national cases and a comparative examination of the mechanisms utilised and the results obtained would be fruitful. A comparison of the experiences of countries in Latin America and in Asia might throw up interesting leads, and contribute to an improved understanding of the relationship between exports and development, as well as avoid excessive trust in export promotion as a unilateral motor of growth.

3 INTERNATIONAL CAPITAL MARKETS AND THEIR INFLUENCE ON THE PERIPHERY

The re-emergence of international markets for private financial capital has perhaps been the most important structural change in the world economy over the last decade. Many countries in Latin America and elsewhere in the Third World have made considerable use of this source of financial resources. Knowledge of precisely how these markets operate is, however, limited. A number of studies relating to this field could be undertaken. One group would include the analysis of what might be called the 'industrial organisation' of Eurocurrency markets and national capital markets in the leading industrial nations. This would involve the investigation of the identity of the major actors in the demand for and supply of credit, the degree of competition which exists, the independence of creditors from the IMF, the structure and range of interest rates and periods of repayment, gaps which exist in these markets for long-term loans and fixed rates of interest, etc. It would be particularly important to examine the sensitivity of the sums loaned to Latin America to the stage of the economic cycle faced by the industrialised nations, and the response of interest rates and repayment periods to changes in the forces behind inflation. A sounder understanding of how these markets have functioned is essential if we are to predict their evolution in the future and prepare better bargaining positions.

Two features of the situation which are particularly relevant are the proposals for the 'regulation' of Eurocurrency markets and the possibility that a recovery in the industrialised nations might make access to these markets abruptly more difficult for LDCs. A further group of themes concerns the study of how the internal policies of debtor countries have been influenced by their participation in these markets, and the analysis of the costs and benefits of that participation in terms of the different national development objectives. To what extent, one might ask, has the use of these external credits affected savings and national capital markets? What kinds of economic actors have been favoured by the opportunities opened up by international capital markets? One possible hypothesis is that the large public enterprises (when allowed to do so), the major banks and the transnational corporations have been the economic agents to benefit most. The techniques used by governments to manage and control their external debt and their international reserves (and the links between the two) are also worth investigating.

A point of departure for such research would be to examine the experiences of a sample of countries with varying characteristics: large, medium-sized and small; some who have managed their debts successfully, and some who have been obliged to renegotiate them in difficult conditions. Some instances in which foreign debt has been rescheduled and consolidated merit special attention.

4 INTERNATIONAL MARKETS FOR PRIMARY COMMODITIES

The instability and the long-term trends of commodity prices have been much discussed, but little detailed attention has been given to international markets in these goods, beyond simple hypotheses regarding stylised supply and demand. Here, too, there is a need to devote more attention to the 'industrial organisation', indentifying key actors, oligopolistic interdependency, information networks and their imperfections. The field of study would include not only production and final consumption, but also the processing, transport and refining of commodities, and would seek to distinguish between quasi-rents and components representing a real cost.

In the field of minerals and of energy, international markets have evolved in significant ways in recent years, with new actors such as public enterprises in producer countries breaking into them. The organisation and behaviour of these public enterprises, their links with TNCs, their capacity to manage existing mines and to undertake new projects of exploration and exploitation are themes of singular importance.

As in previous cases, the research proposed would help us not only to understand the past but also to design policies which would allow us to face an uncertain future and improve the bargaining capacity of the Latin American countries. For example, dissatisfaction with the present functioning of international markets, particularly for mineral products, is shared by 'Northerners' and 'Southerners', although the discontent has different roots. There is talk of new forms of functioning for major projects which will supply future trade flows, involving TNCs, the World Bank, regional banks and LDCs. A more profound understanding of the changing reality of international markets would be a very useful contribution to attempts to reach stable agreements beneficial to all parties.

5 SHORT- AND MEDIUM-TERM MACROECONOMIC MODELS

The many experiments with anti-inflationary programmes in different Latin American countries and the reactions of their economies to 'shocks' originating in international markets have led many observers to doubt the explanatory capacity of 'Northern' macroeconomic models,

models which have certainly entered into a state of crisis along with the countries in which they originated. This provides motivation for the search for alternative models better able to orient analysis of the cyclical ups and downs and the changes in development strategies in semi-industrialised open economies, of the type frequently found in Latin America and in other parts of the Third World.

A satisfactory empirical analysis should be carried out in the framework of a coherent conceptualisation of the global functioning of the economy, or a 'model' in the broad sense of the word. In developing these models, one should emphasise variables and relationships ignored or neglected in the models currently most popular in the Northern economies, such as chronic inflation, unemployment and under-employment, income distribution and the multiple relationships between international markets and domestic economies. The models should use categories and degrees of disaggregation which seek to reflect, in a stylised form, the structural heterogeneity of countries with open and semi-industrialised economies. For example, it is likely that investment functions would be different in these models, both as regards the relevant disaggregations and the key economic agents, from formulations appropriate for more developed countries or from the traditional models of competitive equilibrium.

The construction of these models should be closely linked to the study of the experiences, in macroeconomic terms, of a number of Latin American countries over the last fifteen years, and a comparison of the explanatory power of new models as against those currently better known. Without doubt, the development of research about the degrees and alternative forms of opening an economy to world markets and its consequences could make a significant contribution to the formulation of a more relevant conceptual framework. The task could prove important not only for the design of macroeconomic policies, but also as an additional contribution to the reconstruction of macroeconomic theory, now under way in various academic centres throughout the world.

Index